# GNU Octave

A high-level interactive language for numerical computations
Octave version 2.0.17 (stable)

John W. Eaton

A catalogue record for this book is available from the British Library.

First Printing, February 2002. Edited for publication.
Second Printing, June 2005. Additional corrections.

Published by Network Theory Limited.
15 Royal Park, Bristol BS8 3AL, United Kingdom
Email: info@network-theory.co.uk

ISBN 0-9541617-2-6

Original cover design by David Nicholls.

Further information about this book is available from
http://www.network-theory.co.uk/octave/manual/

This book has an unconditional guarantee. If you are not fully satisfied
with your purchase for any reason, please contact the publisher at the
address above.

This documentation is consistent with version 2.0.17 of Octave, the current stable release at time of publication.

# Table of Contents

# Publisher's Preface

This manual documents the use of GNU Octave, an interactive environment for numerical computation.

GNU Octave is *free software*. The term "free software" is sometimes misunderstood—it has nothing to do with price. It is about freedom. It refers to your freedom to run, copy, distribute, study, change and improve the software. With GNU Octave you have all these freedoms.

GNU Octave is part of the GNU Project. The GNU Project was launched in 1984 to develop a complete Unix-like operating system which is free software: the GNU system. It was conceived as a way of bringing back the cooperative spirit that prevailed in the computing community in earlier days, by removing the obstacles to cooperation imposed by the owners of proprietary software.

The Free Software Foundation is a tax-exempt charity that raises funds for work on the GNU Project and is dedicated to promoting the freedom to modify and redistribute computer programs. You can support the GNU Project by becoming an associate member of the Free Software Foundation and paying regular membership dues. For more information, visit the website www.fsf.org.

Brian Gough
Publisher
June 2005

# Author's Preface

Octave was originally intended to be companion software for an undergraduate-level textbook on chemical reactor design being written by James B. Rawlings of the University of Wisconsin-Madison and John G. Ekerdt of the University of Texas.

Clearly, Octave is now much more than just another 'courseware' package with limited utility beyond the classroom. Although our initial goals were somewhat vague, we knew that we wanted to create something that would enable students to solve realistic problems, and that they could use for many things other than chemical reactor design problems.

There are those who would say that we should be teaching the students Fortran instead, because that is the computer language of engineering, but every time we have tried that, the students have spent far too much time trying to figure out why their Fortran code crashes and not enough time learning about chemical engineering. With Octave, most students pick up the basics quickly, and are using it confidently in just a few hours.

Although it was originally intended to be used to teach reactor design, it has been used in several other undergraduate and graduate courses in the Chemical Engineering Department at the University of Texas, and the math department at the University of Texas has been using it for teaching differential equations and linear algebra as well. If you find it useful, please let us know. We are always interested to find out how Octave is being used in other places.

Virtually everyone thinks that the name Octave has something to do with music, but it is actually the name of a former professor of mine who wrote a famous textbook on chemical reaction engineering, and who was also well known for his ability to do quick 'back of the envelope' calculations. We hope that this software will make it possible for many people to do more ambitious computations just as easily.

Everyone is encouraged to share this software with others under the terms of the GNU General Public License (see Appendix E [Copying], page 281) as described at the beginning of this manual. You are also encouraged to help make Octave more useful by writing and contributing additional functions for it, and by reporting any problems you may have.

## Acknowledgements

Many people have already contributed to Octave's development. In addition to John W. Eaton, the following people have helped write parts of Octave or helped out in various other ways.

- Thomas Baier baier@ci.tuwien.ac.at wrote the original versions of popen, pclose, execute, sync_system, and async_system.

- Karl Berry karl@cs.umb.edu wrote the kpathsea library that allows Octave to recursively search directory paths for function and script files.

- Georg Beyerle gbeyerle@awi-potsdam.de contributed code to save values in MATLAB's '.mat'-file format, and has provided many useful bug reports and suggestions.

- John Campbell jcc@bevo.che.wisc.edu wrote most of the file and C-style input and output functions.

- Brian Fox bfox@gnu.org wrote the readline library used for command history editing, and the portion of this manual that documents it.

- Klaus Gebhardt gebhardt@crunch.ikp.physik.th-darmstadt.de ported Octave to OS/2.

- A. Scottedward Hodel A.S.Hodel@eng.auburn.edu contributed a number of functions including expm, qzval, qzhess, syl, lyap, and balance.

- Kurt Hornik Kurt.Hornik@ci.tuwien.ac.at provided the corrcoef, cov, fftconv, fftfilt, gcd, lcd, kurtosis, null, orth, poly, polyfit, roots, and skewness functions, supplied documentation for these and numerous other functions, rewrote the Emacs mode for editing Octave code and provided its documentation, and has helped tremendously with testing. He has also been a constant source of new ideas for improving Octave.

- Phil Johnson johnsonp@nicco.sscnet.ucla.edu has helped to make Linux releases available.

- Friedrich Leisch leisch@ci.tuwien.ac.at provided the mahalanobis function.

- Ken Neighbors wkn@leland.stanford.edu has provided many useful bug reports and comments on MATLAB compatibility.

- Rick Niles niles@axp745.gsfc.nasa.gov rewrote Octave's plotting functions to add line styles and the ability to specify an unlimited number of lines in a single call. He also continues to track down odd incompatibilities and bugs.

- Mark Odegard meo@sugarland.unocal.com provided the initial implementation of fread, fwrite, feof, and ferror.

- Tony Richardson arichard@stark.cc.oh.us wrote Octave's image processing functions as well as most of the original polynomial functions.

- R. Bruce Tenison Bruce.Tenison@eng.auburn.edu wrote the hess and schur functions.

- Teresa Twaroch twaroch@ci.tuwien.ac.at provided the functions gls and ols.

- Andreas Weingessel Andreas.Weingessel@ci.tuwien.ac.at wrote the audio functions lin2mu, loadaudio, mu2lin, playaudio, record, saveaudio, and setaudio.

- Fook Fah Yap ffy@eng.cam.ac.uk provided the fft and ifft functions and valuable bug reports for early versions.

Special thanks to the following people and organizations for supporting the development of Octave:

- Digital Equipment Corporation, for an equipment grant as part of their External Research Program.

- Sun Microsystems, Inc., for an Academic Equipment grant.

- International Business Machines, Inc., for providing equipment as part of a grant to the University of Texas College of Engineering.

- Texaco Chemical Company, for providing funding to continue the development of this software.

- The University of Texas College of Engineering, for providing a Challenge for Excellence Research Supplement, and for providing an Academic Development Funds grant.

- The State of Texas, for providing funding through the Texas Advanced Technology Program under Grant No. 003658-078.

- Noel Bell, Senior Engineer, Texaco Chemical Company, Austin Texas.

- James B. Rawlings, Professor, University of Wisconsin-Madison, Department of Chemical Engineering.

- Richard Stallman, for writing GNU.

This project would not have been possible without the GNU software used in and used to produce Octave.

## How You Can Contribute to Octave

There are a number of ways that you can contribute to help make Octave a better system. Perhaps the most important way to contribute is to write high-quality code for solving new problems, and to make your code freely available for others to use.

If you find Octave useful, consider providing additional funding to continue its development. Even a modest amount of additional funding could make a significant difference in the amount of time that is available for development and support.

If you cannot provide funding or contribute code, you can still help make Octave better and more reliable by reporting any bugs you find and by offering suggestions for ways to improve Octave. See Appendix B [Trouble], page 251, for tips on how to write useful bug reports.

# Distribution

Octave is *free* software. This means that everyone is free to use it and free to redistribute it on certain conditions. Octave is not in the public domain. It is copyrighted and there are restrictions on its distribution, but the restrictions are designed to ensure that others will have the same freedom to use and redistribute Octave that you have. The precise conditions can be found in the GNU General Public License that comes with Octave and that also appears in Appendix E [Copying], page 281.

Octave is available on CD-ROM with various collections of other free software, and from the Free Software Foundation. Ordering a copy of Octave from the Free Software Foundation helps to fund the development of more free software. For more information, write to

Free Software Foundation
59 Temple Place—Suite 330
Boston, MA 02111–1307
USA

Octave is also available on the Internet from `ftp://ftp.che.wisc.edu/pub/octave`, and additional information is available from `http://www.octave.org/`.

# 1 A Brief Introduction to Octave

This manual documents how to run, install and port GNU Octave, and how to report bugs.

GNU Octave is a high-level language, primarily intended for numerical computations. It provides a convenient command line interface for solving linear and nonlinear problems numerically, and for performing other numerical experiments. It may also be used as a batch-oriented language.

GNU Octave is also freely redistributable software. You may redistribute it and/or modify it under the terms of the GNU General Public License as published by the Free Software Foundation. The GPL is included in this manual in Appendix E [Copying], page 281.

This document corresponds to Octave version 2.0.17.

## 1.1 Running Octave

On most systems, the way to invoke Octave is with the shell command 'octave'. Octave displays an initial message and then a prompt indicating it is ready to accept input. You can begin typing Octave commands immediately afterward.

If you get into trouble, you can usually interrupt Octave by typing *Control-C* (usually written *C-c* for short). *C-c* gets its name from the fact that you type it by holding down (CTRL) and then pressing ©. Doing this will normally return you to Octave's prompt.

To exit Octave, type *quit*, or *exit* at the Octave prompt.

On systems that support job control, you can suspend Octave by sending it a SIGTSTP signal, usually by typing *C-z*.

## 1.2 Simple Examples

The following chapters describe all of Octave's features in detail, but before doing that, it might be helpful to give a sampling of some of its capabilities.

If you are new to Octave, I recommend that you try these examples to begin learning Octave by using it. Lines marked with 'octave:13>' are lines you type, ending each with a carriage return. Octave will respond with an answer, or by displaying a graph.

### Creating a Matrix

To create a new matrix and store it in a variable so that it you can refer to it later, type the command

```
octave:1> a = [ 1, 1, 2; 3, 5, 8; 13, 21, 34 ]
```
Octave will respond by printing the matrix in neatly aligned columns.
Ending a command with a semicolon tells Octave to not print the result
of a command. For example
```
octave:2> b = rand (3, 2);
```
will create a 3 row, 2 column matrix with each element set to a random
value between zero and one.

To display the value of any variable, simply type the name of the
variable. For example, to display the value stored in the matrix b, type
the command
```
octave:3> b
```

## Matrix Arithmetic

Octave has a convenient operator notation for performing matrix arithmetic. For example, to multiply the matrix a by a scalar value, type the
command
```
octave:4> 2 * a
```
To multiply the two matrices a and b, type the command
```
octave:5> a * b
```
To form the matrix product $a^T a$, type the command
```
octave:6> a' * a
```

## Solving Linear Equations

To solve the set of linear equations ax = b, use the left division operator, '\':
```
octave:7> a \ b
```
This is conceptually equivalent to $a^{-1}b$, but avoids computing the inverse
of a matrix directly.

If the coefficient matrix is singular, Octave will print a warning message and compute a minimum norm solution.

## Integrating Differential Equations

Octave has built-in functions for solving nonlinear differential equations of the form

$$\frac{dx}{dt} = f(x,t), \qquad x(t = t_0) = x_0$$

For Octave to integrate equations of this form, you must first provide
a definition of the function $f(x,t)$. This is straightforward, and may be

accomplished by entering the function body directly on the command line. For example, the following commands define the right hand side function for an interesting pair of nonlinear differential equations. Note that while you are entering a function, Octave responds with a different prompt, to indicate that it is waiting for you to complete your input.

```
octave:8> function xdot = f (x, t)
>
>   r = 0.25;
>   k = 1.4;
>   a = 1.5;
>   b = 0.16;
>   c = 0.9;
>   d = 0.8;
>
>   xdot(1) = r*x(1)*(1 - x(1)/k) - a*x(1)*x(2)/(1 + b*x(1));
>   xdot(2) = c*a*x(1)*x(2)/(1 + b*x(1)) - d*x(2);
>
> endfunction
```

Given the initial condition

```
x0 = [1; 2];
```

and the set of output times as a column vector (note that the first output time corresponds to the initial condition given above)

```
t = linspace (0, 50, 200)';
```

it is easy to integrate the set of differential equations:

```
x = lsode ("f", x0, t);
```

The function lsode uses the Livermore Solver for Ordinary Differential Equations, described in A. C. Hindmarsh, *ODEPACK, a Systematized Collection of ODE Solvers*, in: Scientific Computing, R. S. Stepleman et al. (Eds.), North-Holland, Amsterdam, 1983, pages 55–64.

## Producing Graphical Output

To display the solution of the previous example graphically, use the command

```
plot (t, x)
```

If you are using the X Window System, Octave will automatically create a separate window to display the plot. If you are using a terminal that supports some other graphics commands, you will need to tell Octave what kind of terminal you have. Type the command

```
gset term
```

to see a list of the supported terminal types. Octave uses gnuplot to display graphics, and can display graphics on any terminal that is supported by gnuplot.

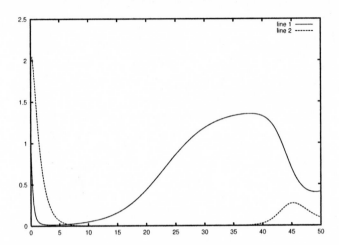

To capture the output of the plot command in a file rather than sending the output directly to your terminal, you can use a set of commands like this

```
gset term postscript
gset output "foo.ps"
replot
```

This will work for other types of output devices as well. Octave's gset command is really just piped to the gnuplot subprocess, so that once you have a plot on the screen that you like, you should be able to do something like this to create an output file suitable for your graphics printer.

Or, you can eliminate the intermediate file by using commands like this

```
gset term postscript
gset output "|lpr -Pname_of_your_graphics_printer"
replot
```

## Editing What You Have Typed

At the Octave prompt, you can recall, edit, and reissue previous commands using Emacs- or vi-style editing commands. The default keybindings use Emacs-style commands. For example, to recall the previous command, type *Control-p* (usually written *C-p* for short). *C-p* gets its name from the fact that you type it by holding down (CTRL) and then pressing

ⓟ. Doing this will normally bring back the previous line of input. *C-n* will bring up the next line of input, *C-b* will move the cursor backward on the line, *C-f* will move the cursor forward on the line, etc.

A complete description of the command line editing capability is given in this manual in Section 2.4 [Command Line Editing], page 23.

## Getting Help

Octave has an extensive help facility. The same documentation that is available in printed form is also available from the Octave prompt, because both forms of the documentation are created from the same input file.

In order to get good help you first need to know the name of the command that you want to use. This name of the function may not always be obvious, but a good place to start is to just type help. This will show you all the operators, reserved words, functions, built-in variables, and function files. You can then get more help on anything that is listed by simply including the name as an argument to help. For example,

    help plot

will display the help text for the plot function.

Octave sends output that is too long to fit on one screen through a pager like less or more. Type a (RET) to advance one line, a (SPC) to advance one page, and ⓠ to exit the pager.

The part of Octave's help facility that allows you to read the complete text of the printed manual from within Octave normally uses a separate program called Info. When you invoke Info you will be put into a menu driven program that contains the entire Octave manual. Help for using Info is provided in this manual in Section 2.3 [Getting Help], page 22.

## 1.3 Conventions

This section explains the notational conventions that are used in this manual. You may want to skip this section and refer back to it later.

### 1.3.1 Fonts

Examples of Octave code appear in this font or form: svd (a). Names that represent arguments or metasyntactic variables appear in this font or form: *first-number*. Commands that you type at the shell prompt sometimes appear in this font or form: 'octave --no-init-file'. Commands that you type at the Octave prompt sometimes appear in this font or form: *foo --bar --baz*. Specific keys on your keyboard appear in this font or form: (ANY).

## 1.3.2 Evaluation Notation

In the examples in this manual, results from expressions that you evaluate are indicated with '⇒'. For example,

```
sqrt (2)
    ⇒ 1.4142
```

You can read this as "sqrt (2) evaluates to 1.4142".

In some cases, matrix values that are returned by expressions are displayed like this

```
[1, 2; 3, 4] == [1, 3; 2, 4]
    ⇒ [ 1, 0; 0, 1 ]
```

and in other cases, they are displayed like this

```
eye (3)
    ⇒   1   0   0
        0   1   0
        0   0   1
```

in order to clearly show the structure of the result.

Sometimes to help describe one expression, another expression is shown that produces identical results. The exact equivalence of expressions is indicated with '≡'. For example,

```
rot90 ([1, 2; 3, 4], -1)
≡
rot90 ([1, 2; 3, 4], 3)
≡
rot90 ([1, 2; 3, 4], 7)
```

## 1.3.3 Printing Notation

Many of the examples in this manual print text when they are evaluated. Examples in this manual indicate printed text with ' ⊣ '. The value that is returned by evaluating the expression (here 1) is displayed with '⇒' and follows on a separate line.

```
printf ("foo %s\n", "bar")
    ⊣ foo bar
    ⇒ 1
```

## 1.3.4 Error Messages

Some examples signal errors. This normally displays an error message on your terminal. Error messages are shown on a line starting with error:.

```
struct_elements ([1, 2; 3, 4])
error: struct_elements: wrong type argument 'matrix'
```

## 1.3.5 Format of Descriptions

Functions, commands, and variables are described in this manual in a uniform format. The first line of a description contains the name of the item followed by its arguments, if any. The category—function, variable, or whatever—is printed next to the right margin. The description follows on succeeding lines, sometimes with examples.

## 1.3.5.1 A Sample Function Description

In a function description, the name of the function being described appears first. It is followed on the same line by a list of parameters. The names used for the parameters are also used in the body of the description.

Here is a description of an imaginary function foo:

**foo** $(x, y, \ldots)$                                                           Function

The function foo subtracts $x$ from $y$, then adds the remaining arguments to the result. If $y$ is not supplied, then the number 19 is used by default.

```
foo (1, [3, 5], 3, 9)
     ⇒ [ 14, 16 ]
foo (5)
     ⇒ 14
```

More generally,

```
foo (w, x, y, ...)
     ≡
x - w + y + ...
```

Any parameter whose name contains the name of a type (e.g., *integer*, *integer1* or *matrix*) is expected to be of that type. Parameters named *object* may be of any type. Parameters with other sorts of names (e.g., *new_file*) are discussed specifically in the description of the function. In some sections, features common to parameters of several functions are described at the beginning.

Functions in Octave may be defined in several different ways. The category name for functions may include another name that indicates the way that the function is defined. These additional tags include

Built-in Function

The function described is written in a language like C++, C, or Fortran, and is part of the compiled Octave binary.

Loadable Function

> The function described is written in a language like C++,
> C, or Fortran. On systems that support dynamic linking of
> user-supplied functions, it may be automatically linked while
> Octave is running, but only if it is needed. See Section 11.8
> [Dynamically Linked Functions], page 113.

Function File

> The function described is defined using Octave commands
> stored in a text file. See Section 11.6 [Function Files],
> page 109.

Mapping Function

> The function described works element-by-element for matrix
> and vector arguments.

## 1.3.5.2 A Sample Command Description

Command descriptions have a format similar to function descriptions,
except that the word 'Function' is replaced by 'Command. Commands are
functions that may called without surrounding their arguments in parentheses. For example, here is the description for Octave's cd command:

**cd** *dir*                                                          Command
**chdir** *dir*                                                       Command

> Change the current working directory to *dir*. For example, *cd*
> *~/octave* changes the current working directory to '~/octave'. If the
> directory does not exist, an error message is printed and the working
> directory is not changed.

## 1.3.5.3 A Sample Variable Description

A *variable* is a name that can hold a value. Although any variable can
be set by the user, *built-in variables* typically exist specifically so that
users can change them to alter the way Octave behaves (built-in variables
are also sometimes called *user options*). Ordinary variables and built-in
variables are described using a format like that for functions except that
there are no arguments.

Here is a description of the imaginary variable do_what_i_mean_not_
what_i_say.

**do_what_i_mean_not_what_i_say**                         Built-in Variable

> If the value of this variable is nonzero, Octave will do what you actually
> wanted, even if you have typed a completely different and meaningless
> list of commands.

Other variable descriptions have the same format, but 'Built-in Variable' is replaced by 'Variable', for ordinary variables, or 'Constant' for symbolic constants whose values cannot be changed.

# 2 Getting Started

This chapter explains some of Octave's basic features, including how to start an Octave session, get help at the command prompt, edit the command line, and write Octave programs that can be executed as commands from your shell.

## 2.1 Invoking Octave

Normally, Octave is used interactively by running the program 'octave' without any arguments. Once started, Octave reads commands from the terminal until you tell it to exit.

You can also specify the name of a file on the command line, and Octave will read and execute the commands from the named file and then exit when it is finished.

You can further control how Octave starts by using the command-line options described in the next section, and Octave itself can remind you of the options available. Type 'octave --help' to display all available options and briefly describe their use ('octave -h' is a shorter equivalent).

### 2.1.1 Command Line Options

Here is a complete list of all the command line options that Octave accepts.

--debug
-d              Enter parser debugging mode. Using this option will cause
                Octave's parser to print a lot of information about the com-
                mands it reads, and is probably only useful if you are actually
                trying to debug the parser.

--echo-commands
-x              Echo commands as they are executed.

--exec-path *path*
                Specify the path to search for programs to run. The value of
                *path* specified on the command line will override any value of
                OCTAVE_EXEC_PATH found in the environment, but not any
                commands in the system or user startup files that set the
                built-in variable EXEC_PATH.

--help
-h
-?              Print short help message and exit.

`--info-file` *filename*

> Specify the name of the info file to use. The value of *filename* specified on the command line will override any value of `OCTAVE_INFO_FILE` found in the environment, but not any commands in the system or user startup files that set the built-in variable `INFO_FILE`.

`--info-program` *program*

> Specify the name of the info program to use. The value of *program* specified on the command line will override any value of `OCTAVE_INFO_PROGRAM` found in the environment, but not any commands in the system or user startup files that set the built-in variable `INFO_PROGRAM`.

`--interactive`

`-i`

> Force interactive behavior. This can be useful for running Octave via a remote shell command or inside an Emacs shell buffer. For another way to run Octave within Emacs, see Appendix D [Emacs], page 269.

`--no-init-file`

> Don't read the '`~/.octaverc`' or '`.octaverc`' files.

`--no-line-editing`

> Disable command-line editing.

`--no-site-file`

> Don't read the site-wide 'octaverc' file.

`--norc`

`-f`

> Don't read any of the system or user initialization files at startup. This is equivalent to using both of the options `--no-init-file` and `--no-site-file`.

`--path` *path*

`-p` *path*

> Specify the path to search for function files. The value of *path* specified on the command line will override any value of `OCTAVE_PATH` found in the environment, but not any commands in the system or user startup files that set the built-in variable `LOADPATH`.

`--silent`

`--quiet`

`-q`

> Don't print the usual greeting and version message at startup.

```
--traditional
--braindead
```
Set initial values for user-preference variables to the following values for compatibility with MATLAB.

| | |
|---|---|
| PS1 | = ">> " |
| PS2 | = "" |
| beep_on_error | = 1 |
| default_save_format | = "mat-binary" |
| define_all_return_values | = 1 |
| do_fortran_indexing | = 1 |
| crash_dumps_octave_core | = 0 |
| empty_list_elements_ok | = 1 |
| implicit_str_to_num_ok | = 1 |
| ok_to_lose_imaginary_part | = 1 |
| page_screen_output | = 0 |
| prefer_column_vectors | = 0 |
| print_empty_dimensions | = 0 |
| treat_neg_dim_as_zero | = 1 |
| warn_function_name_clash | = 0 |
| whitespace_in_literal_matrix | = "traditional" |

```
--verbose
-V
```
Turn on verbose output.

```
--version
-v
```
Print the program version number and exit.

*file*          Execute commands from *file*.

Octave also includes several built-in variables that contain information about the command line, including the number of arguments and all of the options.

**argv**                                                    Built-in Variable

The command line arguments passed to Octave are available in this variable. For example, if you invoked Octave using the command

```
octave --no-line-editing --silent
```

argv would be a string vector with the elements --no-line-editing and --silent.

If you write an executable Octave script, argv will contain the list of arguments passed to the script. see Section 2.6 [Executable Octave Programs], page 32.

**program_invocation_name**                             Built-in Variable
**program_name**                                        Built-in Variable

When Octave starts, the value of the built-in variable `program_`
`invocation_name` is automatically set to the name that was typed at
the shell prompt to run Octave, and the value of `program_name` is automatically set to the final component of `program_invocation_name`.
For example, if you typed '/usr/local/bin/octave' to start Octave,
`program_invocation_name` would have the value "/usr/local/bin/
octave", and `program_name` would have the value "octave".

If executing a script from the command line (e.g., `octave foo.m`) or
using an executable Octave script, the program name is set to the name
of the script. See Section 2.6 [Executable Octave Programs], page 32
for an example of how to create an executable Octave script.

Here is an example of using these variables to reproduce Octave's
command line.

```
printf ("%s", program_name);
for i = 1:nargin
  printf (" %s", argv(i,:));
endfor
printf ("\n");
```

See Section 8.1 [Index Expressions], page 71 for an explanation of how
to properly index arrays of strings and substrings in Octave, and See
Section 11.1 [Defining Functions], page 101 for information about the
variable `nargin`.

## 2.1.2 Startup Files

When Octave starts, it looks for commands to execute from the following files:

*octave-home*/share/octave/site/m/startup/octaverc
> Where *octave-home* is the directory in which all of Octave is
> installed (the default is '/usr/local'). This file is provided
> so that changes to the default Octave environment can be
> made globally for all users at your site for all versions of
> Octave you have installed. Some care should be taken when
> making changes to this file, since all users of Octave at your
> site will be affected.

*octave-home*/share/octave/*version*/m/startup/octaverc
> Where *octave-home* is the directory in which all of Octave is
> installed (the default is '/usr/local'), and *version* is the ver-
> sion number of Octave. This file is provided so that changes

to the default Octave environment can be made globally for all users for a particular version of Octave. Some care should be taken when making changes to this file, since all users of Octave at your site will be affected.

~/.octaverc

This file is normally used to make personal changes to the default Octave environment.

.octaverc    This file can be used to make changes to the default Octave environment for a particular project. Octave searches for this file in the current directory after it reads '~/.octaverc'. Any use of the cd command in the '~/.octaverc' file will affect the directory that Octave searches for the file '.octaverc'.

If you start Octave in your home directory, commands from from the file '~/.octaverc' will only be executed once.

A message will be displayed as each of the startup files is read if you invoke Octave with the --verbose option but without the --silent option.

Startup files may contain any valid Octave commands, including function definitions.

## 2.2  Quitting Octave

**exit** (*status*)                                                Built-in Function
**quit** (*status*)                                                Built-in Function
    Exit the current Octave session. If the optional integer value *status* is supplied, pass that value to the operating system as the Octave's exit status.

**atexit** (*fcn*)                                                 Built-in Function
    Register function to be called when Octave exits. For example,

```
function print_flops_at_exit ()
  printf ("\n%s\n", system ("fortune"));
  fflush (stdout);
endfunction
atexit ("print_flops_at_exit");
```

    will print a message when Octave exits.

# 2.3  Commands for Getting Help

The entire text of this manual is available from the Octave prompt
via the command *help -i*. In addition, the documentation for individual
user-written functions and variables is also available via the *help* command. This section describes the commands used for reading the manual
and the documentation strings for user-supplied functions and variables.
See Section 11.6 [Function Files], page 109, for more information about
how to document the functions you write.

**help**                                                   Command

Octave's help command can be used to print brief usage-style messages, or to display information directly from an on-line version of the
printed manual, using the GNU Info browser. If invoked without any
arguments, help prints a list of all the available operators, functions,
and built-in variables. If the first argument is -i, the help command
searches the index of the on-line version of this manual for the given
topics.

For example, the command *help help* prints a short message describing the help command, and *help -i help* starts the GNU Info browser
at this node in the on-line version of the manual.

Once the GNU Info browser is running, help for using it is available
using the command *C-h*.

The help command can give you information about operators, but not
the comma and semicolons that are used as command separators. To get
help for those, you must type *help comma* or *help semicolon*.

**INFO_FILE**                                         Built-in Variable

The variable INFO_FILE names the location of the Octave info file. The
default value is "*octave-home*/info/octave.info", where *octave-
home* is the directory where all of Octave is installed.

**INFO_PROGRAM**                                      Built-in Variable

The variable INFO_PROGRAM names the info program to run.  Its
initial value is "*octave-home*/libexec/octave/*version*/exec/*arch*/
info", where *octave-home* is the directory where all of Octave is installed, *version* is the Octave version number, and *arch* is the machine
type. The value of INFO_PROGRAM can be overridden by the environment variable OCTAVE_INFO_PROGRAM, or the command line argument
--info-program NAME, or by setting the value of the built-in variable
INFO_PROGRAM in a startup script.

**suppress_verbose_help_message**                           Built-in Variable

If the value of `suppress_verbose_help_message` is nonzero, Octave will not add additional help information to the end of the output from the `help` command and usage messages for built-in commands.

# 2.4 Command Line Editing

Octave uses the GNU readline library to provide an extensive set of command-line editing and history features. Only the most common features are described in this manual. Please see The GNU Readline Library manual for more information.

To insert printing characters (letters, digits, symbols, etc.), simply type the character. Octave will insert the character at the cursor and advance the cursor forward.

Many of the command-line editing functions operate using control characters. For example, the character `Control-a` moves the cursor to the beginning of the line. To type `C-a`, hold down (CTRL) and then press (a). In the following sections, control characters such as `Control-a` are written as `C-a`.

Another set of command-line editing functions use Meta characters. On some terminals, you type `M-u` by holding down (META) and pressing (u). If your terminal does not have a (META) key, you can still type Meta characters using two-character sequences starting with *ESC*. Thus, to enter `M-u`, you could type (ESC)(u). The *ESC* character sequences are also allowed on terminals with real Meta keys. In the following sections, Meta characters such as `Meta-u` are written as `M-u`.

## 2.4.1 Cursor Motion

The following commands allow you to position the cursor.

`C-b`        Move back one character.

`C-f`        Move forward one character.

(DEL)        Delete the character to the left of the cursor.

`C-d`        Delete the character underneath the cursor.

`M-f`        Move forward a word.

`M-b`        Move backward a word.

`C-a`        Move to the start of the line.

`C-e`        Move to the end of the line.

`C-l`        Clear the screen, reprinting the current line at the top.

C-_  
C-/         Undo the last thing that you did. You can undo all the way  
            back to an empty line.

M-r         Undo all changes made to this line. This is like typing the  
            'undo' command enough times to get back to the beginning.

The above table describes the most basic possible keystrokes that you need in order to do editing of the input line. On most terminals, you can also use the arrow keys in place of C-f and C-b to move forward and backward.

Notice how C-f moves forward a character, while M-f moves forward a word. It is a loose convention that control keystrokes operate on characters while meta keystrokes operate on words.

There is also a function available so that you can clear the screen from within Octave programs.

clc ()                                              Built-in Function  
home ()                                             Built-in Function  
     Clear the terminal screen and move the cursor to the upper left corner.

## 2.4.2 Killing and Yanking

*Killing* text means to delete the text from the line, but to save it away for later use, usually by *yanking* it back into the line. If the description for a command says that it 'kills' text, then you can be sure that you can get the text back in a different (or the same) place later.

Here is the list of commands for killing text.

C-k         Kill the text from the current cursor position to the end of  
            the line.

M-d         Kill from the cursor to the end of the current word, or if  
            between words, to the end of the next word.

M-⟨DEL⟩     Kill from the cursor to the start of the previous word, or if  
            between words, to the start of the previous word.

C-w         Kill from the cursor to the previous whitespace. This is  
            different than M-⟨DEL⟩ because the word boundaries differ.

And, here is how to *yank* the text back into the line. Yanking means to copy the most-recently-killed text from the kill buffer.

C-y         Yank the most recently killed text back into the buffer at  
            the cursor.

| | |
|---|---|
| *M-y* | Rotate the kill-ring, and yank the new top. You can only do this if the prior command is *C-y* or *M-y*. |

When you use a kill command, the text is saved in a *kill-ring*. Any number of consecutive kills save all of the killed text together, so that when you yank it back, you get it in one clean sweep. The kill ring is not line specific; the text that you killed on a previously typed line is available to be yanked back later, when you are typing another line.

## 2.4.3 Commands For Changing Text

The following commands can be used for entering characters that would otherwise have a special meaning (e.g., *TAB*, *C-q*, etc.), or for quickly correcting typing mistakes.

| | |
|---|---|
| *C-q* | |
| *C-v* | Add the next character that you type to the line verbatim. This is how to insert things like *C-q* for example. |
| *M-*(TAB) | Insert a tab character. |
| *C-t* | Drag the character before the cursor forward over the character at the cursor, also moving the cursor forward. If the cursor is at the end of the line, then transpose the two characters before it. |
| *M-t* | Drag the word behind the cursor past the word in front of the cursor moving the cursor over that word as well. |
| *M-u* | Uppercase the characters following the cursor to the end of the current (or following) word, moving the cursor to the end of the word. |
| *M-l* | Lowercase the characters following the cursor to the end of the current (or following) word, moving the cursor to the end of the word. |
| *M-c* | Uppercase the character following the cursor (or the beginning of the next word if the cursor is between words), moving the cursor to the end of the word. |

## 2.4.4 Letting Readline Type For You

The following commands allow Octave to complete command and variable names for you.

| | |
|---|---|
| (TAB) | Attempt to do completion on the text before the cursor. Octave can complete the names of commands and variables. |
| *M-?* | List the possible completions of the text before the cursor. |

**completion_append_char**                                         Built-in Variable

   The value of `completion_append_char` is used as the character to
   append to successful command-line completion attempts. The default
   value is " " (a single space).

**completion_matches** (*hint*)                                   Built-in Function

   Generate possible completions given *hint*.

   This function is provided for the benefit of programs like Emacs which
   might be controlling Octave and handling user input. The current
   command number is not incremented when this function is called. This
   is a feature, not a bug.

## 2.4.5  Commands For Manipulating The History

   Octave normally keeps track of the commands you type so that you
can recall previous commands to edit or execute them again. When you
exit Octave, the most recent commands you have typed, up to the number
specified by the variable `history_size`, are saved in a file. When Octave
starts, it loads an initial list of commands from the file named by the
variable `history_file`.

   Here are the commands for simple browsing and searching the history
list.

⟨LFD⟩
⟨RET⟩          Accept the line regardless of where the cursor is. If this
              line is non-empty, add it to the history list. If this line was a
              history line, then restore the history line to its original state.

*C-p*          Move 'up' through the history list.

*C-n*          Move 'down' through the history list.

*M-<*          Move to the first line in the history.

*M->*          Move to the end of the input history, i.e., the line you are
              entering!

*C-r*          Search backward starting at the current line and moving 'up'
              through the history as necessary. This is an incremental
              search.

*C-s*          Search forward starting at the current line and moving
              'down' through the history as necessary.

   On most terminals, you can also use the arrow keys in place of *C-p*
and *C-n* to move through the history list.

In addition to the keyboard commands for moving through the history list, Octave provides three functions for viewing, editing, and re-running chunks of commands from the history list.

**history** *options*                                                      Command
If invoked with no arguments, history displays a list of commands that you have executed. Valid options are:

-w *file*          Write the current history to the file *file*. If the name is omitted, use the default history file (normally '~/.octave_hist').

-r *file*          Read the file *file*, replacing the current history list with its contents. If the name is omitted, use the default history file (normally '~/.octave_hist').

*N*          Only display the most recent *N* lines of history.

-q          Don't number the displayed lines of history. This is useful for cutting and pasting commands if you are using the X Window System.

For example, to display the five most recent commands that you have typed without displaying line numbers, use the command *history -q 5*.

**edit_history** *options*                                                 Command
If invoked with no arguments, edit_history allows you to edit the history list using the editor named by the variable EDITOR. The commands to be edited are first copied to a temporary file. When you exit the editor, Octave executes the commands that remain in the file. It is often more convenient to use edit_history to define functions rather than attempting to enter them directly on the command line. By default, the block of commands is executed as soon as you exit the editor. To avoid executing any commands, simply delete all the lines from the buffer before exiting the editor.

The edit_history command takes two optional arguments specifying the history numbers of first and last commands to edit. For example, the command

```
edit_history 13
```

extracts all the commands from the 13th through the last in the history list. The command

```
edit_history 13 169
```

only extracts commands 13 through 169. Specifying a larger number for the first command than the last command reverses the list of commands before placing them in the buffer to be edited. If both arguments are omitted, the previous command in the history list is used.

**run_history**                                                    Command
A
Similar to edit_history, except that the editor is not invoked, and the commands are simply executed as they appear in the history list.

**EDITOR**                                              Built-in Variable
A string naming the editor to use with the edit_history command. If the environment variable EDITOR is set when Octave starts, its value is used as the default. Otherwise, EDITOR is set to "emacs".

**history_file**                                        Built-in Variable
This variable specifies the name of the file used to store command history. The default value is "~/.octave_hist", but may be overridden by the environment variable OCTAVE_HISTFILE.

**history_size**                                        Built-in Variable
This variable specifies how many entries to store in the history file. The default value is 1024, but may be overridden by the environment variable OCTAVE_HISTSIZE.

**saving_history**                                      Built-in Variable
If the value of saving_history is nonzero, command entered on the command line are saved in the file specified by the variable history_file.

## 2.4.6 Customizing the Prompt

The following variables are available for customizing the appearance of the command-line prompts. Octave allows the prompt to be customized by inserting a number of backslash-escaped special characters that are decoded as follows:

'\t'        The time.

'\d'        The date.

'\n'        Begins a new line by printing the equivalent of a carriage return followed by a line feed.

'\s'        The name of the program (usually just 'octave').

'\w'        The current working directory.

'\W'            The basename of the current working directory.

'\u'            The username of the current user.

'\h'            The hostname, up to the first '.'.

'\H'            The hostname.

'\#'            The command number of this command, counting from when
                Octave starts.

'\!'            The history number of this command. This differs from '\#'
                by the number of commands in the history list when Octave
                starts.

'\$'            If the effective UID is 0, a '#', otherwise a '$'.

'\nnn'          The character whose character code in octal is *nnn*.

'\\'            A backslash.

**PS1**                                                        Built-in Variable
    The primary prompt string.  When executing interactively, Octave
    displays the primary prompt PS1 when it is ready to read a command.
    The default value of PS1 is "\s:\#> ". To change it, use a command
    like

        octave:13> PS1 = "\\u@\\H> "

    which will result in the prompt 'boris@kremvax> ' for the user 'boris'
    logged in on the host 'kremvax.kgb.su'. Note that two backslashes
    are required to enter a backslash into a string. See Chapter 5 [Strings],
    page 47.

**PS2**                                                        Built-in Variable
    The secondary prompt string, which is printed when Octave is ex-
    pecting additional input to complete a command. For example, when
    defining a function over several lines, Octave will print the value of
    PS1 at the beginning of each line after the first. The default value of
    PS2 is "> ".

**PS4**                                                        Built-in Variable
    If Octave is invoked with the --echo-input option, the value of PS4
    is printed before each line of input that is echoed. The default value
    of PS4 is "+ ". See Section 2.1 [Invoking Octave], page 17, for a de-
    scription of --echo-input.

## 2.4.7  Diary and Echo Commands

Octave's diary feature allows you to keep a log of all or part of an interactive session by recording the input you type and the output that Octave produces in a separate file.

**diary** *options*                                          Command
> Create a list of all commands *and* the output they produce, mixed together just as you see them on your terminal. Valid options are:
>
> on          Start recording your session in a file called 'diary' in your current working directory.
>
> off         Stop recording your session in the diary file.
>
> *file*        Record your session in the file named *file*.
>
> Without any arguments, diary toggles the current diary state.

Sometimes it is useful to see the commands in a function or script as they are being evaluated. This can be especially helpful for debugging some kinds of problems.

**echo** *options*                                          Command
> Control whether commands are displayed as they are executed. Valid options are:
>
> on          Enable echoing of commands as they are executed in script files.
>
> off         Disable echoing of commands as they are executed in script files.
>
> on all      Enable echoing of commands as they are executed in script files and functions.
>
> off all     Disable echoing of commands as they are executed in script files and functions.
>
> If invoked without any arguments, echo toggles the current echo state.

**echo_executing_commands**                              Built-in Variable
> This variable may also be used to control the echo state. It may be the sum of the following values:
>
> 1           Echo commands read from script files.
>
> 2           Echo commands from functions.
>
> 4           Echo commands read from command line.

More than one state can be active at once. For example, a value of 3 is equivalent to the command *echo on all*.

The value of echo_executing_commands is set by the *echo* command and the command line option --echo-input.

## 2.5 How Octave Reports Errors

Octave reports two kinds of errors for invalid programs.

A *parse error* occurs if Octave cannot understand something you have typed. For example, if you misspell a keyword,

```
octave:13> functon y = f (x) y = x^2; endfunction
```

Octave will respond immediately with a message like this:

```
parse error:

    functon y = f (x) y = x^2; endfunction
                ^
```

For most parse errors, Octave uses a caret ('^') to mark the point on the line where it was unable to make sense of your input. In this case, Octave generated an error message because the keyword function was misspelled. Instead of seeing 'function f', Octave saw two consecutive variable names, which is invalid in this context. It marked the error at y because the first name by itself was accepted as valid input.

Another class of error message occurs at evaluation time. These errors are called *run-time errors*, or sometimes *evaluation errors* because they occur when your program is being *run*, or *evaluated*. For example, if after correcting the mistake in the previous function definition, you type

```
octave:13> f ()
```

Octave will respond with

```
error: 'x' undefined near line 1 column 24
error: evaluating expression near line 1, column 24
error: evaluating assignment expression near line 1, column 22
error: called from 'f'
```

This error message has several parts, and gives you quite a bit of information to help you locate the source of the error. The messages are generated from the point of the innermost error, and provide a traceback of enclosing expressions and function calls.

In the example above, the first line indicates that a variable named 'x' was found to be undefined near line 1 and column 24 of some function or expression. For errors occurring within functions, lines are counted from the beginning of the file containing the function definition. For errors occurring at the top level, the line number indicates the input line number, which is usually displayed in the prompt string.

The second and third lines in the example indicate that the error occurred within an assignment expression, and the last line of the error message indicates that the error occurred within the function f. If the function f had been called from another function, for example, g, the list of errors would have ended with one more line:

```
error: called from 'g'
```

These lists of function calls usually make it fairly easy to trace the path your program took before the error occurred, and to correct the error before trying again.

## 2.6  Executable Octave Programs

Once you have learned Octave, you may want to write self-contained Octave scripts, using the '#!' script mechanism. You can do this on GNU systems and on many Unix systems[1]

For example, you could create a text file named 'hello', containing the following lines:

```
#! octave-interpreter-name -qf
# a sample Octave program
printf ("Hello, world!\n");
```

(where *octave-interpreter-name* should be replaced with the full file name for your Octave binary). After making this file executable (with the chmod command), you can simply type:

```
hello
```

at the shell, and the system will arrange to run Octave as if you had typed:

```
octave hello
```

The line beginning with '#!' lists the full file name of an interpreter to be run, and an optional initial command line argument to pass to that interpreter. The operating system then runs the interpreter with the given argument and the full argument list of the executed program. The first argument in the list is the full file name of the Octave program. The rest of the argument list will either be options to Octave, or data files, or both. The '-qf' option is usually specified in stand-alone Octave programs to prevent them from printing the normal startup message, and to keep them from behaving differently depending on the contents of a particular user's

---

[1] The '#!' mechanism works on Unix systems derived from Berkeley Unix, System V Release 4, and some System V Release 3 systems.

'~/.octaverc' file. See Section 2.1 [Invoking Octave], page 17. Note that some operating systems may place a limit on the number of characters that are recognized after '#!'.

Self-contained Octave scripts are useful when you want to write a program which users can invoke without knowing that the program is written in the Octave language.

If you invoke an executable Octave script with command line arguments, the arguments are available in the built-in variable argv. See Section 2.1.1 [Command Line Options], page 17. For example, the following program will reproduce the command line that is used to execute it.

```
#! /bin/octave -qf
printf ("%s", program_name);
for i = 1:nargin
  printf (" %s", argv(i,:));
endfor
printf ("\n");
```

## 2.7  Comments in Octave Programs

A *comment* is some text that is included in a program for the sake of human readers, and that is not really part of the program. Comments can explain what the program does, and how it works. Nearly all programming languages have provisions for comments, because programs are typically hard to understand without them.

In the Octave language, a comment starts with either the sharp sign character, '#', or the percent symbol '%' and continues to the end of the line. The Octave interpreter ignores the rest of a line following a sharp sign or percent symbol. For example, we could have put the following into the function f:

```
function xdot = f (x, t)

# usage: f (x, t)
#
# This function defines the right hand
# side functions for a set of nonlinear
# differential equations.

  r = 0.25;
  ...
endfunction
```

The `help` command (see Section 2.3 [Getting Help], page 22) is able
to find the first block of comments in a function (even those that are
composed directly on the command line). This means that users of Octave
can use the same commands to get help for built-in functions, and for
functions that you have defined. For example, after defining the function
`f` above, the command *help f* produces the output

```
usage: f (x, t)

This function defines the right hand
side functions for a set of nonlinear
differential equations.
```

Although it is possible to put comment lines into keyboard-composed
throw-away Octave programs, it usually isn't very useful, because the
purpose of a comment is to help you or another person understand the
program at a later time.

# 3 Data Types

All versions of Octave include a number of built-in data types, including real and complex scalars and matrices, character strings, and a data structure type.

It is also possible to define new specialized data types by writing a small amount of C++ code. On some systems, new data types can be loaded dynamically while Octave is running, so it is not necessary to recompile all of Octave just to add a new type. See Section 11.8 [Dynamically Linked Functions], page 113 for more information about Octave's dynamic linking capabilities. Section 3.2 [User-defined Data Types], page 36 describes what you must do to define a new data type for Octave.

## 3.1 Built-in Data Types

The standard built-in data types are real and complex scalars and matrices, ranges, character strings, and a data structure type. Additional built-in data types may be added in future versions. If you need a specialized data type that is not currently provided as a built-in type, you are encouraged to write your own user-defined data type and contribute it for distribution in a future release of Octave.

### 3.1.1 Numeric Objects

Octave's built-in numeric objects include real and complex scalars and matrices. All built-in numeric data is currently stored as double precision numbers. On systems that use the IEEE floating point format, values in the range of approximately $2.2251 \times 10^{-308}$ to $1.7977 \times 10^{308}$ can be stored, and the relative precision is approximately $2.2204 \times 10^{-16}$. The exact values are given by the variables realmin, realmax, and eps, respectively.

Matrix objects can be of any size, and can be dynamically reshaped and resized. It is easy to extract individual rows, columns, or submatrices using a variety of powerful indexing features. See Section 8.1 [Index Expressions], page 71.

See Chapter 4 [Numeric Data Types], page 39, for more information.

### 3.1.2 String Objects

A character string in Octave consists of a sequence of characters enclosed in either double-quote or single-quote marks. Internally, Octave currently stores strings as matrices of characters. All the indexing operations that work for matrix objects also work for strings.

See Chapter 5 [Strings], page 47, for more information.

### 3.1.3 Data Structure Objects

Octave's data structure type can help you to organize related objects of
different types. The current implementation uses an associative array with
indices limited to strings, but the syntax is more like C-style structures.

See Chapter 6 [Data Structures], page 55, for more information.

## 3.2 User-defined Data Types

Someday I hope to expand this to include a complete description of
Octave's mechanism for managing user-defined data types. Until this
feature is documented here, you will have to make do by reading the code
in the 'ov.h', 'ops.h', and related files from Octave's 'src' directory.

## 3.3 Object Sizes

The following functions allow you to determine the size of a variable
or expression. These functions are defined for all objects. They return
−1 when the operation doesn't make sense. For example, Octave's data
structure type doesn't have rows or columns, so the rows and columns
functions return −1 for structure arguments.

**columns** (a)                                           Function File
> Return the number of columns of a.

**rows** (a)                                              Function File
> Return the number of rows of a.

**length** (a)                                            Function File
> Return the number of rows of a or the number of columns of a,
> whichever is larger.

**size** (a, n)                                           Function File
> Return the number rows and columns of a.
>
> With one input argument and one output argument, the result is re-
> turned in a 2 element row vector. If there are two output arguments,
> the number of rows is assigned to the first, and the number of columns
> to the second. For example,

```
    size ([1, 2; 3, 4; 5, 6])
       ⇒ [ 3, 2 ]

    [nr, nc] = size ([1, 2; 3, 4; 5, 6])
```

$\Rightarrow$ nr = 3

$\Rightarrow$ nc = 2

If given a second argument of either 1 or 2, size will return only the row or column dimension. For example

size ([1, 2; 3, 4; 5, 6], 2)

$\Rightarrow$ 2

returns the number of columns in the given matrix.

**isempty** (a)                                               Function File

Return 1 if a is an empty matrix (either the number of rows, or the number of columns, or both are zero). Otherwise, return 0.

# 4 Numeric Data Types

A *numeric constant* may be a scalar, a vector, or a matrix, and it may contain complex values.

The simplest form of a numeric constant, a scalar, is a single number that can be an integer, a decimal fraction, a number in scientific (exponential) notation, or a complex number. Note that all numeric constants are represented within Octave in double-precision floating point format (complex constants are stored as pairs of double-precision floating point values). Here are some examples of real-valued numeric constants, which all have the same value:

```
105
1.05e+2
1050e-1
```

To specify complex constants, you can write an expression of the form

```
3 + 4i
3.0 + 4.0i
0.3e1 + 40e-1i
```

all of which are equivalent. The letter 'i' in the previous example stands for the pure imaginary constant, defined as $\sqrt{-1}$.

For Octave to recognize a value as the imaginary part of a complex constant, a space must not appear between the number and the 'i'. If it does, Octave will print an error message, like this:

```
octave:13> 3 + 4 i

parse error:

   3 + 4 i
         ^
```

You may also use 'j', 'I', or 'J' in place of the 'i' above. All four forms are equivalent.

## 4.1 Matrices

It is easy to define a matrix of values in Octave. The size of the matrix is determined automatically, so it is not necessary to explicitly state the dimensions. The expression

```
a = [1, 2; 3, 4]
```

results in the matrix

$$a = \begin{bmatrix} 1 & 2 \\ 3 & 4 \end{bmatrix}$$

Elements of a matrix may be arbitrary expressions, provided that the dimensions all make sense when combining the various pieces. For example, given the above matrix, the expression

```
[ a, a ]
```
produces the matrix

```
ans =

   1   2   1   2
   3   4   3   4
```
but the expression

```
[ a, 1 ]
```
produces the error

```
error: number of rows must match near line 13, column 6
```
(assuming that this expression was entered as the first thing on line 13, of course).

Inside the square brackets that delimit a matrix expression, Octave looks at the surrounding context to determine whether spaces and newline characters should be converted into element and row separators, or simply ignored, so commands like

```
[ linspace (1, 2) ]
```
and

```
a = [ 1 2
      3 4 ]
```
will work. However, some possible sources of confusion remain. For example, in the expression

```
[ 1 - 1 ]
```
the '-' is treated as a binary operator and the result is the scalar 0, but in the expression

```
[ 1 -1 ]
```
the '-' is treated as a unary operator and the result is the vector [ 1, -1 ].

Given a = 1, the expression

```
[ 1 a' ]
```
results in the single quote character ''' being treated as a transpose operator and the result is the vector [ 1, 1 ], but the expression

```
[ 1 a ' ]
```
produces the error message

```
error: unterminated string constant
```

because to not do so would make it impossible to correctly parse the valid expression

```
[ a 'foo' ]
```

For clarity, it is probably best to always use commas and semicolons to separate matrix elements and rows. It is possible to enforce this style by setting the built-in variable whitespace_in_literal_matrix to "ignore".

**whitespace_in_literal_matrix**                              Built-in Variable

This variable allows some control over how Octave decides to convert spaces to commas and semicolons in matrix expressions like [m (1)] or

```
[ 1, 2,
  3, 4 ]
```

If the value of whitespace_in_literal_matrix is "ignore", Octave will never insert a comma or a semicolon in a literal matrix list. For example, the expression [1 2] will result in an error instead of being treated the same as [1, 2], and the expression

```
[ 1, 2,
  3, 4 ]
```

will result in the vector [ 1, 2, 3, 4 ] instead of a matrix.

If the value of whitespace_in_literal_matrix is "traditional", Octave will convert spaces to a comma between identifiers and '('. For example, given the matrix

```
m = [3 2]
```

the expression

```
[m (1)]
```

will be parsed as

```
[m, (1)]
```

and will result in

```
[3 2 1]
```

and the expression

```
[ 1, 2,
  3, 4 ]
```

will result in a matrix because the newline character is converted to a semicolon (row separator) even though there is a comma at the end of the first line (trailing commas or semicolons are ignored). This is apparently how MATLAB behaves.

Any other value for whitespace_in_literal_matrix results in behavior that is the same as traditional, except that Octave does not convert spaces to a comma between identifiers and '('. For example, the expression

```
[m (1)]
```

will produce '3'. This is the way Octave has always behaved.

When you type a matrix or the name of a variable whose value is a matrix, Octave responds by printing the matrix in with neatly aligned rows and columns. If the rows of the matrix are too large to fit on the screen, Octave splits the matrix and displays a header before each section to indicate which columns are being displayed. You can use the following variables to control the format of the output.

**output_max_field_width**                                    Built-in Variable
This variable specifies the maximum width of a numeric output field. The default value is 10.

**output_precision**                                          Built-in Variable
This variable specifies the minimum number of significant figures to display for numeric output. The default value is 5.

It is possible to achieve a wide range of output styles by using different values of output_precision and output_max_field_width. Reasonable combinations can be set using the format function. See Section 13.1 [Basic Input and Output], page 124.

**split_long_rows**                                           Built-in Variable
For large matrices, Octave may not be able to display all the columns of a given row on one line of your screen. This can result in missing information or output that is nearly impossible to decipher, depending on whether your terminal truncates or wraps long lines.

If the value of split_long_rows is nonzero, Octave will display the matrix in a series of smaller pieces, each of which can fit within the limits of your terminal width. Each set of rows is labeled so that you can easily see which columns are currently being displayed. For example:

```
octave:13> rand (2,10)
ans =

Columns 1 through 6:

  0.75883  0.93290  0.40064  0.43818  0.94958  0.16467
  0.75697  0.51942  0.40031  0.61784  0.92309  0.40201
```

Columns 7 through 10:

```
0.90174   0.11854   0.72313   0.73326
0.44672   0.94303   0.56564   0.82150
```

The default value of split_long_rows is nonzero.

Octave automatically switches to scientific notation when values become very large or very small. This guarantees that you will see several significant figures for every value in a matrix. If you would prefer to see all values in a matrix printed in a fixed point format, you can set the built-in variable fixed_point_format to a nonzero value. But doing so is not recommended, because it can produce output that can easily be misinterpreted.

fixed_point_format                                                      Built-in Variable
   If the value of this variable is nonzero, Octave will scale all values in a matrix so that the largest may be written with one leading digit. The scaling factor is printed on the first line of output. For example,

```
octave:1> logspace (1, 7, 5)'
ans =

   1.0e+07  *

   0.00000
   0.00003
   0.00100
   0.03162
   1.00000
```

   Notice that first value appears to be zero when it is actually 1. For this reason, you should be careful when setting fixed_point_format to a nonzero value.

   The default value of fixed_point_format is 0.

## 4.1.1 Empty Matrices

   A matrix may have one or both dimensions zero, and operations on empty matrices are handled as described by Carl de Boor in *An Empty Exercise*, SIGNUM, Volume 25, pages 2–6, 1990 and C. N. Nett and W. M. Haddad, in *A System-Theoretic Appropriate Realization of the Empty Matrix Concept*, IEEE Transactions on Automatic Control, Volume 38, Number 5, May 1993. Briefly, given a scalar $s$, an $m \times n$ matrix $M_{m \times n}$, and an $m \times n$ empty matrix $[\,]_{m \times n}$ (with either one or both dimensions equal to zero), the following are true:

$$s \cdot []_{m \times n} = []_{m \times n} \cdot s = []_{m \times n}$$
$$[]_{m \times n} + []_{m \times n} = []_{m \times n}$$
$$[]_{0 \times m} \cdot M_{m \times n} = []_{0 \times n}$$
$$M_{m \times n} \cdot []_{n \times 0} = []_{m \times 0}$$
$$[]_{m \times 0} \cdot []_{0 \times n} = 0_{m \times n}$$

By default, dimensions of the empty matrix are printed along with the empty matrix symbol, '[]'. The built-in variable print_empty_dimensions controls this behavior.

**print_empty_dimensions**                             Built-in Variable

If the value of print_empty_dimensions is nonzero, the dimensions of empty matrices are printed along with the empty matrix symbol, '[]'. For example, the expression

```
zeros (3, 0)
```

will print

```
ans = [] (3x0)
```

Empty matrices may also be used in assignment statements as a convenient way to delete rows or columns of matrices. See Section 8.6 [Assignment Expressions], page 81.

Octave will normally issue a warning if it finds an empty matrix in the list of elements that make up another matrix. You can use the variable empty_list_elements_ok to suppress the warning or to treat it as an error.

**empty_list_elements_ok**                             Built-in Variable

This variable controls whether Octave ignores empty matrices in a matrix list.

For example, if the value of empty_list_elements_ok is nonzero, Octave will ignore the empty matrices in the expression

```
a = [1, [], 3, [], 5]
```

and the variable a will be assigned the value [ 1, 3, 5 ].

The default value is "warn".

When Octave parses a matrix expression, it examines the elements of the list to determine whether they are all constants. If they are, it replaces the list with a single matrix constant.

**propagate_empty_matrices**                                    Built-in Variable

    If the value of `propagate_empty_matrices` is nonzero, functions like `inverse` and `svd` will return an empty matrix if they are given one as an argument. The default value is 1.

## 4.2 Ranges

    A *range* is a convenient way to write a row vector with evenly spaced elements. A range expression is defined by the value of the first element in the range, an optional value for the increment between elements, and a maximum value which the elements of the range will not exceed. The base, increment, and limit are separated by colons (the ':' character) and may contain any arithmetic expressions and function calls. If the increment is omitted, it is assumed to be 1. For example, the range

    1 : 5

defines the set of values '[ 1, 2, 3, 4, 5 ]', and the range

    1 : 3 : 5

defines the set of values '[ 1, 4 ]'.

    Although a range constant specifies a row vector, Octave does *not* convert range constants to vectors unless it is necessary to do so. This allows you to write a constant like '1 : 10000' without using 80,000 bytes of storage on a typical 32-bit workstation.

    Note that the upper (or lower, if the increment is negative) bound on the range is not always included in the set of values, and that ranges defined by floating point values can produce surprising results because Octave uses floating point arithmetic to compute the values in the range. If it is important to include the endpoints of a range and the number of elements is known, you should use the `linspace` function instead (see Section 15.3 [Special Utility Matrices], page 168).

    When Octave parses a range expression, it examines the elements of the expression to determine whether they are all constants. If they are, it replaces the range expression with a single range constant.

## 4.3 Predicates for Numeric Objects

**is_matrix** (*a*)                                              Function File

    Return 1 if *a* is a matrix. Otherwise, return 0.

**is_vector** (*a*)                                              Function File

    Return 1 if *a* is a vector. Otherwise, return 0.

**is_scalar** (a)                                                    Function File
    Return 1 if a is a scalar. Otherwise, return 0.

**is_square** (x)                                                    Function File
    If x is a square matrix, then return the dimension of x. Otherwise,
    return 0.

**is_symmetric** (x, tol)                                            Function File
    If x is symmetric within the tolerance specified by tol, then return the
    dimension of x. Otherwise, return 0. If tol is omitted, use a tolerance
    equal to the machine precision.

# 5  Strings

A *string constant* consists of a sequence of characters enclosed in either double-quote or single-quote marks. For example, both of the following expressions

    "parrot"
    'parrot'

represent the string whose contents are 'parrot'. Strings in Octave can be of any length.

Since the single-quote mark is also used for the transpose operator (see Section 8.3 [Arithmetic Ops], page 76) but double-quote marks have no other purpose in Octave, it is best to use double-quote marks to denote strings.

Some characters cannot be included literally in a string constant. You represent them instead with *escape sequences*, which are character sequences beginning with a backslash ('\').

One use of an escape sequence is to include a double-quote (single-quote) character in a string constant that has been defined using double-quote (single-quote) marks. Since a plain double-quote would end the string, you must use '\"' to represent a single double-quote character as a part of the string. The backslash character itself is another character that cannot be included normally. You must write '\\' to put one backslash in the string. Thus, the string whose contents are the two characters '"\' may be written "\"\\" or '"\\'. Similarly, the string whose contents are the two characters ''\' may be written '\'\\' or "'\\".

Another use of backslash is to represent unprintable characters such as newline. While there is nothing to stop you from writing most of these characters directly in a string constant, they may look ugly.

Here is a table of all the escape sequences used in Octave. They are the same as those used in the C programming language.

\\          Represents a literal backslash, '\'.

\"          Represents a literal double-quote character, '"'.

\'          Represents a literal single-quote character, '''.

\a          Represents the "alert" character, control-g, ASCII code 7.

\b          Represents a backspace, control-h, ASCII code 8.

\f          Represents a formfeed, control-l, ASCII code 12.

\n          Represents a newline, control-j, ASCII code 10.

\r          Represents a carriage return, control-m, ASCII code 13.

\t                Represents a horizontal tab, control-i, ASCII code 9.

\v                Represents a vertical tab, control-k, ASCII code 11.

Strings may be concatenated using the notation for defining matrices.
For example, the expression

        [ "foo" , "bar" , "baz" ]

produces the string whose contents are 'foobarbaz'. See Chapter 4 [Numeric Data Types], page 39 for more information about creating matrices.

# 5.1 Creating Strings

blanks (*n*)                                                    Function File
    Return a string of *n* blanks.

int2str (*n*)                                                   Function File
num2str (*x*)                                                   Function File
    Convert a number to a string. These functions are not very flexible,
    but are provided for compatibility with MATLAB. For better control
    over the results, use sprintf (see Section 13.2.4 [Formatted Output],
    page 133).

setstr (*x*)                                                 Built-in Function
    Convert a matrix to a string. Each element of the matrix is converted
    to the corresponding ASCII character. For example,

        setstr ([97, 98, 99])
            ⇒ "abc"

strcat (*s1, s2, ...*)                                          Function File
    Return a string containing all the arguments concatenated. For exam-
    ple,

        s = [ "ab"; "cde" ];
        strcat (s, s, s)
            ⇒ "ab ab ab "
                "cdecdecde"

string_fill_char                                             Built-in Variable
    The value of this variable is used to pad all strings in a string matrix
    to the same length. It should be a single character. The default value
    is " " (a single space). For example,

```
string_fill_char = "X";
[ "these"; "are"; "strings" ]
    ⇒ "theseXX"
      "areXXXX"
      "strings"
```

**str2mat** (*s_1*, ..., *s_n*)                                    Function File

Return a matrix containing the strings *s_1*, ..., *s_n* as its rows. Each string is padded with blanks in order to form a valid matrix.

**Note:** This function is modelled after MATLAB. In Octave, you can create a matrix of strings by [*s_1*; ...; *s_n*] even if the strings are not all the same length.

**isstr** (*a*)                                                Built-in Function

Return 1 if *a* is a string. Otherwise, return 0.

# 5.2 Searching and Replacing

**deblank** (*s*)                                                 Function File

Removes the trailing blanks from the string *s*.

**findstr** (*s*, *t*, *overlap*)                                 Function File

Return the vector of all positions in the longer of the two strings *s* and *t* where an occurrence of the shorter of the two starts. If the optional argument *overlap* is nonzero, the returned vector can include overlapping positions (this is the default). For example,

```
findstr ("ababab", "a")
    ⇒ [ 1, 3, 5 ]
findstr ("abababa", "aba", 0)
    ⇒ [ 1, 5 ]
```

**index** (*s*, *t*)                                               Function File

Return the position of the first occurrence of the string *t* in the string *s*, or 0 if no occurrence is found. For example,

```
index ("Teststring", "t")
    ⇒ 4
```

**Note:** This function does not work for arrays of strings.

**rindex** (*s*, *t*)                                              Function File

Return the position of the last occurrence of the string *t* in the string *s*, or 0 if no occurrence is found. For example,

```
rindex ("Teststring", "t")
    ⇒ 6
```

**Note:** This function does not work for arrays of strings.

**split** (*s*, *t*)                                          Function File
Divides the string *s* into pieces separated by *t*, returning the result in a string array (padded with blanks to form a valid matrix). For example,

```
split ("Test string", "t")
    ⇒ "Tes "
      " s  "
      "ring"
```

**strcmp** (*s1*, *s2*)                                       Function File
Compares two strings, returning 1 if they are the same, and 0 otherwise.

**Note:** For compatibility with MATLAB, Octave's strcmp function returns 1 if the strings are equal, and 0 otherwise. This is just the opposite of the corresponding C library function.

**strrep** (*s*, *x*, *y*)                                    Function File
Replaces all occurrences of the substring *x* of the string *s* with the string *y*. For example,

```
strrep ("This is a test string", "is", "&%$")
    ⇒ "Th&%$ &%$ a test string"
```

**substr** (*s*, *beg*, *len*)                                Function File
Return the substring of *s* which starts at character number *beg* and is *len* characters long. For example,

```
substr ("This is a test string", 6, 9)
    ⇒ "is a test"
```

**Note:** This function is patterned after AWK. You can get the same result by *s* (*beg* : (*beg* + *len* - 1)).

## 5.3 String Conversions

**bin2dec** (*s*)                                             Function File
Return a decimal number corresponding to the binary number represented as a string of zeros and ones. For example,

```
bin2dec ("1110")
    ⇒ 14
```

**dec2bin** (*n*)                                            Function File
Return a binary number corresponding the nonnegative decimal number *n*, as a string of ones and zeros. For example,

```
dec2bin (14)
    ⇒ "1110"
```

**dec2hex** (*n*)                                            Function File
Return the hexadecimal number corresponding to the nonnegative decimal number *n*, as a string. For example,

```
dec2hex (2748)
    ⇒ "abc"
```

**hex2dec** (*s*)                                            Function File
Return the decimal number corresponding to the hexadecimal number stored in the string *s*. For example,

```
hex2dec ("12B")
    ⇒ 299
hex2dec ("12b")
    ⇒ 299
```

**str2num** (*s*)                                            Function File
Convert the string *s* to a number.

**toascii** (*s*)                                            Function File
Return ASCII representation of *s* in a matrix. For example,

```
toascii ("ASCII")
    ⇒ [ 65, 83, 67, 73, 73 ]
```

**tolower** (*s*)                                            Function File
Return a copy of the string *s*, with each upper-case character replaced by the corresponding lower-case one; nonalphabetic characters are left unchanged. For example,

```
tolower ("MiXeD cAsE 123")
    ⇒ "mixed case 123"
```

**toupper** (*s*)                                            Function File
Return a copy of the string *s*, with each lower-case character replaced by the corresponding upper-case one; nonalphabetic characters are left unchanged. For example,

```
toupper ("MiXeD cAsE 123")
    ⇒ "MIXED CASE 123"
```

**undo_string_escapes** (*s*)                                      Built-in Function
Converts special characters in strings back to their escaped forms. For example, the expression

```
bell = "\a";
```

assigns the value of the alert character (control-g, ASCII code 7) to the string variable bell. If this string is printed, the system will ring the terminal bell (if it is possible). This is normally the desired outcome. However, sometimes it is useful to be able to print the original representation of the string, with the special characters replaced by their escape sequences. For example,

```
octave:13> undo_string_escapes (bell)
ans = \a
```

replaces the unprintable alert character with its printable representation.

**implicit_num_to_str_ok**                                        Built-in Variable
If the value of implicit_num_to_str_ok is nonzero, implicit conversions of numbers to their ASCII character equivalents are allowed when strings are constructed using a mixture of strings and numbers in matrix notation. Otherwise, an error message is printed and control is returned to the top level. The default value is 0. For example,

```
[ "f", 111, 111 ]
     ⇒ "foo"
```

**implicit_str_to_num_ok**                                        Built-in Variable
If the value of implicit_str_to_num_ok is nonzero, implicit conversions of strings to their numeric ASCII equivalents are allowed. Otherwise, an error message is printed and control is returned to the top level. The default value is 0.

## 5.4 Character Class Functions

Octave also provides the following character class test functions patterned after the functions in the standard C library. They all operate on string arrays and return matrices of zeros and ones. Elements that are nonzero indicate that the condition was true for the corresponding character in the string array. For example,

```
isalpha ("!Q@WERT^Y&")
     ⇒ [ 0, 1, 0, 1, 1, 1, 1, 0, 1, 0 ]
```

**isalnum** (*s*)                                           Mapping Function
Return 1 for characters that are letters or digits (isalpha (a) or isdigit () is true).

**isalpha** (*s*)                                           Mapping Function
Return true for characters that are letters (isupper (a) or islower () is true).

**isascii** (*s*)                                           Mapping Function
Return 1 for characters that are ASCII (in the range 0 to 127 decimal).

**iscntrl** (*s*)                                           Mapping Function
Return 1 for control characters.

**isdigit** (*s*)                                           Mapping Function
Return 1 for characters that are decimal digits.

**isgraph** (*s*)                                           Mapping Function
Return 1 for printable characters (but not the space character).

**islower** (*s*)                                           Mapping Function
Return 1 for characters that are lower case letters.

**isprint** (*s*)                                           Mapping Function
Return 1 for printable characters (including the space character).

**ispunct** (*s*)                                           Mapping Function
Return 1 for punctuation characters.

**isspace** (*s*)                                           Mapping Function
Return 1 for whitespace characters (space, formfeed, newline, carriage return, tab, and vertical tab).

**isupper** (*s*)                                           Mapping Function
Return 1 for upper case letters.

**isxdigit** (*s*)                                          Mapping Function
Return 1 for characters that are hexadecimal digits.

# 6 Data Structures

Octave includes support for organizing data in structures. The current implementation uses an associative array with indices limited to strings, but the syntax is more like C-style structures. Here are some examples of using data structures in Octave.

Elements of structures can be of any value type. For example, the three expressions

```
x.a = 1
x.b = [1, 2; 3, 4]
x.c = "string"
```

create a structure with three elements. To print the value of the structure, you can type its name, just as for any other variable:

```
octave:2> x
x =
{
  a = 1
  b =

    1  2
    3  4

  c = string
}
```

Note that Octave may print the elements in any order.

Structures may be copied.

```
octave:1> y = x
y =
{
  a = 1
  b =

    1  2
    3  4

  c = string
}
```

Since structures are themselves values, structure elements may reference other structures. The following statements change the value of the element b of the structure x to be a data structure containing the single element d, which has a value of 3.

```
octave:1> x.b.d = 3
x.b.d = 3
octave:2> x.b
ans =
{
  d = 3
}
octave:3> x
x =
{
  a = 1
  b =
  {
    d = 3
  }

  c = string
}
```

Note that when Octave prints the value of a structure that contains
other structures, only a few levels are displayed. For example,

```
octave:1> a.b.c.d.e = 1;
octave:2> a
a =
{
  b =
  {
    c = <structure>
  }
}
```

This prevents long and confusing output from large deeply nested structures.

**struct_levels_to_print**                            Built-in Variable
    You can tell Octave how many structure levels to display by setting
    the built-in variable struct_levels_to_print. The default value is
    2.

    Functions can return structures. For example, the following function
separates the real and complex parts of a matrix and stores them in two
elements of the same structure variable.

```
octave:1> function y = f (x)
> y.re = real (x);
```

```
> y.im = imag (x);
> endfunction
```

When called with a complex-valued argument, f returns the data structure containing the real and imaginary parts of the original function argument.

```
octave:2> f (rand (2) + rand (2) * I);
ans =
{
  im =

    0.26475   0.14828
    0.18436   0.83669

  re =

    0.040239   0.242160
    0.238081   0.402523
}
```

Function return lists can include structure elements, and they may be indexed like any other variable. For example,

```
octave:1> [ x.u, x.s(2:3,2:3), x.v ] = svd ([1, 2; 3, 4])
x.u =

  -0.40455   -0.91451
  -0.91451    0.40455

x.s =

   0.00000   0.00000   0.00000
   0.00000   5.46499   0.00000
   0.00000   0.00000   0.36597

x.v =

  -0.57605    0.81742
  -0.81742   -0.57605
```

It is also possible to cycle through all the elements of a structure in a loop, using a special form of the for statement (see Section 10.4 [The for Statement], page 94)

The following functions are available to give you information about structures.

**is_struct** (*expr*)                                      Built-in Function
   Return 1 if the value of the expression *expr* is a structure.

**struct_contains** (*expr, name*)                          Built-in Function
   Return 1 if the expression *expr* is a structure and it includes an element
   named *name*. The first argument must be a structure and the second
   must be a string.

**struct_elements** (*struct*)                              Built-in Function
   Return a list of strings naming the elements of the structure *struct*. It
   is an error to call `struct_elements` with an argument that is not a
   structure.

# 7 Variables

Variables let you give names to values and refer to them later. You have already seen variables in many of the examples. The name of a variable must be a sequence of letters, digits and underscores, but it may not begin with a digit. Octave does not enforce a limit on the length of variable names, but it is seldom useful to have variables with names longer than about 30 characters. The following are all valid variable names

```
x
x15
__foo_bar_baz__
fucnrdthsucngtagdjb
```

However, names like `__foo_bar_baz__` that begin and end with two underscores are understood to be reserved for internal use by Octave. You should not use them in code you write, except to access Octave's documented internal variables and built-in symbolic constants.

Case is significant in variable names. The symbols a and A are distinct variables.

A variable name is a valid expression by itself. It represents the variable's current value. Variables are given new values with *assignment operators* and *increment operators*. See Section 8.6 [Assignment Expressions], page 81.

A number of variables have special built-in meanings. For example, ans holds the most recently computed result, and pi names the ratio of the circumference of a circle to its diameter. See Section 7.3 [Summary of Built-in Variables], page 63, for a list of all the predefined variables. Some of these built-in symbols are constants and may not be changed. Others can be used and assigned just like all other variables, but their values are also used or changed automatically by Octave.

Variables in Octave do not have fixed types, so it is possible to first store a numeric value in a variable and then to later use the same name to hold a string value in the same program. Variables may not be used before they have been given a value. Doing so results in an error.

## 7.1 Global Variables

A variable that has been declared *global* may be accessed from within a function body without having to pass it as a formal parameter.

A variable may be declared global using a `global` declaration statement. The following statements are all global declarations.

```
global a
```

```
global b = 2
global c = 3, d, e = 5
```

It is necessary declare a variable as global within a function body in order to access it. For example,

```
global x
function f ()
  x = 1;
endfunction
f ()
```

does *not* set the value of the global variable x to 1. In order to change the value of the global variable x, you must also declare it to be global within the function body, like this

```
function f ()
  global x;
  x = 1;
endfunction
```

Passing a global variable in a function parameter list will make a local copy and not modify the global value. For example, given the function

```
function f (x)
  x = 0
endfunction
```

and the definition of x as a global variable at the top level,

```
global x = 13
```

the expression

```
f (x)
```

will display the value of x from inside the function as 0, but the value of x at the top level remains unchanged, because the function works with a *copy* of its argument.

**warn_comma_in_global_decl**                                Built-in Variable

If the value of warn_comma_in_global_decl is nonzero, a warning is issued for statements like

```
global a = 1, b
```

which makes the variables a and b global and assigns the value 1 to the variable a, because in this context, the comma is not interpreted as a statement separator.

The default value of warn_comma_in_global_decl is nonzero.

**initialize_global_variables**                          Built-in Variable
> If the value of `initialize_global_variables` is nonzero, global variables are initialized to the value of the built-in variable `default_global_variable_value`.
>
> the default value of `initialize_global_variables` is zero.

**default_global_variable_value**                          Built-in Variable
> If `initialize_global_variables` is nonzero, the value of `default_global_variable_value` is used as the initial value of global variables that are not explicitly initialized. for example,
>
> ```
> initialize_global_variables = 1;
> default_global_variable_value = 13;
> global foo;
> foo
>     ⇒ 13
> ```
>
> the variable `default_global_variable_value` is initially undefined.

**is_global** (*name*)                          Built-in Function
> Return 1 if *name* is globally visible. Otherwise, return 0. For example,
>
> ```
> global x
> is_global ("x")
>     ⇒ 1
> ```

## 7.2  Status of Variables

**clear** *options pattern* ...                          Command
> Delete the names matching the given patterns from the symbol table. The pattern may contain the following special characters:

?               Match any single character.

*               Match zero or more characters.

[ *list* ]      Match the list of characters specified by *list*. If the first character is ! or ^, match all characters except those specified by *list*. For example, the pattern '[a-zA-Z]' will match all lower and upper case alphabetic characters.

> For example, the command
>
> ```
> clear foo b*r
> ```
>
> clears the name `foo` and all names that begin with the letter b and end with the letter r.

If `clear` is called without any arguments, all user-defined variables (local and global) are cleared from the symbol table. If `clear` is called with at least one argument, only the visible names matching the arguments are cleared. For example, suppose you have defined a function foo, and then hidden it by performing the assignment foo = 2. Executing the command *clear foo* once will clear the variable definition and restore the definition of foo as a function. Executing *clear foo* a second time will clear the function definition.

This command may not be used within a function body.

**who** *options pattern ...*                                      Command
**whos** *options pattern ...*                                     Command

    List currently defined symbols matching the given patterns. The following are valid options. They may be shortened to one character but may not be combined.

    `-all`      List all currently defined symbols.

    `-builtins`  List built-in variables and functions. This includes all currently compiled function files, but does not include all function files that are in the LOADPATH.

    `-functions`

              List user-defined functions.

    `-long`    Print a long listing including the type and dimensions of any symbols. The symbols in the first column of output indicate whether it is possible to redefine the symbol, and whether it is possible for it to be cleared.

    `-variables`

              List user-defined variables.

    Valid patterns are the same as described for the `clear` command above. If no patterns are supplied, all symbols from the given category are listed. By default, only user defined functions and variables visible in the local scope are displayed.

    The command *whos* is equivalent to *who -long*.

**exist** (*name*)                                             Built-in Function

    Return 1 if the name exists as a variable, 2 if the name (after appending '.m') is a function file in the path, 3 if the name is a '.oct' file in the path, or 5 if the name is a built-in function. Otherwise, return 0.

**document** (*symbol, text*)                                  Built-in Function

    Set the documentation string for *symbol* to *text*.

**type** *options name* . . .                                           Command
> Display the definition of each *name* that refers to a function.
>
> Normally also displays if each *name* is user-defined or builtin; the -q option suppresses this behaviour.
>
> Currently, Octave can only display functions that can be compiled cleanly, because it uses its internal representation of the function to recreate the program text.
>
> Comments are not displayed because Octave's parser currently discards them as it converts the text of a function file to its internal representation. This problem may be fixed in a future release.

**which** *name* . . .                                                  Command
> Display the type of each *name*. If *name* is defined from a function file, the full name of the file is also displayed.

# 7.3 Summary of Built-in Variables

Here is a summary of all of Octave's built-in variables along with cross references to additional information and their default values. In the following table *octave-home* stands for the root directory where all of Octave is installed (the default is '/usr/local', *version* stands for the Octave version number (for example, 2.0.17) and *arch* stands for the type of system for which Octave was compiled (for example, i586-pc-linux-gnu).

DEFAULT_LOADPATH
> See Section 11.6 [Function Files], page 109.
>
> Default value: ".:*octave-home*/lib/*version*".

EDITOR        See Section 2.4.5 [Commands For History], page 26.
> Default value: "emacs".

EXEC_PATH     See Section 29.3 [Controlling Subprocesses], page 234.
> Default value: ":$PATH".

INFO_FILE     See Section 2.3 [Getting Help], page 22.
> Default value: "*octave-home*/info/octave.info".

INFO_PROGRAM
> See Section 2.3 [Getting Help], page 22.
>
> Default value:   "*octave-home*/libexec/octave/*version*/exec/*arch*/info".

LOADPATH     See Section 11.6 [Function Files], page 109.

             Default value: ":", which tells Octave to use the directories
             specified by the built-in variable DEFAULT_LOADPATH.

OCTAVE_HOME
             Default value: "/usr/local".

PAGER        See Chapter 13 [Input and Output], page 123.

             Default value: "less", or "more".

PS1          See Section 2.4.6 [Customizing the Prompt], page 28.

             Default value: "\s:\#> ".

PS2          See Section 2.4.6 [Customizing the Prompt], page 28.

             Default value: "> ".

PS4          See Section 2.4.6 [Customizing the Prompt], page 28.

             Default value: "+ ".

auto_unload_dot_oct_files
             See Section 11.8 [Dynamically Linked Functions], page 113.

             Default value: 0.

automatic_replot
             See Section 14.1 [Two-Dimensional Plotting], page 149.

             Default value: 0.

beep_on_error
             See Chapter 12 [Error Handling], page 119.

             Default value: 0.

completion_append_char
             See Section 2.4.4 [Commands For Completion], page 25.

             Default value: " ".

default_eval_print_flag
             See Chapter 9 [Evaluation], page 87.

             Default value: 1.

default_return_value
             See Section 11.2 [Multiple Return Values], page 104.

             Default value: [].

`default_save_format`
> See Section 13.1.3 [Simple File I/O], page 128.
>
> Default value: `"ascii"`.

`do_fortran_indexing`
> See Section 8.1 [Index Expressions], page 71.
>
> Default value: 0.

`crash_dumps_octave_core`
> See Section 13.1.3 [Simple File I/O], page 128.
>
> Default value: 1.

`define_all_return_values`
> See Section 11.2 [Multiple Return Values], page 104.
>
> Default value: 0.

`empty_list_elements_ok`
> See Section 4.1.1 [Empty Matrices], page 43.
>
> Default value: `"warn"`.

`fixed_point_format`
> See Section 4.1 [Matrices], page 39
>
> Default value: 0.

`gnuplot_binary`
> See Section 14.3 [Three-Dimensional Plotting], page 157.
>
> Default value: `"gnuplot"`.

`history_file`
> See Section 2.4.5 [Commands For History], page 26.
>
> Default value: `"~/.octave_hist"`.

`history_size`
> See Section 2.4.5 [Commands For History], page 26.
>
> Default value: 1024.

`ignore_function_time_stamp`
> See Section 11.6 [Function Files], page 109.
>
> Default value: `"system"`.

`implicit_num_to_str_ok`
> See Section 5.3 [String Conversions], page 50.
>
> Default value: 0.

`implicit_str_to_num_ok`
> See Section 5.3 [String Conversions], page 50.
>
> Default value: 0.

`max_recursion_depth`
> See Section 8.2.2 [Recursion], page 76.
>
> Default value: 256.

`ok_to_lose_imaginary_part`
> See Section 15.3 [Special Utility Matrices], page 168.
>
> Default value: "warn".

`output_max_field_width`
> See Section 4.1 [Matrices], page 39.
>
> Default value: 10.

`output_precision`
> See Section 4.1 [Matrices], page 39.
>
> Default value: 5.

`page_screen_output`
> See Chapter 13 [Input and Output], page 123.
>
> Default value: 1.

`prefer_column_vectors`
> See Section 8.1 [Index Expressions], page 71.
>
> Default value: 1.

`print_answer_id_name`
> See Section 13.1.1 [Terminal Output], page 124.
>
> Default value: 1.

`print_empty_dimensions`
> See Section 4.1.1 [Empty Matrices], page 43.
>
> Default value: 1.

`resize_on_range_error`
> See Section 8.1 [Index Expressions], page 71.
>
> Default value: 1.

`return_last_computed_value`
> See Section 11.5 [Returning From a Function], page 108.
>
> Default value: 0.

`save_precision`
> See Section 13.1.3 [Simple File I/O], page 128.
>
> Default value: 17.

`saving_history`
> See Section 2.4.5 [Commands For History], page 26.
>
> Default value: 1.

`silent_functions`
> See Section 11.1 [Defining Functions], page 101.
>
> Default value: 0.

`split_long_rows`
> See Section 4.1 [Matrices], page 39.
>
> Default value: 1.

`struct_levels_to_print`
> See Chapter 6 [Data Structures], page 55.
>
> Default value: 2.

`suppress_verbose_help_message`
> See Section 2.3 [Getting Help], page 22.
>
> Default value: 1.

`treat_neg_dim_as_zero`
> See Section 15.3 [Special Utility Matrices], page 168.
>
> Default value: 0.

`warn_assign_as_truth_value`
> See Section 10.1 [The if Statement], page 89.
>
> Default value: 1.

`warn_comma_in_global_decl`
> See Section 7.1 [Global Variables], page 59.
>
> Default value: 1.

`warn_divide_by_zero`
> See Section 8.3 [Arithmetic Ops], page 76.
>
> Default value: 1.

`warn_function_name_clash`
> See Section 11.6 [Function Files], page 109.
>
> Default value: 1.

```
warn_reload_forces_clear
```
See Section 11.8 [Dynamically Linked Functions], page 113.

Default value: 1.

```
warn_variable_switch_label
```
See Section 10.2 [The switch Statement], page 92.

Default value: 0.

```
whitespace_in_literal_matrix
```
See Section 4.1 [Matrices], page 39.

Default value: "".

## 7.4 Defaults from the Environment

Octave uses the values of the following environment variables to set the default values for the corresponding built-in variables. In addition, the values from the environment may be overridden by command-line arguments. See Section 2.1.1 [Command Line Options], page 17.

`EDITOR`        See Section 2.4.5 [Commands For History], page 26.

Built-in variable: `EDITOR`.

`OCTAVE_EXEC_PATH`

See Section 29.3 [Controlling Subprocesses], page 234.

Built-in variable: `EXEC_PATH`. Command-line argument: `--exec-path`.

`OCTAVE_PATH`

See Section 11.6 [Function Files], page 109.

Built-in variable: `LOADPATH`. Command-line argument: `--path`.

`OCTAVE_INFO_FILE`

See Section 2.3 [Getting Help], page 22.

Built-in variable: `INFO_FILE`. Command-line argument: `--info-file`.

`OCTAVE_INFO_PROGRAM`

See Section 2.3 [Getting Help], page 22.

Built-in variable: `INFO_PROGRAM`. Command-line argument: `--info-program`.

`OCTAVE_HISTSIZE`

See Section 2.4.5 [Commands For History], page 26.

Built-in variable: `history_size`.

OCTAVE_HISTFILE
> See Section 2.4.5 [Commands For History], page 26.
>
> Built-in variable: `history_file`.

# 8 Expressions

Expressions are the basic building block of statements in Octave. An expression evaluates to a value, which you can print, test, store in a variable, pass to a function, or assign a new value to a variable with an assignment operator.

An expression can serve as a statement on its own. Most other kinds of statements contain one or more expressions which specify data to be operated on. As in other languages, expressions in Octave include variables, array references, constants, and function calls, as well as combinations of these with various operators.

## 8.1 Index Expressions

An *index expression* allows you to reference or extract selected elements of a matrix or vector.

Indices may be scalars, vectors, ranges, or the special operator ':', which may be used to select entire rows or columns.

Vectors are indexed using a single expression. Matrices require two indices unless the value of the built-in variable do_fortran_indexing is nonzero, in which case matrices may also be indexed by a single expression.

**do_fortran_indexing**                                   Built-in Variable

If the value of do_fortran_indexing is nonzero, Octave allows you to select elements of a two-dimensional matrix using a single index by treating the matrix as a single vector created from the columns of the matrix. The default value is 0.

Given the matrix

    a = [1, 2; 3, 4]

all of the following expressions are equivalent

    a (1, [1, 2])
    a (1, 1:2)
    a (1, :)

and select the first row of the matrix.

A special form of indexing may be used to select elements of a matrix or vector. If the indices are vectors made up of only ones and zeros, the result is a new matrix whose elements correspond to the elements of the index vector that are equal to one. For example,

    a = [1, 2; 3, 4];
    a ([1, 0], :)

selects the first row of the matrix a.

This operation can be useful for selecting elements of a matrix based on some condition, since the comparison operators return matrices of ones and zeros.

This special zero-one form of indexing leads to a conflict with the standard indexing operation. For example, should the following statements

```
a = [1, 2; 3, 4];
a ([1, 1], :)
```

return the original matrix, or the matrix formed by selecting the first row twice? Although this conflict is not likely to arise very often in practice, you may select the behavior you prefer by setting the built-in variable prefer_zero_one_indexing.

**prefer_zero_one_indexing**                           Built-in Variable

If the value of prefer_zero_one_indexing is nonzero, Octave will perform zero-one style indexing when there is a conflict with the normal indexing rules. See Section 8.1 [Index Expressions], page 71. For example, given a matrix

```
a = [1, 2, 3, 4]
```

with prefer_zero_one_indexing is set to nonzero, the expression

```
a ([1, 1, 1, 1])
```

results in the matrix [ 1, 2, 3, 4 ]. If the value of prefer_zero_one_indexing set to 0, the result would be the matrix [ 1, 1, 1, 1 ].

In the first case, Octave is selecting each element corresponding to a '1' in the index vector. In the second, Octave is selecting the first element multiple times.

The default value for prefer_zero_one_indexing is 0.

Finally, indexing a scalar with a vector of ones can be used to create a vector the same size as the index vector, with each element equal to the value of the original scalar. For example, the following statements

```
a = 13;
a ([1, 1, 1, 1])
```

produce a vector whose four elements are all equal to 13.

Similarly, indexing a scalar with two vectors of ones can be used to create a matrix. For example the following statements

```
a = 13;
a ([1, 1], [1, 1, 1])
```

create a 2 by 3 matrix with all elements equal to 13.

This is an obscure notation and should be avoided. It is better to use the function ones to generate a matrix of the appropriate size whose elements are all one, and then to scale it to produce the desired result. See Section 15.3 [Special Utility Matrices], page 168.

**prefer_column_vectors**                                    Built-in Variable

If prefer_column_vectors is nonzero, operations like

```
for i = 1:10
  a (i) = i;
endfor
```

(for a previously undefined) produce column vectors. Otherwise, row vectors are preferred. The default value is 1.

If a variable is already defined to be a vector (a matrix with a single row or column), the original orientation is respected, regardless of the value of prefer_column_vectors.

**resize_on_range_error**                                    Built-in Variable

If the value of resize_on_range_error is nonzero, expressions like

```
for i = 1:10
  a (i) = sqrt (i);
endfor
```

(for a previously undefined) result in the variable a being resized to be just large enough to hold the new value. New elements that have not been given a value are set to zero. If the value of resize_on_range_error is 0, an error message is printed and control is returned to the top level. The default value is 1.

Note that it is quite inefficient to create a vector using a loop like the one shown in the example above. In this particular case, it would have been much more efficient to use the expression

```
a = sqrt (1:10);
```

thus avoiding the loop entirely. In cases where a loop is still required, or a number of values must be combined to form a larger matrix, it is generally much faster to set the size of the matrix first, and then insert elements using indexing commands. For example, given a matrix a,

```
[nr, nc] = size (a);
x = zeros (nr, n * nc);
for i = 1:n
  x(:,(i-1)*n+1:i*n) = a;
endfor
```

is considerably faster than

```
x = a;
for i = 1:n-1
  x = [x, a];
endfor
```

particularly for large matrices because Octave does not have to repeatedly resize the result.

## 8.2  Calling Functions

A *function* is a name for a particular calculation. Because it has a name, you can ask for it by name at any point in the program. For example, the function sqrt computes the square root of a number.

A fixed set of functions are *built-in*, which means they are available in every Octave program. The sqrt function is one of these. In addition, you can define your own functions. See Chapter 11 [Functions and Scripts], page 101, for information about how to do this.

The way to use a function is with a *function call* expression, which consists of the function name followed by a list of *arguments* in parentheses. The arguments are expressions which give the raw materials for the calculation that the function will do. When there is more than one argument, they are separated by commas. If there are no arguments, you can omit the parentheses, but it is a good idea to include them anyway, to clearly indicate that a function call was intended. Here are some examples:

```
sqrt (x^2 + y^2)      # One argument
ones (n, m)           # Two arguments
rand ()               # No arguments
```

Each function expects a particular number of arguments. For example, the sqrt function must be called with a single argument, the number to take the square root of:

```
sqrt (argument)
```

Some of the built-in functions take a variable number of arguments, depending on the particular usage, and their behavior is different depending on the number of arguments supplied.

Like every other expression, the function call has a value, which is computed by the function based on the arguments you give it. In this example, the value of sqrt (*argument*) is the square root of the argument. A function can also have side effects, such as assigning the values of certain variables or doing input or output operations.

Unlike most languages, functions in Octave may return multiple values. For example, the following statement

```
[u, s, v] = svd (a)
```

computes the singular value decomposition of the matrix a and assigns the three result matrices to u, s, and v.

The left side of a multiple assignment expression is itself a list of expressions, and is allowed to be a list of variable names or index expressions. See also Section 8.1 [Index Expressions], page 71, and Section 8.6 [Assignment Ops], page 81.

## 8.2.1 Call by Value

In Octave, unlike Fortran, function arguments are passed by value, which means that each argument in a function call is evaluated and assigned to a temporary location in memory before being passed to the function. There is currently no way to specify that a function parameter should be passed by reference instead of by value. This means that it is impossible to directly alter the value of function parameter in the calling function. It can only change the local copy within the function body. For example, the function

```
function f (x, n)
  while (n-- > 0)
    disp (x);
  endwhile
endfunction
```

displays the value of the first argument $n$ times. In this function, the variable $n$ is used as a temporary variable without having to worry that its value might also change in the calling function. Call by value is also useful because it is always possible to pass constants for any function parameter without first having to determine that the function will not attempt to modify the parameter.

The caller may use a variable as the expression for the argument, but the called function does not know this: it only knows what value the argument had. For example, given a function called as

```
foo = "bar";
fcn (foo)
```

you should not think of the argument as being "the variable foo." Instead, think of the argument as the string value, "bar".

Even though Octave uses pass-by-value semantics for function arguments, values are not copied unnecessarily. For example,

```
x = rand (1000);
f (x);
```

does not actually force two 1000 by 1000 element matrices to exist *unless* the function f modifies the value of its argument. Then Octave must

create a copy to avoid changing the value outside the scope of the function
f, or attempting (and probably failing!) to modify the value of a constant
or the value of a temporary result.

## 8.2.2 Recursion

With some restrictions[1], recursive function calls are allowed. A *recursive function* is one which calls itself, either directly or indirectly. For
example, here is an inefficient[2] way to compute the factorial of a given
integer:

```
function retval = fact (n)
  if (n > 0)
    retval = n * fact (n-1);
  else
    retval = 1;
  endif
endfunction
```

This function is recursive because it calls itself directly. It eventually
terminates because each time it calls itself, it uses an argument that is
one less than was used for the previous call. Once the argument is no
longer greater than zero, it does not call itself, and the recursion ends.

The built-in variable max_recursion_depth specifies a limit to the
recursion depth and prevents Octave from recursing infinitely.

**Limit** the number of times a function may be                 max_recursion_depth
            called recursively.

If the limit is exceeded, an error message is printed and control returns
to the top level.

The default value is 256.

## 8.3 Arithmetic Operators

The following arithmetic operators are available, and work on scalars
and matrices.

---

[1] Some of Octave's function are implemented in terms of functions that cannot
be called recursively. For example, the ODE solver lsode is ultimately
implemented in a Fortran subroutine that cannot be called recursively, so
lsode should not be called either directly or indirectly from within the user-
supplied function that lsode requires. Doing so will result in undefined
behavior.

[2] It would be much better to use prod (1:n), or gamma (n+1) instead, after
first checking to ensure that the value n is actually a positive integer.

| | |
|---|---|
| *x* + *y* | Addition. If both operands are matrices, the number of rows and columns must both agree. If one operand is a scalar, its value is added to all the elements of the other operand. |
| *x* .+ *y* | Element by element addition. This operator is equivalent to +. |
| *x* - *y* | Subtraction. If both operands are matrices, the number of rows and columns of both must agree. |
| *x* .- *y* | Element by element subtraction. This operator is equivalent to -. |
| *x* * *y* | Matrix multiplication. The number of columns of *x* must agree with the number of rows of *y*. |
| *x* .* *y* | Element by element multiplication. If both operands are matrices, the number of rows and columns must both agree. |
| *x* / *y* | Right division. This is conceptually equivalent to the expression |

```
(inverse (y') * x')'
```

but it is computed without forming the inverse of *y*'.

If the system is not square, or if the coefficient matrix is singular, a minimum norm solution is computed.

| | |
|---|---|
| *x* ./ *y* | Element by element right division. |
| *x* \ *y* | Left division. This is conceptually equivalent to the expression |

```
inverse (x) * y
```

but it is computed without forming the inverse of *x*.

If the system is not square, or if the coefficient matrix is singular, a minimum norm solution is computed.

| | |
|---|---|
| *x* .\ *y* | Element by element left division. Each element of *y* is divided by each corresponding element of *x*. |
| *x* ^ *y*<br>*x* ** *y* | Power operator. If *x* and *y* are both scalars, this operator returns *x* raised to the power *y*. If *x* is a scalar and *y* is a square matrix, the result is computed using an eigenvalue expansion. If *x* is a square matrix. the result is computed by repeated multiplication if *y* is an integer, and by an eigenvalue expansion if *y* is not an integer. An error results if both *x* and *y* are matrices. |

The implementation of this operator needs to be improved.

*x* .^ *y*

*x* .** *y*      Element by element power operator. If both operands are
                matrices, the number of rows and columns must both agree.

-*x*            Negation.

+*x*            Unary plus. This operator has no effect on the operand.

*x* '           Complex conjugate transpose. For real arguments, this op-
                erator is the same as the transpose operator. For complex
                arguments, this operator is equivalent to the expression

                    conj (x.')

*x*.'           Transpose.

    Note that because Octave's element by element operators begin with
a '.', there is a possible ambiguity for statements like

        1./m

because the period could be interpreted either as part of the constant or as
part of the operator. To resolve this conflict, Octave treats the expression
as if you had typed

        (1) ./ m

and not

        (1.) / m

Although this is inconsistent with the normal behavior of Octave's lexer,
which usually prefers to break the input into tokens by preferring the
longest possible match at any given point, it is more useful in this case.

---

warn_divide_by_zero                                      Built-in Variable
    If the value of warn_divide_by_zero is nonzero, a warning is issued
    when Octave encounters a division by zero. If the value is 0, the
    warning is omitted. The default value is 1.

## 8.4 Comparison Operators

    *Comparison operators* compare numeric values for relationships such
as equality. They are written using *relational operators*.

    All of Octave's comparison operators return a value of 1 if the com-
parison is true, or 0 if it is false. For matrix values, they all work on an
element-by-element basis. For example,

        [1, 2; 3, 4] == [1, 3; 2, 4]
            ⇒   1   0
                0   1

If one operand is a scalar and the other is a matrix, the scalar is compared to each element of the matrix in turn, and the result is the same size as the matrix.

$x < y$        True if $x$ is less than $y$.

$x <= y$      True if $x$ is less than or equal to $y$.

$x == y$      True if $x$ is equal to $y$.

$x >= y$      True if $x$ is greater than or equal to $y$.

$x > y$        True if $x$ is greater than $y$.

$x \mathrel{!}= y$
$x \mathrel{\tilde{}}= y$
$x <> y$      True if $x$ is not equal to $y$.

String comparisons may also be performed with the strcmp function, not with the comparison operators listed above. See Chapter 5 [Strings], page 47.

# 8.5 Boolean Expressions

## 8.5.1 Element-by-element Boolean Operators

An *element-by-element boolean expression* is a combination of comparison expressions using the boolean operators "or" ('|'), "and" ('&'), and "not" ('!'), along with parentheses to control nesting. The truth of the boolean expression is computed by combining the truth values of the corresponding elements of the component expressions. A value is considered to be false if it is zero, and true otherwise.

Element-by-element boolean expressions can be used wherever comparison expressions can be used. They can be used in if and while statements. However, if a matrix value used as the condition in an if or while statement is only true if *all* of its elements are nonzero.

Like comparison operations, each element of an element-by-element boolean expression also has a numeric value (1 if true, 0 if false) that comes into play if the result of the boolean expression is stored in a variable, or used in arithmetic.

Here are descriptions of the three element-by-element boolean operators.

*boolean1* & *boolean2*
> Elements of the result are true if both corresponding elements of *boolean1* and *boolean2* are true.

*boolean1* | *boolean2*

> Elements of the result are true if either of the corresponding elements of *boolean1* or *boolean2* is true.

! *boolean*

~ *boolean*      Each element of the result is true if the corresponding element of *boolean* is false.

For matrix operands, these operators work on an element-by-element basis. For example, the expression

```
[1, 0; 0, 1] & [1, 0; 2, 3]
```

returns a two by two identity matrix.

For the binary operators, the dimensions of the operands must conform if both are matrices. If one of the operands is a scalar and the other a matrix, the operator is applied to the scalar and each element of the matrix.

For the binary element-by-element boolean operators, both subexpressions *boolean1* and *boolean2* are evaluated before computing the result. This can make a difference when the expressions have side effects. For example, in the expression

```
a & b++
```

the value of the variable *b* is incremented even if the variable *a* is zero.

This behavior is necessary for the boolean operators to work as described for matrix-valued operands.

## 8.5.2 Short-circuit Boolean Operators

Combined with the implicit conversion to scalar values in if and while conditions, Octave's element-by-element boolean operators are often sufficient for performing most logical operations. However, it is sometimes desirable to stop evaluating a boolean expression as soon as the overall truth value can be determined. Octave's *short-circuit* boolean operators work this way.

*boolean1* && *boolean2*

> The expression *boolean1* is evaluated and converted to a scalar using the equivalent of the operation all (all (*boolean1*)). If it is false, the result of the overall expression is 0. If it is true, the expression *boolean2* is evaluated and converted to a scalar using the equivalent of the operation all (all (*boolean1*)). If it is true, the result of the overall expression is 1. Otherwise, the result of the overall expression is 0.

*boolean1* || *boolean2*

> The expression *boolean1* is evaluated and converted to
> a scalar using the equivalent of the operation all (all
> (*boolean1*)). If it is true, the result of the overall expres-
> sion is 1. If it is false, the expression *boolean2* is evaluated
> and converted to a scalar using the equivalent of the oper-
> ation all (all (*boolean1*)). If it is true, the result of the
> overall expression is 1. Otherwise, the result of the overall
> expression is 0.

The fact that both operands may not be evaluated before determining
the overall truth value of the expression can be important. For example,
in the expression

```
a && b++
```

the value of the variable *b* is only incremented if the variable *a* is nonzero.

This can be used to write somewhat more concise code. For example,
it is possible write

```
function f (a, b, c)
  if (nargin > 2 && isstr (c))
    . . .
```

instead of having to use two if statements to avoid attempting to evaluate
an argument that doesn't exist. For example, without the short-circuit
feature, it would be necessary to write

```
function f (a, b, c)
  if (nargin > 2)
    if (isstr (c))
      . . .
```

Writing

```
function f (a, b, c)
  if (nargin > 2 & isstr (c))
    . . .
```

would result in an error if f were called with one or two arguments because
Octave would be forced to try to evaluate both of the operands for the
operator '&'.

# 8.6 Assignment Expressions

An *assignment* is an expression that stores a new value into a variable.
For example, the following expression assigns the value 1 to the variable
z:

```
z = 1
```

After this expression is executed, the variable z has the value 1. Whatever old value z had before the assignment is forgotten. The '=' sign is called an *assignment operator*.

Assignments can store string values also. For example, the following expression would store the value "this food is good" in the variable message:

```
thing = "food"
predicate = "good"
message = [ "this " , thing , " is " , predicate ]
```

(This also illustrates concatenation of strings.)

Most operators (addition, concatenation, and so on) have no effect except to compute a value. If you ignore the value, you might as well not use the operator. An assignment operator is different. It does produce a value, but even if you ignore the value, the assignment still makes itself felt through the alteration of the variable. We call this a *side effect*.

The left-hand operand of an assignment need not be a variable (see Chapter 7 [Variables], page 59). It can also be an element of a matrix (see Section 8.1 [Index Expressions], page 71) or a list of return values (see Section 8.2 [Calling Functions], page 74). These are all called *lvalues*, which means they can appear on the left-hand side of an assignment operator. The right-hand operand may be any expression. It produces the new value which the assignment stores in the specified variable, matrix element, or list of return values.

It is important to note that variables do *not* have permanent types. The type of a variable is simply the type of whatever value it happens to hold at the moment. In the following program fragment, the variable foo has a numeric value at first, and a string value later on:

```
octave:13> foo = 1
foo = 1
octave:13> foo = "bar"
foo = bar
```

When the second assignment gives foo a string value, the fact that it previously had a numeric value is forgotten.

Assignment of a scalar to an indexed matrix sets all of the elements that are referenced by the indices to the scalar value. For example, if a is a matrix with at least two columns,

```
a(:, 2) = 5
```

sets all the elements in the second column of a to 5.

Assigning an empty matrix '[]' works in most cases to allow you to delete rows or columns of matrices and vectors. See Section 4.1.1 [Empty Matrices], page 43. For example, given a 4 by 5 matrix $A$, the assignment

```
A (3, :) = []
```
deletes the third row of $A$, and the assignment
```
A (:, 1:2:5) = []
```
deletes the first, third, and fifth columns.

An assignment is an expression, so it has a value. Thus, z = 1 as an expression has the value 1. One consequence of this is that you can write multiple assignments together:
```
x = y = z = 0
```
stores the value 0 in all three variables. It does this because the value of z = 0, which is 0, is stored into y, and then the value of y = z = 0, which is 0, is stored into x.

This is also true of assignments to lists of values, so the following is a valid expression
```
[a, b, c] = [u, s, v] = svd (a)
```
that is exactly equivalent to
```
[u, s, v] = svd (a)
a = u
b = s
c = v
```
In expressions like this, the number of values in each part of the expression need not match. For example, the expression
```
[a, b, c, d] = [u, s, v] = svd (a)
```
is equivalent to the expression above, except that the value of the variable 'd' is left unchanged, and the expression
```
[a, b] = [u, s, v] = svd (a)
```
is equivalent to
```
[u, s, v] = svd (a)
a = u
b = s
```
You can use an assignment anywhere an expression is called for. For example, it is valid to write x != (y = 1) to set y to 1 and then test whether x equals 1. But this style tends to make programs hard to read. Except in a one-shot program, you should rewrite it to get rid of such nesting of assignments. This is never very hard.

## 8.7 Increment Operators

*Increment operators* increase or decrease the value of a variable by 1. The operator to increment a variable is written as '++'. It may be used to increment a variable either before or after taking its value.

For example, to pre-increment the variable x, you would write ++x. This would add one to x and then return the new value of x as the result of the expression. It is exactly the same as the expression x = x + 1.

To post-increment a variable x, you would write x++. This adds one to the variable x, but returns the value that x had prior to incrementing it. For example, if x is equal to 2, the result of the expression x++ is 2, and the new value of x is 3.

For matrix and vector arguments, the increment and decrement operators work on each element of the operand.

Here is a list of all the increment and decrement expressions.

++x          This expression increments the variable x. The value of the expression is the *new* value of x. It is equivalent to the expression x = x + 1.

--x          This expression decrements the variable x. The value of the expression is the *new* value of x. It is equivalent to the expression x = x - 1.

x++          This expression causes the variable x to be incremented. The value of the expression is the *old* value of x.

x--          This expression causes the variable x to be decremented. The value of the expression is the *old* value of x.

It is not currently possible to increment index expressions. For example, you might expect that the expression v(4)++ would increment the fourth element of the vector v, but instead it results in a parse error. This problem may be fixed in a future release of Octave.

# 8.8 Operator Precedence

*Operator precedence* determines how operators are grouped, when different operators appear close by in one expression. For example, '*' has higher precedence than '+'. Thus, the expression a + b * c means to multiply b and c, and then add a to the product (i.e., a + (b * c)).

You can overrule the precedence of the operators by using parentheses. You can think of the precedence rules as saying where the parentheses are assumed if you do not write parentheses yourself. In fact, it is wise to use parentheses whenever you have an unusual combination of operators, because other people who read the program may not remember what the precedence is in this case. You might forget as well, and then you too could make a mistake. Explicit parentheses will help prevent any such mistake.

When operators of equal precedence are used together, the leftmost operator groups first, except for the assignment and exponentiation operators, which group in the opposite order. Thus, the expression a - b + c groups as (a - b) + c, but the expression a = b = c groups as a = (b = c).

The precedence of prefix unary operators is important when another operator follows the operand. For example, -x^2 means -(x^2), because '-' has lower precedence than '^'.

Here is a table of the operators in Octave, in order of increasing precedence.

statement separators
        ';', ','.

assignment
        '='. This operator groups right to left.

logical "or" and "and"
        '||', '&&'.

element-wise "or" and "and"
        '|', '&'.

relational
        '<', '<=', '==', '>=', '>', '!=', '~=', '<>'.

colon        ':'.

add, subtract
        '+', '-'.

multiply, divide
        '*', '/', '\', '.\', '.*', './'.

transpose    '\'', '.\''

unary plus, minus, increment, decrement, and ''not''
        '+', '-', '++', '--', '!', '~'.

exponentiation
        '^', '**', '.^', '.**'.

# 9 Evaluation

Normally, you evaluate expressions simply by typing them at the Octave prompt, or by asking Octave to interpret commands that you have saved in a file.

Sometimes, you may find it necessary to evaluate an expression that has been computed and stored in a string, or use a string as the name of a function to call. The eval and feval functions allow you to do just that, and are necessary in order to evaluate commands that are not known until run time, or to write functions that will need to call user-supplied functions.

**eval** (*command*)                                          Built-in Function

   Parse the string *command* and evaluate it as if it were an Octave program, returning the last value computed. The *command* is evaluated in the current context, so any results remain available after eval returns. For example,

```
eval ("a = 13")
   ⊣ a = 13
   ⇒ 13
```

In this case, the value of the evaluated expression is printed and it is also returned returned from eval. Just as with any other expression, you can turn printing off by ending the expression in a semicolon. For example,

```
eval ("a = 13;")
   ⇒ 13
```

In this example, the variable a has been given the value 13, but the value of the expression is not printed. You can also turn off automatic printing for all expressions executed by eval using the variable default_eval_print_flag.

**default_eval_print_flag**                                   Built-in Variable

   If the value of this variable is nonzero, Octave prints the results of commands executed by eval that do not end with semicolons. If it is zero, automatic printing is suppressed. The default value is 1.

**feval** (*name*, ...)                                       Built-in Function

   Evaluate the function named *name*. Any arguments after the first are passed on to the named function. For example,

```
feval ("acos", -1)
   ⇒ 3.1416
```

calls the function acos with the argument '-1'.

The function feval is necessary in order to be able to write functions
that call user-supplied functions, because Octave does not have a way
to declare a pointer to a function (like C) or to declare a special kind of
variable that can be used to hold the name of a function (like EXTERNAL
in Fortran). Instead, you must refer to functions by name, and use
feval to call them.

Here is a simple-minded function using feval that finds the root of a
user-supplied function of one variable using Newton's method.

```
function result = newtroot (fname, x)
# usage: newtroot (fname, x)
#
#    fname : a string naming a function f(x).
#    x     : initial guess
  delta = tol = sqrt (eps);
  maxit = 200;
  fx = feval (fname, x);
  for i = 1:maxit
    if (abs (fx) < tol)
      result = x;
      return;
    else
      fx_new = feval (fname, x + delta);
      deriv = (fx_new - fx) / delta;
      x = x - fx / deriv;
      fx = fx_new;
    endif
  endfor

  result = x;

endfunction
```

Note that this is only meant to be an example of calling user-supplied
functions and should not be taken too seriously. In addition to using a
more robust algorithm, any serious code would check the number and
type of all the arguments, ensure that the supplied function really was
a function, etc. See See Section 4.3 [Predicates for Numeric Objects],
page 45, for example, for a list of predicates for numeric objects, and See
Section 7.2 [Status of Variables], page 61, for a description of the exist
function.

# 10  Statements

Statements may be a simple constant expression or a complicated list of nested loops and conditional statements.

*Control statements* such as if, while, and so on control the flow of execution in Octave programs. All the control statements start with special keywords such as if and while, to distinguish them from simple expressions. Many control statements contain other statements; for example, the if statement contains another statement which may or may not be executed.

Each control statement has a corresponding *end* statement that marks the end of the end of the control statement. For example, the keyword endif marks the end of an if statement, and endwhile marks the end of a while statement. You can use the keyword end anywhere a more specific end keyword is expected, but using the more specific keywords is preferred because if you use them, Octave is able to provide better diagnostics for mismatched or missing end tokens.

The list of statements contained between keywords like if or while and the corresponding end statement is called the *body* of a control statement.

## 10.1  The if Statement

The if statement is Octave's decision-making statement. There are three basic forms of an if statement. In its simplest form, it looks like this:

```
if (condition)
    then-body
endif
```

*condition* is an expression that controls what the rest of the statement will do. The *then-body* is executed only if *condition* is true.

The condition in an if statement is considered true if its value is non-zero, and false if its value is zero. If the value of the conditional expression in an if statement is a vector or a matrix, it is considered true only if *all* of the elements are non-zero.

The second form of an if statement looks like this:

```
if (condition)
    then-body
else
    else-body
endif
```

If *condition* is true, *then-body* is executed; otherwise, *else-body* is executed.

Here is an example:

```
if (rem (x, 2) == 0)
   printf ("x is even\n");
else
   printf ("x is odd\n");
endif
```

In this example, if the expression rem (x, 2) == 0 is true (that is, the value of x is divisible by 2), then the first printf statement is evaluated, otherwise the second printf statement is evaluated.

The third and most general form of the if statement allows multiple decisions to be combined in a single statement. It looks like this:

```
if (condition)
   then-body
elseif (condition)
   elseif-body
else
   else-body
endif
```

Any number of elseif clauses may appear. Each condition is tested in turn, and if one is found to be true, its corresponding *body* is executed. If none of the conditions are true and the else clause is present, its body is executed. Only one else clause may appear, and it must be the last part of the statement.

In the following example, if the first condition is true (that is, the value of x is divisible by 2), then the first printf statement is executed. If it is false, then the second condition is tested, and if it is true (that is, the value of x is divisible by 3), then the second printf statement is executed. Otherwise, the third printf statement is performed.

```
if (rem (x, 2) == 0)
   printf ("x is even\n");
elseif (rem (x, 3) == 0)
   printf ("x is odd and divisible by 3\n");
else
   printf ("x is odd\n");
endif
```

Note that the elseif keyword must not be spelled else if, as is allowed in Fortran. If it is, the space between the else and if will tell Octave to treat this as a new if statement within another if statement's else clause. For example, if you write

```
if (c1)
  body-1
else if (c2)
  body-2
endif
```

Octave will expect additional input to complete the first if statement. If you are using Octave interactively, it will continue to prompt you for additional input. If Octave is reading this input from a file, it may complain about missing or mismatched end statements, or, if you have not used the more specific end statements (endif, endfor, etc.), it may simply produce incorrect results, without producing any warning messages.

It is much easier to see the error if we rewrite the statements above like this,

```
if (c1)
  body-1
else
  if (c2)
    body-2
  endif
```

using the indentation to show how Octave groups the statements. See Chapter 11 [Functions and Scripts], page 101.

**warn_assign_as_truth_value**                                Built-in Variable

If the value of warn_assign_as_truth_value is nonzero, a warning is issued for statements like

```
if (s = t)
  ...
```

since such statements are not common, and it is likely that the intent was to write

```
if (s == t)
  ...
```

instead.

There are times when it is useful to write code that contains assignments within the condition of a while or if statement. For example, statements like

```
while (c = getc())
  ...
```

are common in C programming.

It is possible to avoid all warnings about such statements by setting warn_assign_as_truth_value to 0, but that may also let real errors like

```
if (x = 1)  # intended to test (x == 1)!
   ...
```

slip by.

In such cases, it is possible suppress errors for specific statements by writing them with an extra set of parentheses. For example, writing the previous example as

```
while ((c = getc()))
   ...
```

will prevent the warning from being printed for this statement, while allowing Octave to warn about other assignments used in conditional contexts.

The default value of `warn_assign_as_truth_value` is 1.

## 10.2 The switch Statement

The `switch` statement was introduced in Octave 2.0.5. It should be considered experimental, and details of the implementation may change slightly in future versions of Octave. If you have comments or would like to share your experiences in trying to use this new command in real programs, please send them to `maintainers@octave.org`. (But if you think you've found a bug, please report it to `bug@octave.org`.

The general form of the `switch` statement is

```
switch expression
  case label
      command_list
  case label
      command_list
  ...

  otherwise
      command_list
endswitch
```

- The identifiers `switch`, `case`, `otherwise`, and `endswitch` are now keywords.

- The *label* may be any expression.

- Duplicate *label* values are not detected. The *command_list* corresponding to the first match will be executed.

- You must have at least one `case` *label command_list* clause.

- The `otherwise` *command_list* clause is optional.

- As with all other specific end keywords, endswitch may be replaced by end, but you can get better diagnostics if you use the specific forms.

- Cases are exclusive, so they don't 'fall through' as do the cases in the switch statement of the C language.

- The *command_list* elements are not optional. Making the list optional would have meant requiring a separator between the label and the command list. Otherwise, things like

```
switch (foo)
  case (1) -2
  . . .
```

would produce surprising results, as would

```
switch (foo)
  case (1)
  case (2)
    doit ();
    . . .
```

particularly for C programmers.

- The implementation is simple-minded and currently offers no real performance improvement over an equivalent if block, even if all the labels are integer constants. Perhaps a future variation on this could detect all constant integer labels and improve performance by using a jump table.

**warn_variable_switch_label**                                Built-in Variable
If the value of this variable is nonzero, Octave will print a warning if a switch label is not a constant or constant expression

## 10.3 The while Statement

In programming, a *loop* means a part of a program that is (or at least can be) executed two or more times in succession.

The while statement is the simplest looping statement in Octave. It repeatedly executes a statement as long as a condition is true. As with the condition in an if statement, the condition in a while statement is considered true if its value is non-zero, and false if its value is zero. If the value of the conditional expression in a while statement is a vector or a matrix, it is considered true only if *all* of the elements are non-zero.

Octave's while statement looks like this:

```
while (condition)
```

    *body*
    `endwhile`

Here *body* is a statement or list of statements that we call the *body* of the loop, and *condition* is an expression that controls how long the loop keeps running.

    The first thing the `while` statement does is test *condition*. If *condition* is true, it executes the statement *body*. After *body* has been executed, *condition* is tested again, and if it is still true, *body* is executed again. This process repeats until *condition* is no longer true. If *condition* is initially false, the body of the loop is never executed.

    This example creates a variable `fib` that contains the first ten elements of the Fibonacci sequence.

```
fib = ones (1, 10);
i = 3;
while (i <= 10)
  fib (i) = fib (i-1) + fib (i-2);
  i++;
endwhile
```

Here the body of the loop contains two statements.

    The loop works like this: first, the value of i is set to 3. Then, the `while` tests whether i is less than or equal to 10. This is the case when i equals 3, so the value of the i-th element of `fib` is set to the sum of the previous two values in the sequence. Then the i++ increments the value of i and the loop repeats. The loop terminates when i reaches 11.

    A newline is not required between the condition and the body; but using one makes the program clearer unless the body is very simple.

    See Section 10.1 [The if Statement], page 89 for a description of the variable `warn_assign_as_truth_value`.

## 10.4 The `for` Statement

    The `for` statement makes it more convenient to count iterations of a loop. The general form of the `for` statement looks like this:

```
for var = expression
  body
endfor
```

where *body* stands for any statement or list of statements, *expression* is any valid expression, and *var* may take several forms. Usually it is a simple variable name or an indexed variable. If the value of *expression* is a structure, *var* may also be a list. See Section 10.4.1 [Looping Over Structure Elements], page 95, below.

The assignment expression in the for statement works a bit differently than Octave's normal assignment statement. Instead of assigning the complete result of the expression, it assigns each column of the expression to var in turn. If *expression* is a range, a row vector, or a scalar, the value of var will be a scalar each time the loop body is executed. If var is a column vector or a matrix, var will be a column vector each time the loop body is executed.

The following example shows another way to create a vector containing the first ten elements of the Fibonacci sequence, this time using the for statement:

```
fib = ones (1, 10);
for i = 3:10
  fib (i) = fib (i-1) + fib (i-2);
endfor
```

This code works by first evaluating the expression 3:10, to produce a range of values from 3 to 10 inclusive. Then the variable i is assigned the first element of the range and the body of the loop is executed once. When the end of the loop body is reached, the next value in the range is assigned to the variable i, and the loop body is executed again. This process continues until there are no more elements to assign.

Although it is possible to rewrite all for loops as while loops, the Octave language has both statements because often a for loop is both less work to type and more natural to think of. Counting the number of iterations is very common in loops and it can be easier to think of this counting as part of looping rather than as something to do inside the loop.

## 10.4.1 Looping Over Structure Elements

A special form of the for statement allows you to loop over all the elements of a structure:

```
for [ val, key ] = expression
  body
endfor
```

In this form of the for statement, the value of *expression* must be a structure. If it is, *key* and *val* are set to the name of the element and the corresponding value in turn, until there are no more elements. For example,

```
x.a = 1
x.b = [1, 2; 3, 4]
x.c = "string"
for [val, key] = x
  key
```

```
    val
  endfor
```

```
        ⊣ key = a
        ⊣ val = 1
        ⊣ key = b
        ⊣ val =
        ⊣
        ⊣   1  2
        ⊣   3  4
        ⊣
        ⊣ key = c
        ⊣ val = string
```

The elements are not accessed in any particular order. If you need to cycle through the list in a particular way, you will have to use the function struct_elements and sort the list yourself.

The *key* variable may also be omitted. If it is, the brackets are also optional. This is useful for cycling through the values of all the structure elements when the names of the elements do not need to be known.

## 10.5 The break Statement

The break statement jumps out of the innermost for or while loop that encloses it. The break statement may only be used within the body of a loop. The following example finds the smallest divisor of a given integer, and also identifies prime numbers:

```
num = 103;
div = 2;
while (div*div <= num)
  if (rem (num, div) == 0)
    break;
  endif
  div++;
endwhile
if (rem (num, div) == 0)
  printf ("Smallest divisor of %d is %d\n", num, div)
else
  printf ("%d is prime\n", num);
endif
```

When the remainder is zero in the first while statement, Octave immediately *breaks out* of the loop. This means that Octave proceeds immediately to the statement following the loop and continues processing. (This is very different from the exit statement which stops the entire Octave program.)

Here is another program equivalent to the previous one. It illustrates how the *condition* of a while statement could just as well be replaced with a break inside an if:

```
num = 103;
div = 2;
while (1)
  if (rem (num, div) == 0)
    printf ("Smallest divisor of %d is %d\n", num, div);
    break;
  endif
  div++;
  if (div*div > num)
    printf ("%d is prime\n", num);
    break;
  endif
endwhile
```

## 10.6 The continue Statement

The continue statement, like break, is used only inside for or while loops. It skips over the rest of the loop body, causing the next cycle around the loop to begin immediately. Contrast this with break, which jumps out of the loop altogether. Here is an example:

```
# print elements of a vector of random
# integers that are even.

# first, create a row vector of 10 random
# integers with values between 0 and 100:

vec = round (rand (1, 10) * 100);

# print what we're interested in:

for x = vec
  if (rem (x, 2) != 0)
    continue;
  endif
  printf ("%d\n", x);
```

```
endfor
```

If one of the elements of *vec* is an odd number, this example skips the print statement for that element, and continues back to the first statement in the loop.

This is not a practical example of the continue statement, but it should give you a clear understanding of how it works. Normally, one would probably write the loop like this:

```
for x = vec
  if (rem (x, 2) == 0)
    printf ("%d\n", x);
  endif
endfor
```

## 10.7  The unwind_protect Statement

Octave supports a limited form of exception handling modelled after the unwind-protect form of Lisp.

The general form of an unwind_protect block looks like this:

```
unwind_protect
  body
unwind_protect_cleanup
  cleanup
end_unwind_protect
```

Where *body* and *cleanup* are both optional and may contain any Octave expressions or commands. The statements in *cleanup* are guaranteed to be executed regardless of how control exits *body*.

This is useful to protect temporary changes to global variables from possible errors. For example, the following code will always restore the original value of the built-in variable do_fortran_indexing even if an error occurs while performing the indexing operation.

```
save_do_fortran_indexing = do_fortran_indexing;
unwind_protect
  do_fortran_indexing = 1;
  elt = a (idx)
unwind_protect_cleanup
  do_fortran_indexing = save_do_fortran_indexing;
end_unwind_protect
```

Without unwind_protect, the value of *do_fortran_indexing* would not be restored if an error occurs while performing the indexing operation because evaluation would stop at the point of the error and the statement to restore the value would not be executed.

# 10.8 The try Statement

In addition to unwind_protect, Octave supports another limited form of exception handling.

The general form of a try block looks like this:

```
try
    body
catch
    cleanup
end_try_catch
```

Where *body* and *cleanup* are both optional and may contain any Octave expressions or commands. The statements in *cleanup* are only executed if an error occurs in *body*.

No warnings or error messages are printed while *body* is executing. If an error does occur during the execution of *body*, *cleanup* can access the text of the message that would have been printed in the builtin constant __error_text__. This is the same as eval (*try*, *catch*) (which may now also use __error_text__) but it is more efficient since the commands do not need to be parsed each time the *try* and *catch* statements are evaluated. See Chapter 12 [Error Handling], page 119, for more information about the __error_text__ variable.

Octave's *try* block is a very limited variation on the Lisp condition-case form (limited because it cannot handle different classes of errors separately). Perhaps at some point Octave can have some sort of classification of errors and try-catch can be improved to be as powerful as condition-case in Lisp.

# 10.9 Continuation Lines

In the Octave language, most statements end with a newline character and you must tell Octave to ignore the newline character in order to continue a statement from one line to the next. Lines that end with the characters ... or \ are joined with the following line before they are divided into tokens by Octave's parser. For example, the lines

```
x = long_variable_name ...
    + longer_variable_name \
    - 42
```

form a single statement. The backslash character on the second line above is interpreted a continuation character, *not* as a division operator.

For continuation lines that do not occur inside string constants, whitespace and comments may appear between the continuation marker and the newline character. For example, the statement

```
x = long_variable_name ...      # comment one
    + longer_variable_name \    # comment two
    - 42                        # last comment
```

is equivalent to the one shown above. Inside string constants, the continuation marker must appear at the end of the line just before the newline character.

Input that occurs inside parentheses can be continued to the next line without having to use a continuation marker. For example, it is possible to write statements like

```
if (fine_dining_destination == on_a_boat
    || fine_dining_destination == on_a_train)
  suess (i, will, not, eat, them, sam, i, am, i,
         will, not, eat, green, eggs, and, ham);
endif
```

without having to add to the clutter with continuation markers.

# 11 Functions and Script Files

Complicated Octave programs can often be simplified by defining functions. Functions can be defined directly on the command line during interactive Octave sessions, or in external files, and can be called just like built-in functions.

## 11.1 Defining Functions

In its simplest form, the definition of a function named *name* looks like this:

```
function name
   body
endfunction
```

A valid function name is like a valid variable name: a sequence of letters, digits and underscores, not starting with a digit. Functions share the same pool of names as variables.

The function *body* consists of Octave statements. It is the most important part of the definition, because it says what the function should actually *do*.

For example, here is a function that, when executed, will ring the bell on your terminal (assuming that it is possible to do so):

```
function wakeup
   printf ("\a");
endfunction
```

The printf statement (see Chapter 13 [Input and Output], page 123) simply tells Octave to print the string "\a". The special character '\a' stands for the alert character (ASCII 7). See Chapter 5 [Strings], page 47.

Once this function is defined, you can ask Octave to evaluate it by typing the name of the function.

Normally, you will want to pass some information to the functions you define. The syntax for passing parameters to a function in Octave is

```
function name (arg-list)
   body
endfunction
```

where *arg-list* is a comma-separated list of the function's arguments. When the function is called, the argument names are used to hold the argument values given in the call. The list of arguments may be empty, in which case this form is equivalent to the one shown above.

To print a message along with ringing the bell, you might modify the beep to look like this:

```
function wakeup (message)
  printf ("\a%s\n", message);
endfunction
```

Calling this function using a statement like this

```
wakeup ("Rise and shine!");
```

will cause Octave to ring your terminal's bell and print the message 'Rise
and shine!', followed by a newline character (the '\n' in the first argument to the printf statement).

In most cases, you will also want to get some information back from
the functions you define. Here is the syntax for writing a function that
returns a single value:

```
function ret-var = name (arg-list)
  body
endfunction
```

The symbol *ret-var* is the name of the variable that will hold the value
to be returned by the function. This variable must be defined before the
end of the function body in order for the function to return a value.

Variables used in the body of a function are local to the function.
Variables named in *arg-list* and *ret-var* are also local to the function.
See Section 7.1 [Global Variables], page 59, for information about how to
access global variables inside a function.

For example, here is a function that computes the average of the elements of a vector:

```
function retval = avg (v)
  retval = sum (v) / length (v);
endfunction
```

If we had written avg like this instead,

```
function retval = avg (v)
  if (is_vector (v))
    retval = sum (v) / length (v);
  endif
endfunction
```

and then called the function with a matrix instead of a vector as the
argument, Octave would have printed an error message like this:

```
error: 'retval' undefined near line 1 column 10
error: evaluating index expression near line 7, column 1
```

because the body of the if statement was never executed, and retval
was never defined. To prevent obscure errors like this, it is a good idea to
always make sure that the return variables will always have values, and to

produce meaningful error messages when problems are encountered. For example, avg could have been written like this:

```
function retval = avg (v)
  retval = 0;
  if (is_vector (v))
    retval = sum (v) / length (v);
  else
    error ("avg: expecting vector argument");
  endif
endfunction
```

There is still one additional problem with this function. What if it is called without an argument? Without additional error checking, Octave will probably print an error message that won't really help you track down the source of the error. To allow you to catch errors like this, Octave provides each function with an automatic variable called nargin. Each time a function is called, nargin is automatically initialized to the number of arguments that have actually been passed to the function. For example, we might rewrite the avg function like this:

```
function retval = avg (v)
  retval = 0;
  if (nargin != 1)
    usage ("avg (vector)");
  endif
  if (is_vector (v))
    retval = sum (v) / length (v);
  else
    error ("avg: expecting vector argument");
  endif
endfunction
```

Although Octave does not automatically report an error if you call a function with more arguments than expected, doing so probably indicates that something is wrong. Octave also does not automatically report an error if a function is called with too few arguments, but any attempt to use a variable that has not been given a value will result in an error. To avoid such problems and to provide useful messages, we check for both possibilities and issue our own error message.

nargin                                              Automatic Variable
    When a function is called, this local variable is automatically initialized
    to the number of arguments passed to the function. At the top level,
    nargin holds the number of command line arguments that were passed
    to Octave.

silent_functions                                          Built-in Variable

If the value of silent_functions is nonzero, internal output from a
function is suppressed. Otherwise, the results of expressions within a
function body that are not terminated with a semicolon will have their
values printed. The default value is 0.

For example, if the function

```
function f ()
  2 + 2
endfunction
```

is executed, Octave will either print 'ans = 4' or nothing depending on
the value of silent_functions.

warn_missing_semicolon                                    Built-in Variable

If the value of this variable is nonzero, Octave will warn when statements in function definitions don't end in semicolons. The default
value is 0.

## 11.2  Multiple Return Values

Unlike many other computer languages, Octave allows you to define
functions that return more than one value. The syntax for defining functions that return multiple values is

```
function [ret-list] = name (arg-list)
  body
endfunction
```

where name, arg-list, and body have the same meaning as before, and ret-
list is a comma-separated list of variable names that will hold the values
returned from the function. The list of return values must have at least
one element. If ret-list has only one element, this form of the function
statement is equivalent to the form described in the previous section.

Here is an example of a function that returns two values, the maximum
element of a vector and the index of its first occurrence in the vector.

```
function [max, idx] = vmax (v)
  idx = 1;
  max = v (idx);
  for i = 2:length (v)
    if (v (i) > max)
      max = v (i);
      idx = i;
    endif
  endfor
```

```
endfunction
```

In this particular case, the two values could have been returned as elements of a single array, but that is not always possible or convenient. The values to be returned may not have compatible dimensions, and it is often desirable to give the individual return values distinct names.

In addition to setting nargin each time a function is called, Octave also automatically initializes nargout to the number of values that are expected to be returned. This allows you to write functions that behave differently depending on the number of values that the user of the function has requested. The implicit assignment to the built-in variable ans does not figure in the count of output arguments, so the value of nargout may be zero.

The svd and lu functions are examples of built-in functions that behave differently depending on the value of nargout.

It is possible to write functions that only set some return values. For example, calling the function

```
function [x, y, z] = f ()
  x = 1;
  z = 2;
endfunction
```

as

```
[a, b, c] = f ()
```

produces:

```
a = 1

b = [](0x0)

c = 2
```

provided that the built-in variable define_all_return_values is nonzero and the value of default_return_value is '[]'. See Section 7.3 [Summary of Built-in Variables], page 63.

**nargout** Automatic Variable

When a function is called, this local variable is automatically initialized to the number of arguments expected to be returned. For example,

```
f ()
```

will result in nargout being set to 0 inside the function f and

```
[s, t] = f ()
```

will result in nargout being set to 2 inside the function f.

At the top level, nargout is undefined.

**default_return_value**                              Built-in Variable
The value given to otherwise uninitialized return values if define_
all_return_values is nonzero. The default value is [].

**define_all_return_values**                         Built-in Variable
If the value of define_all_return_values is nonzero, Octave will
substitute the value specified by default_return_value for any return values that remain undefined when a function returns. The default value is 0.

**nargchk** (*nargin_min*, *nargin_max*, *n*)                Function File
If *n* is in the range *nargin_min* through *nargin_max* inclusive, return
the empty matrix. Otherwise, return a message indicating whether *n*
is too large or too small.

This is useful for checking to see that the number of arguments supplied
to a function is within an acceptable range.

# 11.3 Variable-length Argument Lists

Octave has a real mechanism for handling functions that take an unspecified number of arguments, so it is not necessary to place an upper
bound on the number of optional arguments that a function can accept.

Here is an example of a function that uses the new syntax to print a
header followed by an unspecified number of values:

```
function foo (heading, ...)
  disp (heading);
  va_start ();
  ## Pre-decrement to skip 'heading' arg.
  while (--nargin)
    disp (va_arg ());
  endwhile
endfunction
```

The ellipsis that marks the variable argument list may only appear
once and must be the last element in the list of arguments.

**va_start** ()                                       Built-in Function
Position an internal pointer to the first unnamed argument and allows
you to cycle through the arguments more than once. It is not necessary
to call va_start if you do not plan to cycle through the arguments
more than once. This function may only be called inside functions that
have been declared to accept a variable number of input arguments.

va_arg ()                                               Built-in Function

Return the value of the next available argument and move the internal pointer to the next argument. It is an error to call va_arg() when there are no more arguments available.

Sometimes it is useful to be able to pass all unnamed arguments to another function. The keyword *all_va_args* makes this very easy to do. For example,

```
function f (...)
  while (nargin--)
    disp (va_arg ())
  endwhile
endfunction

function g (...)
  f ("begin", all_va_args, "end")
endfunction

g (1, 2, 3)
```

```
     ⊣ begin
     ⊣ 1
     ⊣ 2
     ⊣ 3
     ⊣ end
```

all_va_args                                                      Keyword

This keyword stands for the entire list of optional argument, so it is possible to use it more than once within the same function without having to call va_start. It can only be used within functions that take a variable number of arguments. It is an error to use it in other contexts.

## 11.4 Variable-length Return Lists

Octave also has a real mechanism for handling functions that return an unspecified number of values, so it is no longer necessary to place an upper bound on the number of outputs that a function can produce.

Here is an example of a function that uses a variable-length return list to produce $n$ values:

```
function [...] = f (n, x)
  for i = 1:n
```

```
      vr_val (i * x);
   endfor
endfunction

[dos, quatro] = f (2, 2)
     ⇒ dos = 2
     ⇒ quatro = 4
```

As with variable argument lists, the ellipsis that marks the variable return list may only appear once and must be the last element in the list of returned values.

**vr_val** (*val*)                                          Built-in Function
Each time this function is called, it places the value of its argument at the end of the list of values to return from the current function. Once vr_val has been called, there is no way to go back to the beginning of the list and rewrite any of the return values. This function may only be called within functions that have been declared to return an unspecified number of output arguments (by using the special ellipsis notation described above).

# 11.5 Returning From a Function

The body of a user-defined function can contain a return statement. This statement returns control to the rest of the Octave program. It looks like this:

```
return
```

Unlike the return statement in C, Octave's return statement cannot be used to return a value from a function. Instead, you must assign values to the list of return variables that are part of the function statement. The return statement simply makes it easier to exit a function from a deeply nested loop or conditional statement.

Here is an example of a function that checks to see if any elements of a vector are nonzero.

```
function retval = any_nonzero (v)
   retval = 0;
   for i = 1:length (v)
     if (v (i) != 0)
       retval = 1;
       return;
     endif
   endfor
```

```
    printf ("no nonzero elements found\n");
  endfunction
```

Note that this function could not have been written using the break statement to exit the loop once a nonzero value is found without adding extra logic to avoid printing the message if the vector does contain a nonzero element.

**return**                                                                Keyword
When Octave encounters the keyword return inside a function or script, it returns control to be caller immediately. At the top level, the return statement is ignored. A return statement is assumed at the end of every function definition.

**return_last_computed_value**                              Built-in Variable
If the value of return_last_computed_value is true, and a function is defined without explicitly specifying a return value, the function will return the value of the last expression. Otherwise, no value will be returned. The default value is 0.

For example, the function

```
  function f ()
    2 + 2;
  endfunction
```

will either return nothing, if the value of return_last_computed_value is 0, or 4, if the value of return_last_computed_value is nonzero.

## 11.6 Function Files

Except for simple one-shot programs, it is not practical to have to define all the functions you need each time you need them. Instead, you will normally want to save them in a file so that you can easily edit them, and save them for use at a later time.

Octave does not require you to load function definitions from files before using them. You simply need to put the function definitions in a place where Octave can find them.

When Octave encounters an identifier that is undefined, it first looks for variables or functions that are already compiled and currently listed in its symbol table. If it fails to find a definition there, it searches the list of directories specified by the built-in variable LOADPATH for files ending in '.m' that have the same base name as the undefined identifier.[1] Once

---

[1] The '.m' suffix was chosen for compatibility with MATLAB.

Octave finds a file with a name that matches, the contents of the file are read. If it defines a *single* function, it is compiled and executed. See Section 11.7 [Script Files], page 111, for more information about how you can define more than one function in a single file.

When Octave defines a function from a function file, it saves the full name of the file it read and the time stamp on the file. After that, it checks the time stamp on the file every time it needs the function. If the time stamp indicates that the file has changed since the last time it was read, Octave reads it again.

Checking the time stamp allows you to edit the definition of a function while Octave is running, and automatically use the new function definition without having to restart your Octave session. Checking the time stamp every time a function is used is rather inefficient, but it has to be done to ensure that the correct function definition is used.

To avoid degrading performance unnecessarily by checking the time stamps on functions that are not likely to change, Octave assumes that any function files located in the directory tree '*octave-home*/share/octave/*version*/m' will not change, so it doesn't have to check their time stamps every time the functions defined in those files are used. This is normally a very good assumption and provides a significant improvement in performance for the function files that are distributed with Octave.

If you know that your own function files will not change while you are running Octave, you can improve performance by setting the variable ignore_function_time_stamp to "all", so that Octave will ignore the time stamps for all function files. Setting it to "system" gives the default behavior. If you set it to anything else, Octave will check the time stamps on all function files.

**DEFAULT_LOADPATH**                                   Built-in Variable

A colon separated list of directories in which to search for function files by default. The value of this variable is also automatically substituted for leading, trailing, or doubled colons that appear in the built-in variable LOADPATH.

**LOADPATH**                                           Built-in Variable

A colon separated list of directories in which to search for function files. See Chapter 11 [Functions and Scripts], page 101. The value of LOADPATH overrides the environment variable OCTAVE_PATH. See Appendix C [Installation], page 259.

LOADPATH is now handled in the same way as TeX handles TEXINPUTS. Leading, trailing, or doubled colons that appear in LOADPATH are replaced by the value of DEFAULT_LOADPATH. The default value of LOADPATH is ":", which tells Octave to search in the directories specified by DEFAULT_LOADPATH.

In addition, if any path element ends in '//', that directory and all subdirectories it contains are searched recursively for function files. This can result in a slight delay as Octave caches the lists of files found in the LOADPATH the first time Octave searches for a function. After that, searching is usually much faster because Octave normally only needs to search its internal cache for files.

To improve performance of recursive directory searching, it is best for each directory that is to be searched recursively to contain *either* additional subdirectories *or* function files, but not a mixture of both.

See Section 11.9 [Organization of Functions], page 117 for a description of the function file directories that are distributed with Octave.

**ignore_function_time_stamp**                    Built-in Variable
This variable can be used to prevent Octave from making the system call stat each time it looks up functions defined in function files. If ignore_function_time_stamp to "system", Octave will not automatically recompile function files in subdirectories of '*octave-home*/lib/*version*' if they have changed since they were last compiled, but will recompile other function files in the LOADPATH if they change. If set to "all", Octave will not recompile any function files unless their definitions are removed with clear. For any other value of ignore_function_time_stamp, Octave will always check to see if functions defined in function files need to recompiled. The default value of ignore_function_time_stamp is "system".

**warn_function_name_clash**                    Built-in Variable
If the value of warn_function_name_clash is nonzero, a warning is issued when Octave finds that the name of a function defined in a function file differs from the name of the file. (If the names disagree, the name declared inside the file is ignored.) If the value is 0, the warning is omitted. The default value is 1.

## 11.7 Script Files

A script file is a file containing (almost) any sequence of Octave commands. It is read and evaluated just as if you had typed each command at the Octave prompt, and provides a convenient way to perform a sequence of commands that do not logically belong inside a function.

Unlike a function file, a script file must *not* begin with the keyword function. If it does, Octave will assume that it is a function file, and that it defines a single function that should be evaluated as soon as it is defined.

A script file also differs from a function file in that the variables named in a script file are not local variables, but are in the same scope as the other variables that are visible on the command line.

Even though a script file may not begin with the function keyword, it is possible to define more than one function in a single script file and load (but not execute) all of them at once. To do this, the first token in the file (ignoring comments and other white space) must be something other than function. If you have no other statements to evaluate, you can use a statement that has no effect, like this:

```
# Prevent Octave from thinking that this
# is a function file:

1;

# Define function one:

function one ()
    ...
```

To have Octave read and compile these functions into an internal form, you need to make sure that the file is in Octave's LOADPATH, then simply type the base name of the file that contains the commands. (Octave uses the same rules to search for script files as it does to search for function files.)

If the first token in a file (ignoring comments) is function, Octave will compile the function and try to execute it, printing a message warning about any non-whitespace characters that appear after the function definition.

Note that Octave does not try to look up the definition of any identifier until it needs to evaluate it. This means that Octave will compile the following statements if they appear in a script file, or are typed at the command line,

```
# not a function file:
1;
function foo ()
   do_something ();
endfunction
function do_something ()
   do_something_else ();
endfunction
```

even though the function do_something is not defined before it is referenced in the function foo. This is not an error because Octave does not need to resolve all symbols that are referenced by a function until the function is actually evaluated.

Since Octave doesn't look for definitions until they are needed, the following code will always print 'bar = 3' whether it is typed directly on the command line, read from a script file, or is part of a function body, even if there is a function or script file called 'bar.m' in Octave's LOADPATH.

```
eval ("bar = 3");
bar
```

Code like this appearing within a function body could fool Octave if definitions were resolved as the function was being compiled. It would be virtually impossible to make Octave clever enough to evaluate this code in a consistent fashion. The parser would have to be able to perform the call to eval at compile time, and that would be impossible unless all the references in the string to be evaluated could also be resolved, and requiring that would be too restrictive (the string might come from user input, or depend on things that are not known until the function is evaluated).

Although Octave normally executes commands from script files that have the name 'file.m', you can use the function source to execute commands from any file.

**source** (*file*)                                    Built-in Function
   Parse and execute the contents of *file*. This is equivalent to executing commands from a script file, but without requiring the file to be named '*file*.m'.

# 11.8 Dynamically Linked Functions

On some systems, Octave can dynamically load and execute functions written in C++. Octave can only directly call functions written in C++, but you can also load functions written in other languages by calling them from a simple wrapper function written in C++.

Here is an example of how to write a C++ function that Octave can load, with commentary. The source for this function is included in the source distributions of Octave, in the file 'examples/oregonator.cc'. It defines the same set of differential equations that are used in the example problem of Section 20.1 [Ordinary Differential Equations], page 195. By running that example and this one, we can compare the execution times to see what sort of increase in speed you can expect by using dynamically linked functions.

The function defined in 'oregonator.cc' contains just 8 statements, and is not much different than the code defined in the corresponding M-file (also distributed with Octave in the file 'examples/oregonator.m').

Here is the complete text of 'oregonator.cc':

```
#include <octave/oct.h>

DEFUN_DLD (oregonator, args, ,
  "The 'oregonator'.")
{
  ColumnVector dx (3);

  ColumnVector x = args(0).vector_value ();

  dx(0) = 77.27 * (x(1) - x(0)*x(1) + x(0)
                    - 8.375e-06*pow (x(0), 2));

  dx(1) = (x(2) - x(0)*x(1) - x(1)) / 77.27;

  dx(2) = 0.161*(x(0) - x(2));

  return octave_value (dx);
}
```

The first line of the file,

```
#include <octave/oct.h>
```

includes declarations for all of Octave's internal functions that you will need. If you need other functions from the standard C++ or C libraries, you can include the necessary headers here.

The next two lines

```
DEFUN_DLD (oregonator, args, ,
  "The 'oregonator'.")
```

declares the function. The macro DEFUN_DLD and the macros that it depends on are defined in the files 'defun-dld.h', 'defun.h', and 'defun-int.h' (these files are included in the header file 'octave/oct.h').

Note that the third parameter to DEFUN_DLD (nargout) is not used, so it is omitted from the list of arguments to in order to avoid the warning from gcc about an unused function parameter.

simply declares an object to store the right hand sides of the differential equation, and

The statement

```
ColumnVector x = args(0).vector_value ();
```

extracts a column vector from the input arguments. The variable `args` is passed to functions defined with DEFUN_DLD as an `octave_value_list` object, which includes methods for getting the length of the list and extracting individual elements.

In this example, we don't check for errors, but that is not difficult. All of the Octave's built-in functions do some form of checking on their arguments, so you can check the source code for those functions for examples of various strategies for verifying that the correct number and types of arguments have been supplied.

The next statements

```
ColumnVector dx (3);

dx(0) = 77.27 * (x(1) - x(0)*x(1) + x(0)
                 - 8.375e-06*pow (x(0), 2));

dx(1) = (x(2) - x(0)*x(1) - x(1)) / 77.27;

dx(2) = 0.161*(x(0) - x(2));
```

define the right hand side of the differential equation. Finally, we can return dx:

```
return octave_value (dx);
```

The actual return type is `octave_value_list`, but it is only necessary to convert the return type to an `octave_value` because there is a default constructor that can automatically create an object of that type from an `octave_value` object, so we can just use that instead.

To use this file, your version of Octave must support dynamic linking. To find out if it does, type the command *octave_config_info ("dld")* at the Octave prompt. Support for dynamic linking is included if this command returns 1.

To compile the example file, type the command 'mkoctfile oregonator.cc' at the shell prompt. The script mkoctfile should have been installed along with Octave. Running it will create a file called 'oregonator.oct' that can be loaded by Octave. To test the 'oregonator.oct' file, start Octave and type the command

```
oregonator ([1, 2, 3], 0)
```

at the Octave prompt. Octave should respond by printing

```
ans =

   77.269353
   -0.012942
   -0.322000
```

You can now use the 'oregonator.oct' file just as you would the oregonator.m file to solve the set of differential equations.

On a 133 MHz Pentium running Linux, Octave can solve the problem shown in Section 20.1 [Ordinary Differential Equations], page 195 in about 1.4 second using the dynamically linked function, compared to about 19 seconds using the M-file. Similar decreases in execution time can be expected for other functions, particularly those that rely on functions like lsode that require user-supplied functions.

Just as for M-files, Octave will automatically reload dynamically linked functions when the files that define them are more recent than the last time that the function was loaded. Two variables are available to control how Octave behaves when dynamically linked functions are cleared or reloaded.

**auto_unload_dot_oct_files**                                      Built-in Variable
   If the value of auto_unload_dot_oct_files is nonzero, Octave will automatically unload any '.oct' files when there are no longer any functions in the symbol table that reference them.

**warn_reload_forces_clear**                                       Built-in Variable
   If several functions have been loaded from the same file, Octave must clear all the functions before any one of them can be reloaded. If warn_reload_forces_clear, Octave will warn you when this happens, and print a list of the additional functions that it is forced to clear.

Additional examples for writing dynamically linked functions are available in the files in the 'src' directory of the Octave distribution. Currently, this includes the files

| balance.cc | fft2.cc | inv.cc | qzval.cc |
| chol.cc | filter.cc | log.cc | schur.cc |
| colloc.cc | find.cc | lsode.cc | sort.cc |
| dassl.cc | fsolve.cc | lu.cc | svd.cc |
| det.cc | givens.cc | minmax.cc | syl.cc |
| eig.cc | hess.cc | pinv.cc | |
| expm.cc | ifft.cc | qr.cc | |
| fft.cc | ifft2.cc | quad.cc | |

These files use the macro DEFUN_DLD_BUILTIN instead of DEFUN_DLD. The difference between these two macros is just that DEFUN_DLD_BUILTIN can define a built-in function that is not dynamically loaded if the operating system does not support dynamic linking. To define your own dynamically linked functions you should use DEFUN_DLD.

There is currently no detailed description of all the functions that you can call in a built-in function. For the time being, you will have to read the source code for Octave.

# 11.9  Organization of Functions Distributed with Octave

Many of Octave's standard functions are distributed as function files. They are loosely organized by topic, in subdirectories of '*octave-home*/lib/octave/*version*/m', to make it easier to find them.

The following is a list of all the function file subdirectories, and the types of functions you will find there.

'audio'      Functions for playing and recording sounds.

'control'    Functions for design and simulation of automatic control systems.

'elfun'      Elementary functions.

'general'    Miscellaneous matrix manipulations, like flipud, rot90, and triu, as well as other basic functions, like is_matrix, nargchk, etc.

'image'      Image processing tools. These functions require the X Window System.

'io'         Input-output functions.

'linear-algebra'
             Functions for linear algebra.

'miscellaneous'
             Functions that don't really belong anywhere else.

'plot'       A set of functions that implement the MATLAB-like plotting functions.

'polynomial'
             Functions for manipulating polynomials.

'set'        Functions for creating and manipulating sets of unique values.

'signal'     Functions for signal processing applications.

'specfun'    Special functions.

'special-matrix'
             Functions that create special matrix forms.

'startup'        Octave's system-wide startup file.

'statistics'
                 Statistical functions.

'strings'        Miscellaneous string-handling functions.

'time'           Functions related to time keeping.

# 12 Error Handling

Octave includes several functions for printing error and warning messages. When you write functions that need to take special action when they encounter abnormal conditions, you should print the error messages using the functions described in this chapter.

**error** (*template*, ...)                                     Built-in Function

The error function formats the optional arguments under the control of the template string *template* using the same rules as the printf family of functions (see Section 13.2.4 [Formatted Output], page 133). The resulting message is prefixed by the string 'error: ' and printed on the stderr stream.

Calling error also sets Octave's internal error state such that control will return to the top level without evaluating any more commands. This is useful for aborting from functions or scripts.

If the error message does not end with a new line character, Octave will print a traceback of all the function calls leading to the error. For example, given the following function definitions:

```
function f () g () end
function g () h () end
function h () nargin == 1 || error ("nargin != 1"); end
```

calling the function f will result in a list of messages that can help you to quickly locate the exact location of the error:

```
f ()
error: nargin != 1
error: evaluating index expression near line 1, column 30
error: evaluating binary operator '||' near line 1, column 27
error: called from 'h'
error: called from 'g'
error: called from 'f'
```

If the error message ends in a new line character, Octave will print the message but will not display any traceback messages as it returns control to the top level. For example, modifying the error message in the previous example to end in a new line causes Octave to only print a single message:

```
function h () nargin == 1 || error ("nargin != 1\n"); end
f ()
error: nargin != 1
```

**error_text**                                                Built-in Variable
This variable contains the text of error messages that would have been printed in the body of the most recent unwind_protect or try statement or the *try* part of the most recent call to the eval function. Outside of the unwind_protect and try statements or the eval function, or if no error has occurred within them, the value of error_text is guaranteed to be the empty string.

Note that the message does not include the first 'error: ' prefix, so that it may easily be passed to the error function without additional processing[1].

See Section 10.8 [The try Statement], page 99 and Section 10.7 [The unwind_protect Statement], page 98.

**beep_on_error**                                            Built-in Variable
If the value of beep_on_error is nonzero, Octave will try to ring your terminal's bell before printing an error message. The default value is 0.

**warning** (*msg*)                                          Built-in Function
Print a warning message *msg* prefixed by the string 'warning: '. After printing the warning message, Octave will continue to execute commands. You should use this function should when you want to notify the user of an unusual condition, but only when it makes sense for your program to go on.

**usage** (*msg*)                                            Built-in Function
Print the message *msg*, prefixed by the string 'usage: ', and set Octave's internal error state such that control will return to the top level without evaluating any more commands. This is useful for aborting from functions.

After usage is evaluated, Octave will print a traceback of all the function calls leading to the usage message.

You should use this function for reporting problems errors that result from an improper call to a function, such as calling a function with an incorrect number of arguments, or with arguments of the wrong type. For example, most functions distributed with Octave begin with code like this

```
if (nargin != 2)
  usage ("foo (a, b)");
endif
```

to check for the proper number of arguments.

---

[1] Yes, it's a kluge, but it seems to be a reasonably useful one.

The following pair of functions are of limited usefulness, and may be removed from future versions of Octave.

**perror** (*name, num*)                                              Function File
   Print the error message for function *name* corresponding to the error number *num*. This function is intended to be used to print useful error messages for those functions that return numeric error codes.

**strerror** (*name, num*)                                            Function File
   Return the text of an error message for function *name* corresponding to the error number *num*. This function is intended to be used to print useful error messages for those functions that return numeric error codes.

# 13 Input and Output

There are two distinct classes of input and output functions. The first set are modeled after the functions available in MATLAB. The second set are modeled after the standard I/O library used by the C programming language and offer more flexibility and control over the output.

When running interactively, Octave normally sends any output intended for your terminal that is more than one screen long to a paging program, such as less or more. This avoids the problem of having a large volume of output stream by before you can read it. With less (and some versions of more) you can also scan forward and backward, and search for specific items.

Normally, no output is displayed by the pager until just before Octave is ready to print the top level prompt, or read from the standard input (for example, by using the fscanf or scanf functions). This means that there may be some delay before any output appears on your screen if you have asked Octave to perform a significant amount of work with a single command statement. The function fflush may be used to force output to be sent to the pager (or any other stream) immediately.

You can select the program to run as the pager by setting the variable PAGER, and you can turn paging off by setting the value of the variable page_screen_output to 0.

**more**                                                                   Command
**more** *on*                                                              Command
**more** *off*                                                             Command
  Turn output pagination on or off. Without an argument, more toggles the current state.

**PAGER**                                                          Built-in Variable
  The default value is normally "less", "more", or "pg", depending on what programs are installed on your system. See Appendix C [Installation], page 259.

  When running interactively, Octave sends any output intended for your terminal that is more than one screen long to the program named by the value of the variable PAGER.

**page_screen_output**                                              Built-in Variable
  If the value of page_screen_output is nonzero, all output intended for the screen that is longer than one page is sent through a pager. This allows you to view one screenful at a time. Some pagers (such as less—see Appendix C [Installation], page 259) are also capable of moving backward on the output. The default value is 1.

**page_output_immediately**                                    Built-in Variable
  If the value of page_output_immediately is nonzero, Octave sends
  output to the pager as soon as it is available. Otherwise, Octave
  buffers its output and waits until just before the prompt is printed to
  flush it to the pager. The default value is 0.

**fflush** (*fid*)                                             Built-in Function
  Flush output to *fid*. This is useful for ensuring that all pending
  output makes it to the screen before some other event occurs. For
  example, it is always a good idea to flush the standard output
  stream before calling input.

# 13.1  Basic Input and Output

## 13.1.1  Terminal Output

Since Octave normally prints the value of an expression as soon as it
has been evaluated, the simplest of all I/O functions is a simple expression.
For example, the following expression will display the value of pi

    pi
        ⊣ pi = 3.1416

This works well as long as it is acceptable to have the name of the
variable (or 'ans') printed along with the value. To print the value of a
variable without printing its name, use the function disp.

The format command offers some control over the way Octave prints
values with disp and through the normal echoing mechanism.

**ans**                                                       Built-in Variable
  This variable holds the most recently computed result that was not
  explicitly assigned to a variable. For example, after the expression

    3^2 + 4^2

  is evaluated, the value of ans is 25.

**disp** (*x*)                                                Built-in Function
  Display the value of *x*. For example,

        disp ("The value of pi is:"), disp (pi)

            ⊣ the value of pi is:
            ⊣ 3.1416

  Note that the output from disp always ends with a newline.

**format** *options*                                              Command

Control the format of the output produced by disp and Octave's normal echoing mechanism. Valid options are listed in the following table.

short       Octave will try to print numbers with at least 3 significant figures within a field that is a maximum of 8 characters wide.

                  If Octave is unable to format a matrix so that columns line up on the decimal point and all the numbers fit within the maximum field width, it switches to an 'e' format.

long        Octave will try to print numbers with at least 15 significant figures within a field that is a maximum of 24 characters wide.

                  As will the 'short' format, Octave will switch to an 'e' format if it is unable to format a matrix so that columns line up on the decimal point and all the numbers fit within the maximum field width.

long e

short e     The same as 'format long' or 'format short' but always display output with an 'e' format. For example, with the 'short e' format, pi is displayed as 3.14e+00.

long E

short E     The same as 'format long e' or 'format short e' but always display output with an uppercase 'E' format. For example, with the 'long E' format, pi is displayed as 3.14159265358979E+00.

free

none      Print output in free format, without trying to line up columns of matrices on the decimal point. This also causes complex numbers to be formatted like this '(0.604194, 0.607088)' instead of like this '0.60419 + 0.60709i'.

bank       Print in a fixed format with two places to the right of the decimal point.

+            Print a '+' symbol for nonzero matrix elements and a space for zero matrix elements. This format can be very useful for examining the structure of a large matrix.

hex        Print the hexadecimal representation numbers as they are stored in memory. For example, on a workstation which stores 8 byte real values in IEEE format with the least

significant byte first, the value of pi when printed in hex
format is 400921fb54442d18. This format only works for
numeric values.

bit        Print the bit representation of numbers as stored in memory. For example, the value of pi is

    01000000000010010010000111111011
    01010100010001000010110100011000

(shown here in two 32 bit sections for typesetting pur-
poses) when printed in bit format on a workstation which
stores 8 byte real values in IEEE format with the least
significant byte first. This format only works for numeric
types.

By default, Octave will try to print numbers with at least 5 significant
figures within a field that is a maximum of 10 characters wide.

If Octave is unable to format a matrix so that columns line up on the
decimal point and all the numbers fit within the maximum field width,
it switches to an 'e' format.

If format is invoked without any options, the default format state is
restored.

**print_answer_id_name**               Built-in Variable
If the value of print_answer_id_name is nonzero, variable names are
printed along with the result. Otherwise, only the result values are
printed. The default value is 1.

## 13.1.2 Terminal Input

Octave has three functions that make it easy to prompt users for input. The input and menu functions are normally used for managing an
interactive dialog with a user, and the keyboard function is normally used
for doing simple debugging.

**input** (*prompt*)               Built-in Function
**input** (*prompt*, "s")            Built-in Function
Print a prompt and wait for user input. For example,

    input ("Pick a number, any number! ")

prints the prompt

    Pick a number, any number!

and waits for the user to enter a value. The string entered by the user
is evaluated as an expression, so it may be a literal constant, a variable
name, or any other valid expression.

Currently, input only returns one value, regardless of the number of values produced by the evaluation of the expression.

If you are only interested in getting a literal string value, you can call input with the character string "s" as the second argument. This tells Octave to return the string entered by the user directly, without evaluating it first.

Because there may be output waiting to be displayed by the pager, it is a good idea to always call fflush (stdout) before calling input. This will ensure that all pending output is written to the screen before your prompt. See Chapter 13 [Input and Output], page 123.

**menu** (*title, opt1, ...*)                                Function File
Print a title string followed by a series of options. Each option will be printed along with a number. The return value is the number of the option selected by the user. This function is useful for interactive programs. There is no limit to the number of options that may be passed in, but it may be confusing to present more than will fit easily on one screen.

**keyboard** (*prompt*)                                    Built-in Function
This function is normally used for simple debugging. When the keyboard function is executed, Octave prints a prompt and waits for user input. The input strings are then evaluated and the results are printed. This makes it possible to examine the values of variables within a function, and to assign new values to variables. No value is returned from the keyboard function, and it continues to prompt for input until the user types 'quit', or 'exit'.

If keyboard is invoked without any arguments, a default prompt of 'debug> ' is used.

For both input and keyboard, the normal command line history and editing functions are available at the prompt.

Octave also has a function that makes it possible to get a single character from the keyboard without requiring the user to type a carriage return.

**kbhit** ()                                               Built-in Function
Read a single keystroke from the keyboard. For example,

    x = kbhit ();

will set x to the next character typed at the keyboard as soon as it is typed.

# 13.1.3 Simple File I/O

The save and load commands allow data to be written to and read from disk files in various formats. The default format of files written by the save command can be controlled using the built-in variables default_ save_format and save_precision.

Note that Octave can not yet save or load structure variables or any user-defined types.

save *options file v1 v2 . . .*                                    Command

    Save the named variables *v1*, *v2*, . . . in the file *file*. The special file-name '-' can be used to write the output to your terminal. If no variable names are listed, Octave saves all the variables in the current scope. Valid options for the save command are listed in the following table. Options that modify the output format override the format specified by the built-in variable default_save_format.

    -ascii     Save the data in Octave's text data format.

    -binary    Save the data in Octave's binary data format.

    -float-binary

              Save the data in Octave's binary data format but only using single precision. You should use this format only if you know that all the values to be saved can be represented in single precision.

    -mat-binary

              Save the data in MATLAB's binary data format.

    -save-builtins

              Force Octave to save the values of built-in variables too. By default, Octave does not save built-in variables.

The list of variables to save may include wildcard patterns containing the following special characters:

    ?          Match any single character.

    *          Match zero or more characters.

    [ *list* ]   Match the list of characters specified by *list*. If the first character is ! or ^, match all characters except those specified by *list*. For example, the pattern '[a-zA-Z]' will match all lower and upper case alphabetic characters.

Except when using the MATLAB binary data file format, saving global variables also saves the global status of the variable, so that if it is restored at a later time using 'load', it will be restored as a global variable.

The command

```
save -binary data a b*
```

saves the variable 'a' and all variables beginning with 'b' to the file 'data' in Octave's binary format.

There are two variables that modify the behavior of save and one that controls whether variables are saved when Octave exits unexpectedly.

**crash_dumps_octave_core**                                    Built-in Variable

If this variable is set to a nonzero value, Octave tries to save all current variables the the file "octave-core" if it crashes or receives a hangup, terminate or similar signal. The default value is 1.

**default_save_format**                                        Built-in Variable

This variable specifies the default format for the save command. It should have one of the following values: "ascii", "binary", float-binary, or "mat-binary". The initial default save format is Octave's text format.

**save_precision**                                             Built-in Variable

This variable specifies the number of digits to keep when saving data in text format. The default value is 17.

**load** *options file v1 v2 . . .*                                      Command

Load the named variables from the file *file*. As with save, you may specify a list of variables and load will only extract those variables with names that match. For example, to restore the variables saved in the file 'data', use the command

```
load data
```

Octave will refuse to overwrite existing variables unless you use the option '-force'.

If a variable that is not marked as global is loaded from a file when a global symbol with the same name already exists, it is loaded in the global symbol table. Also, if a variable is marked as global in a file and a local symbol exists, the local symbol is moved to the global symbol table and given the value from the file. Since it seems that both of these cases are likely to be the result of some sort of error, they will generate warnings.

The load command can read data stored in Octave's text and binary formats, and MATLAB's binary format. It will automatically detect the type of file and do conversion from different floating point formats (currently only IEEE big and little endian, though other formats may added in the future).

Valid options for load are listed in the following table.

-force      Force variables currently in memory to be overwritten by variables with the same name found in the file.

-ascii      Force Octave to assume the file is in Octave's text format.

-binary     Force Octave to assume the file is in Octave's binary format.

-mat-binary
            Force Octave to assume the file is in MATLAB's binary format.

## 13.2  C-Style I/O Functions

Octave's C-style input and output functions provide most of the functionality of the C programming language's standard I/O library. The argument lists for some of the input functions are slightly different, however, because Octave has no way of passing arguments by reference.

In the following, *file* refers to a file name and fid refers to an integer file number, as returned by fopen.

There are three files that are always available. Although these files can be accessed using their corresponding numeric file ids, you should always use the symbolic names given in the table below, since it will make your programs easier to understand.

**stdin**                                               Built-in Variable
    The standard input stream (file id 0). When Octave is used interactively, this is filtered through the command line editing functions.

**stdout**                                              Built-in Variable
    The standard output stream (file id 1). Data written to the standard output is normally filtered through the pager.

**stderr**                                              Built-in Variable
    The standard error stream (file id 2). Even if paging is turned on, the standard error is not sent to the pager. It is useful for error messages and prompts.

## 13.2.1 Opening and Closing Files

[*fid*, *msg*] = **fopen** (*name*, *mode*, *arch*)       Built-in Function
*fid_list* = **fopen** ("all")       Built-in Function
*file* = **fopen** (*fid*)       Built-in Function

The first form of the fopen function opens the named file with the
specified mode (read-write, read-only, etc.) and architecture interpretation (IEEE big endian, IEEE little endian, etc.), and returns an
integer value that may be used to refer to the file later. If an error
occurs, *fid* is set to −1 and *msg* contains the corresponding system error message. The *mode* is a one or two character string that specifies
whether the file is to be opened for reading, writing, or both.

The second form of the fopen function returns a vector of file ids corresponding to all the currently open files, excluding the stdin, stdout,
and stderr streams.

The third form of the fopen function returns the name of a currently
open file given its file id.

For example,

        myfile = fopen ("splat.dat", "r", "ieee-le");

opens the file 'splat.dat' for reading. If necessary, binary numeric
values will be read assuming they are stored in IEEE format with the
least significant bit first, and then converted to the native representation.

Opening a file that is already open simply opens it again and returns
a separate file id. It is not an error to open a file several times, though
writing to the same file through several different file ids may produce
unexpected results.

The possible values 'mode' may have are

'r'         Open a file for reading.

'w'         Open a file for writing. The previous contents are discarded.

'a'         Open or create a file for writing at the end of the file.

'r+'       Open an existing file for reading and writing.

'w+'       Open a file for reading or writing. The previous contents
are discarded.

'a+'       Open or create a file for reading or writing at the end of
the file.

The parameter *arch* is a string specifying the default data format for
the file. Valid values for *arch* are:

'native' The format of the current machine (this is the default).

'ieee-le' IEEE big endian format.

'ieee-be' IEEE little endian format.

'vaxd' VAX D floating format.

'vaxg' VAX G floating format.

'cray' Cray floating format.

however, conversions are currently only supported for 'native' 'ieee-be', and 'ieee-le' formats.

**fclose** (*fid*)                                          Built-in Function
    Closes the specified file. If an error is encountered while trying to close the file, an error message is printed and fclose returns 0. Otherwise, it returns 1.

## 13.2.2 Simple Output

**fputs** (*fid, string*)                                   Built-in Function
    Write a string to a file with no formatting.

**puts** (*string*)                                         Built-in Function
    Write a string to the standard output with no formatting.

## 13.2.3 Line-Oriented Input

**fgetl** (*fid, len*)                                      Built-in Function
    Read characters from a file, stopping after a newline, or EOF, or *len* characters have been read. The characters read, excluding the possible trailing newline, are returned as a string.

    If *len* is omitted, fgetl reads until the next newline character.

    If there are no more characters to read, fgetl returns −1.

**fgets** (*fid, len*)                                      Built-in Function
    Read characters from a file, stopping after a newline, or EOF, or *len* characters have been read. The characters read, including the possible trailing newline, are returned as a string.

    If *len* is omitted, fgets reads until the next newline character.

    If there are no more characters to read, fgets returns −1.

## 13.2.4 Formatted Output

This section describes how to call printf and related functions.

The following functions are available for formatted output. They are modelled after the C language functions of the same name, but they interpret the format template differently in order to improve the performance of printing vector and matrix values.

printf (*template, ...*)                                             Function File
    The printf function prints the optional arguments under the control of the template string *template* to the stream stdout.

fprintf (*fid, template, ...*)                                   Built-in Function
    This function is just like printf, except that the output is written to the stream *fid* instead of stdout.

sprintf (*template, ...*)                                        Built-in Function
    This is like printf, except that the output is returned as a string. Unlike the C library function, which requires you to provide a suitably sized string as an argument, Octave's sprintf function returns the string, automatically sized to hold all of the items converted.

The printf function can be used to print any number of arguments. The template string argument you supply in a call provides information not only about the number of additional arguments, but also about their types and what style should be used for printing them.

Ordinary characters in the template string are simply written to the output stream as-is, while *conversion specifications* introduced by a '%' character in the template cause subsequent arguments to be formatted and written to the output stream. For example,

```
pct = 37;
filename = "foo.txt";
printf ("Processing of '%s' is %d%% finished.\nPlease wait.\n",
        filename, pct);
```

produces output like

```
Processing of 'foo.txt' is 37% finished.
Please be patient.
```

This example shows the use of the '%d' conversion to specify that a scalar argument should be printed in decimal notation, the '%s' conversion to specify printing of a string argument, and the '%%' conversion to print a literal '%' character.

There are also conversions for printing an integer argument as an unsigned value in octal, decimal, or hexadecimal radix ('%o', '%u', or '%x', respectively); or as a character value ('%c').

Floating-point numbers can be printed in normal, fixed-point notation using the '%f' conversion or in exponential notation using the '%e' conversion. The '%g' conversion uses either '%e' or '%f' format, depending on what is more appropriate for the magnitude of the particular number.

You can control formatting more precisely by writing *modifiers* between the '%' and the character that indicates which conversion to apply. These slightly alter the ordinary behavior of the conversion. For example, most conversion specifications permit you to specify a minimum field width and a flag indicating whether you want the result left- or right-justified within the field.

The specific flags and modifiers that are permitted and their interpretation vary depending on the particular conversion. They're all described in more detail in the following sections.

## 13.2.5 Output Conversion for Matrices

When given a matrix value, Octave's formatted output functions cycle through the format template until all the values in the matrix have been printed. For example,

```
printf ("%4.2f %10.2e %8.4g\n", hilb (3));
```

```
⊣ 1.00    5.00e-01    0.3333
⊣ 0.50    3.33e-01    0.25
⊣ 0.33    2.50e-01    0.2
```

If more than one value is to be printed in a single call, the output functions do not return to the beginning of the format template when moving on from one value to the next. This can lead to confusing output if the number of elements in the matrices are not exact multiples of the number of conversions in the format template. For example,

```
printf ("%4.2f %10.2e %8.4g\n", [1, 2], [3, 4]);
```

```
⊣ 1.00    2.00e+00           3
⊣ 4.00
```

If this is not what you want, use a series of calls instead of just one.

## 13.2.6 Output Conversion Syntax

This section provides details about the precise syntax of conversion specifications that can appear in a printf template string.

Characters in the template string that are not part of a conversion specification are printed as-is to the output stream.

The conversion specifications in a `printf` template string have the general form:

% *flags width* [ . *precision* ] *type conversion*

For example, in the conversion specifier '%-10.8ld', the '-' is a flag, '10' specifies the field width, the precision is '8', the letter '1' is a type modifier, and 'd' specifies the conversion style. (This particular type specifier says to print a numeric argument in decimal notation, with a minimum of 8 digits left-justified in a field at least 10 characters wide.)

In more detail, output conversion specifications consist of an initial '%' character followed in sequence by:

- Zero or more *flag characters* that modify the normal behavior of the conversion specification.

- An optional decimal integer specifying the *minimum field width*. If the normal conversion produces fewer characters than this, the field is padded with spaces to the specified width. This is a *minimum* value; if the normal conversion produces more characters than this, the field is *not* truncated. Normally, the output is right-justified within the field.

  You can also specify a field width of '*'. This means that the next argument in the argument list (before the actual value to be printed) is used as the field width. The value is rounded to the nearest integer. If the value is negative, this means to set the '-' flag (see below) and to use the absolute value as the field width.

- An optional *precision* to specify the number of digits to be written for the numeric conversions. If the precision is specified, it consists of a period ('.') followed optionally by a decimal integer (which defaults to zero if omitted).

  You can also specify a precision of '*'. This means that the next argument in the argument list (before the actual value to be printed) is used as the precision. The value must be an integer, and is ignored if it is negative.

- An optional *type modifier character*. This character is ignored by Octave's `printf` function, but is recognized to provide compatibility with the C language `printf`.

- A character that specifies the conversion to be applied.

The exact options that are permitted and how they are interpreted vary between the different conversion specifiers. See the descriptions of the individual conversions for information about the particular options that they use.

## 13.2.7 Table of Output Conversions

Here is a table summarizing what all the different conversions do:

'%d', '%i'    Print an integer as a signed decimal number. See Section 13.2.8 [Integer Conversions], page 137, for details. '%d' and '%i' are synonymous for output, but are different when used with scanf for input (see Section 13.2.13 [Table of Input Conversions], page 141).

'%o'          Print an integer as an unsigned octal number. See Section 13.2.8 [Integer Conversions], page 137, for details.

'%u'          Print an integer as an unsigned decimal number. See Section 13.2.8 [Integer Conversions], page 137, for details.

'%x', '%X'    Print an integer as an unsigned hexadecimal number. '%x' uses lower-case letters and '%X' uses upper-case. See Section 13.2.8 [Integer Conversions], page 137, for details.

'%f'          Print a floating-point number in normal (fixed-point) notation. See Section 13.2.9 [Floating-Point Conversions], page 137, for details.

'%e', '%E'    Print a floating-point number in exponential notation. '%e' uses lower-case letters and '%E' uses upper-case. See Section 13.2.9 [Floating-Point Conversions], page 137, for details.

'%g', '%G'    Print a floating-point number in either normal (fixed-point) or exponential notation, whichever is more appropriate for its magnitude. '%g' uses lower-case letters and '%G' uses upper-case. See Section 13.2.9 [Floating-Point Conversions], page 137, for details.

'%c'          Print a single character. See Section 13.2.10 [Other Output Conversions], page 138.

'%s'          Print a string. See Section 13.2.10 [Other Output Conversions], page 138.

'%%'          Print a literal '%' character. See Section 13.2.10 [Other Output Conversions], page 138.

If the syntax of a conversion specification is invalid, unpredictable things will happen, so don't do this. If there aren't enough function arguments provided to supply values for all the conversion specifications in the template string, or if the arguments are not of the correct types, the results are unpredictable. If you supply more arguments than conversion specifications, the extra argument values are simply ignored; this is sometimes useful.

## 13.2.8 Integer Conversions

This section describes the options for the '%d', '%i', '%o', '%u', '%x', and '%X' conversion specifications. These conversions print integers in various formats.

The '%d' and '%i' conversion specifications both print an numeric argument as a signed decimal number; while '%o', '%u', and '%x' print the argument as an unsigned octal, decimal, or hexadecimal number (respectively). The '%X' conversion specification is just like '%x' except that it uses the characters 'ABCDEF' as digits instead of 'abcdef'.

The following flags are meaningful:

'−'          Left-justify the result in the field (instead of the normal right-justification).

'+'          For the signed '%d' and '%i' conversions, print a plus sign if the value is positive.

' '          For the signed '%d' and '%i' conversions, if the result doesn't start with a plus or minus sign, prefix it with a space character instead. Since the '+' flag ensures that the result includes a sign, this flag is ignored if you supply both of them.

'#'          For the '%o' conversion, this forces the leading digit to be '0', as if by increasing the precision. For '%x' or '%X', this prefixes a leading '0x' or '0X' (respectively) to the result. This doesn't do anything useful for the '%d', '%i', or '%u' conversions.

'0'          Pad the field with zeros instead of spaces. The zeros are placed after any indication of sign or base. This flag is ignored if the '−' flag is also specified, or if a precision is specified.

If a precision is supplied, it specifies the minimum number of digits to appear; leading zeros are produced if necessary. If you don't specify a precision, the number is printed with as many digits as it needs. If you convert a value of zero with an explicit precision of zero, then no characters at all are produced.

## 13.2.9 Floating-Point Conversions

This section discusses the conversion specifications for floating-point numbers: the '%f', '%e', '%E', '%g', and '%G' conversions.

The '%f' conversion prints its argument in fixed-point notation, producing output of the form [−]ddd.ddd, where the number of digits following the decimal point is controlled by the precision you specify.

The '%e' conversion prints its argument in exponential notation, producing output of the form [-]d.ddde[+|-]dd. Again, the number of digits following the decimal point is controlled by the precision. The exponent always contains at least two digits. The '%E' conversion is similar but the exponent is marked with the letter 'E' instead of 'e'.

The '%g' and '%G' conversions print the argument in the style of '%e' or '%E' (respectively) if the exponent would be less than -4 or greater than or equal to the precision; otherwise they use the '%f' style. Trailing zeros are removed from the fractional portion of the result and a decimal-point character appears only if it is followed by a digit.

The following flags can be used to modify the behavior:

'-'             Left-justify the result in the field. Normally the result is right-justified.

'+'             Always include a plus or minus sign in the result.

' '             If the result doesn't start with a plus or minus sign, prefix it with a space instead. Since the '+' flag ensures that the result includes a sign, this flag is ignored if you supply both of them.

'#'             Specifies that the result should always include a decimal point, even if no digits follow it. For the '%g' and '%G' conversions, this also forces trailing zeros after the decimal point to be left in place where they would otherwise be removed.

'0'             Pad the field with zeros instead of spaces; the zeros are placed after any sign. This flag is ignored if the '-' flag is also specified.

The precision specifies how many digits follow the decimal-point character for the '%f', '%e', and '%E' conversions. For these conversions, the default precision is 6. If the precision is explicitly 0, this suppresses the decimal point character entirely. For the '%g' and '%G' conversions, the precision specifies how many significant digits to print. Significant digits are the first digit before the decimal point, and all the digits after it. If the precision is 0 or not specified for '%g' or '%G', it is treated like a value of 1. If the value being printed cannot be expressed precisely in the specified number of digits, the value is rounded to the nearest number that fits.

## 13.2.10 Other Output Conversions

This section describes miscellaneous conversions for printf.

The '%c' conversion prints a single character. The '-' flag can be used to specify left-justification in the field, but no other flags are defined, and no precision or type modifier can be given. For example:

```
    printf ("%c%c%c%c%c", "h", "e", "l", "l", "o");
```
prints 'hello'.

The '%s' conversion prints a string. The corresponding argument must
be a string. A precision can be specified to indicate the maximum number
of characters to write; otherwise characters in the string up to but not
including the terminating null character are written to the output stream.
The '-' flag can be used to specify left-justification in the field, but no
other flags or type modifiers are defined for this conversion. For example:

```
    printf ("%3s%-6s", "no", "where");
```
prints ' no where ' (note the leading and trailing spaces).

## 13.2.11 Formatted Input

Octave provides the scanf, fscanf, and sscanf functions to read
formatted input. There are two forms of each of these functions. One
can be used to extract vectors of data from a file, and the other is more
'C-like'.

[val, count] = **fscanf** (fid, template, size)          Built-in Function
[v1, v2, ...] = **fscanf** (fid, template, "C")          Built-in Function

In the first form, read from fid according to template, returning the
result in the matrix val.

The optional argument size specifies the amount of data to read and
may be one of

Inf          Read as much as possible, returning a column vector.

nr           Read up to nr elements, returning a column vector.

[nr, Inf]    Read as much as possible, returning a matrix with nr
             rows. If the number of elements read is not an exact
             multiple of nr, the last column is padded with zeros.

[nr, nc]     Read up to nr * nc elements, returning a matrix with
             nr rows. If the number of elements read is not an exact
             multiple of nr, the last column is padded with zeros.

If size is omitted, a value of Inf is assumed.

A string is returned if template specifies only character conversions.

The number of items successfully read is returned in count.

In the second form, read from fid according to template, with each
conversion specifier in template corresponding to a single scalar return
value. This form is more 'C-like', and also compatible with previous
versions of Octave.

[*val, count*] = **sscanf** (*string, template, size*)                Built-in Function
[*v1, v2, ...*] = **sscanf** (*string, template*, "C")                Built-in Function
   This is like fscanf, except that the characters are taken from the
   string *string* instead of from a stream. Reaching the end of the string
   is treated as an end-of-file condition.


[*val, count*] = **scanf** (*template, size*)                         Built-in Function
[*v1, v2, ...*] = **scanf** (*template*, "C")                         Built-in Function
   This is equivalent to calling fscanf with *fid* = stdin.

   It is currently not useful to call scanf in interactive programs.


Calls to scanf are superficially similar to calls to printf in that arbitrary arguments are read under the control of a template string. While
the syntax of the conversion specifications in the template is very similar to that for printf, the interpretation of the template is oriented
more towards free-format input and simple pattern matching, rather than
fixed-field formatting. For example, most scanf conversions skip over
any amount of "white space" (including spaces, tabs, and newlines) in
the input file, and there is no concept of precision for the numeric input
conversions as there is for the corresponding output conversions. Ordi-
narily, non-whitespace characters in the template are expected to match
characters in the input stream exactly.

When a *matching failure* occurs, scanf returns immediately, leaving
the first non-matching character as the next character to be read from the
stream, and scanf returns all the items that were successfully converted.


The formatted input functions are not used as frequently as the formatted output functions. Partly, this is because it takes some care to
use them properly. Another reason is that it is difficult to recover from a
matching error.

## 13.2.12 Input Conversion Syntax

A scanf template string is a string that contains ordinary multibyte
characters interspersed with conversion specifications that start with '%'.

Any whitespace character in the template causes any number of whitespace characters in the input stream to be read and discarded. The whitespace characters that are matched need not be exactly the same whitespace characters that appear in the template string. For example, write '
, ' in the template to recognize a comma with optional whitespace before
and after.

Other characters in the template string that are not part of conversion specifications must match characters in the input stream exactly; if this is not the case, a matching failure occurs.

The conversion specifications in a scanf template string have the general form:

> % flags width type conversion

In more detail, an input conversion specification consists of an initial '%' character followed in sequence by:

- An optional flag character '*', which says to ignore the text read for this specification. When scanf finds a conversion specification that uses this flag, it reads input as directed by the rest of the conversion specification, but it discards this input, does not return any value, and does not increment the count of successful assignments.

- An optional decimal integer that specifies the maximum field width. Reading of characters from the input stream stops either when this maximum is reached or when a non-matching character is found, whichever happens first. Most conversions discard initial whitespace characters, and these discarded characters don't count towards the maximum field width. Conversions that do not discard initial whitespace are explicitly documented.

- An optional type modifier character. This character is ignored by Octave's scanf function, but is recognized to provide compatibility with the C language scanf.

- A character that specifies the conversion to be applied.

The exact options that are permitted and how they are interpreted vary between the different conversion specifiers. See the descriptions of the individual conversions for information about the particular options that they allow.

## 13.2.13 Table of Input Conversions

Here is a table that summarizes the various conversion specifications:

'%d'        Matches an optionally signed integer written in decimal. See Section 13.2.14 [Numeric Input Conversions], page 142.

'%i'        Matches an optionally signed integer in any of the formats that the C language defines for specifying an integer constant. See Section 13.2.14 [Numeric Input Conversions], page 142.

'%o'        Matches an unsigned integer written in octal radix. See Section 13.2.14 [Numeric Input Conversions], page 142.

'%u'            Matches an unsigned integer written in decimal radix. See
                Section 13.2.14 [Numeric Input Conversions], page 142.

'%x', '%X'      Matches an unsigned integer written in hexadecimal radix.
                See Section 13.2.14 [Numeric Input Conversions], page 142.

'%e', '%f', '%g', '%E', '%G'
                Matches an optionally signed floating-point number. See
                Section 13.2.14 [Numeric Input Conversions], page 142.

'%s'            Matches a string containing only non-whitespace characters.
                See Section 13.2.15 [String Input Conversions], page 143.

'%c'            Matches a string of one or more characters; the number of
                characters read is controlled by the maximum field width
                given for the conversion. See Section 13.2.15 [String Input
                Conversions], page 143.

'%%'            This matches a literal '%' character in the input stream. No
                corresponding argument is used.

If the syntax of a conversion specification is invalid, the behavior is
undefined. If there aren't enough function arguments provided to supply
addresses for all the conversion specifications in the template strings that
perform assignments, or if the arguments are not of the correct types,
the behavior is also undefined. On the other hand, extra arguments are
simply ignored.

## 13.2.14 Numeric Input Conversions

This section describes the scanf conversions for reading numeric values.

The '%d' conversion matches an optionally signed integer in decimal radix.

The '%i' conversion matches an optionally signed integer in any of the formats that the C language defines for specifying an integer constant.

For example, any of the strings '10', '0xa', or '012' could be read in as integers under the '%i' conversion. Each of these specifies a number with decimal value 10.

The '%o', '%u', and '%x' conversions match unsigned integers in octal, decimal, and hexadecimal radices, respectively.

The '%X' conversion is identical to the '%x' conversion. They both permit either uppercase or lowercase letters to be used as digits.

Unlike the C language scanf, Octave ignores the 'h', 'l', and 'L' modifiers.

## 13.2.15  String Input Conversions

This section describes the scanf input conversions for reading string and character values: '%s' and '%c'.

The '%c' conversion is the simplest: it matches a fixed number of characters, always. The maximum field with says how many characters to read; if you don't specify the maximum, the default is 1. This conversion does not skip over initial whitespace characters. It reads precisely the next *n* characters, and fails if it cannot get that many.

The '%s' conversion matches a string of non-whitespace characters. It skips and discards initial whitespace, but stops when it encounters more whitespace after having read something.

For example, reading the input:

    hello, world

with the conversion '%10c' produces " hello, wo", but reading the same input with the conversion '%10s' produces "hello,".

## 13.2.16  Binary I/O

Octave can read and write binary data using the functions fread and fwrite, which are patterned after the standard C functions with the same names. The are able to automatically swap the byte order of integer data and convert among ths supported floating point formats as the data are read.

[*val*, *count*] = **fread** (*fid*, *size*, *precision*, *skip*,          Built-in Function
          *arch*)

Read binary data of type *precision* from the specified file ID *fid*.

The optional argument *size* specifies the amount of data to read and may be one of

Inf          Read as much as possible, returning a column vector.

*nr*          Read up to *nr* elements, returning a column vector.

[*nr*, Inf]  Read as much as possible, returning a matrix with *nr* rows. If the number of elements read is not an exact multiple of *nr*, the last column is padded with zeros.

[*nr*, *nc*]  Read up to *nr* * *nc* elements, returning a matrix with *nr* rows. If the number of elements read is not an exact multiple of *nr*, the last column is padded with zeros.

If *size* is omitted, a value of Inf is assumed.

The optional argument *precision* is a string specifying the type of data to read and may be one of

```
"char"
"char*1"
"integer*1"
"int8"        Single character.

"signed char"
"schar"       Signed character.

"unsigned char"
"uchar"       Unsigned character.

"short"       Short integer.

"unsigned short"
"ushort"      Unsigned short integer.

"int"         Integer.

"unsigned int"
"uint"        Unsigned integer.

"long"        Long integer.

"unsigned long"
"ulong"       Unsigned long integer.

"float"
"float32"
"real*4"      Single precision float.

"double"
"float64"
"real*8"      Double precision float.

"integer*2"
"int16"       Two byte integer.

"integer*4"
"int32"       Four byte integer.
```

The default precision is "uchar".

The optional argument *skip* specifies the number of bytes to skip before each element is read. If it is not specified, a value of 0 is assumed.

The optional argument *arch* is a string specifying the data format for the file. Valid values are

```
"native"      The format of the current machine.

"ieee-le"     IEEE big endian.

"ieee-be"     IEEE little endian.
```

| `"vaxd"` | VAX D floating format. |
| `"vaxg"` | VAX G floating format. |
| `"cray"` | Cray floating format. |

Conversions are currently only supported for `"ieee-be"` and `"ieee-le"` formats.

The data read from the file is returned in *val*, and the number of values read is returned in `count`

*count* = **fwrite** (*fid, data, precision, skip, arch*)          Built-in Function
  Write data in binary form of type *precision* to the specified file ID *fid*, returning the number of values successfully written to the file.

  The argument *data* is a matrix of values that are to be written to the file. The values are extracted in column-major order.

  The remaining arguments *precision*, *skip*, and *arch* are optional, and are interpreted as described for `fread`.

  The behavior of `fwrite` is undefined if the values in *data* are too large to fit in the specified precision.

## 13.2.17  Temporary Files

**tmpnam** ()                                              Built-in Function
  Return a unique temporary file name as a string.

  Since the named file is not opened, by `tmpnam`, it is possible (though relatively unlikely) that it will not be available by the time your program attempts to open it.

## 13.2.18  End of File and Errors

**feof** (*fid*)                                           Built-in Function
  Return 1 if an end-of-file condition has been encountered for a given file and 0 otherwise. Note that it will only return 1 if the end of the file has already been encountered, not if the next read operation will result in an end-of-file condition.

**ferror** (*fid*)                                        Built-in Function
  Return 1 if an error condition has been encountered for a given file and 0 otherwise. Note that it will only return 1 if an error has already been encountered, not if the next operation will result in an error condition.

**freport ()**                                    Built-in Function
  Print a list of which files have been opened, and whether they are open
  for reading, writing, or both. For example,

    freport ()

    ⊣  number  mode  name
    ⊣
    ⊣      0      r   stdin
    ⊣      1      w   stdout
    ⊣      2      w   stderr
    ⊣      3      r   myfile

## 13.2.19 File Positioning

  Three functions are available for setting and determining the position
of the file pointer for a given file.

**ftell (*fid*)**                                  Built-in Function
  Return the position of the file pointer as the number of characters from
  the beginning of the file *fid*.

**fseek (*fid*, *offset*, *origin*)**              Built-in Function
  Set the file pointer to any location within the file *fid*. The pointer
  is positioned *offset* characters from the *origin*, which may be one of
  the predefined variables SEEK_CUR (current position), SEEK_SET (beginning), or SEEK_END (end of file). If *origin* is omitted, SEEK_SET is
  assumed. The offset must be zero, or a value returned by ftell (in
  which case *origin* must be SEEK_SET.

**SEEK_SET**                                       Built-in Variable
**SEEK_CUR**                                       Built-in Variable
**SEEK_END**                                       Built-in Variable
  These variables may be used as the optional third argument for the
  function fseek.

**frewind (*fid*)**                                Built-in Function
  Move the file pointer to the beginning of the file *fid*, returning 1 for
  success, and 0 if an error was encountered. It is equivalent to fseek
  (*fid*, 0, SEEK_SET).

  The following example stores the current file position in the variable
marker, moves the pointer to the beginning of the file, reads four characters, and then returns to the original position.

```
marker = ftell (myfile);
frewind (myfile);
fourch = fgets (myfile, 4);
fseek (myfile, marker, SEEK_SET);
```

# 14  Plotting

All of Octave's plotting functions use gnuplot to handle the actual graphics. There are two low-level functions, gplot and gsplot, that behave almost exactly like the corresponding gnuplot functions plot and splot. A number of other higher level plotting functions, patterned after the graphics functions found in MATLAB version 3.5, are also available. These higher level functions are all implemented in terms of the two low-level plotting functions.

## 14.1  Two-Dimensional Plotting

**gplot** *ranges expression using title style*                       Command
Generate a 2-dimensional plot.

The *ranges*, *using*, *title*, and *style* arguments are optional, and the *using*, *title* and *style* qualifiers may appear in any order after the expression. You may plot multiple expressions with a single command by separating them with commas. Each expression may have its own set of qualifiers.

The optional item *ranges* has the syntax

        [ x_lo : x_up ] [ y_lo : y_up ]

and may be used to specify the ranges for the axes of the plot, independent of the actual range of the data. The range for the y axes and any of the individual limits may be omitted. A range [:] indicates that the default limits should be used. This normally means that a range just large enough to include all the data points will be used.

The expression to be plotted must not contain any literal matrices (e.g. [ 1, 2; 3, 4 ]) since it is nearly impossible to distinguish a plot range from a matrix of data.

See the help for gnuplot for a description of the syntax for the optional items.

By default, the gplot command plots the second column of a matrix versus the first. If the matrix only has one column, it is taken as a vector of y-coordinates and the x-coordinate is taken as the element index, starting with zero. For example,

        gplot rand (100,1) with linespoints

will plot 100 random values and connect them with lines.

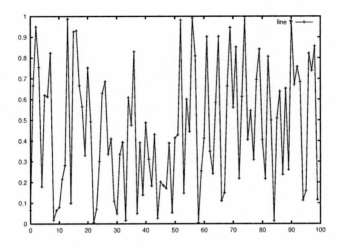

When gplot is used to plot a column vector, the indices of the elements
are taken as x values.

If there are more than two columns, you can choose which columns to
plot with the *using* qualifier. For example, given the data

```
x = (-10:0.1:10)';
data = [x, sin(x), cos(x)];
```

the command

```
gplot [-11:11] [-1.1:1.1] \
    data with lines, data using 1:3 with impulses
```

will plot two lines. The first line is generated by the command data
with lines, and is a graph of the sine function over the range −10 to
10. The data is taken from the first two columns of the matrix because
columns to plot were not specified with the *using* qualifier.

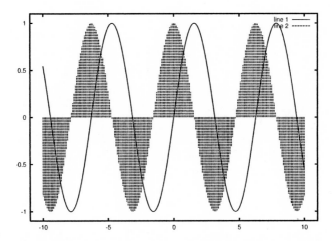

The clause using 1:3 in the second part of this plot command specifies that the first and third columns of the matrix data should be taken as the values to plot.

In this example, the ranges have been explicitly specified to be a bit larger than the actual range of the data so that the curves do not touch the border of the plot.

**gset** *options*                                                        Command
**gshow** *options*                                                       Command
**replot** *options*                                                      Command

In addition to the basic plotting commands, the whole range of gset and gshow commands from gnuplot are available, as is replot.

Note that in Octave 2.0, the set and show commands were renamed to gset and gshow in order to allow for compatibility with the MATLAB graphics and GUI commands in a future version of Octave. (For now, the old set and show commands do work, but they print an annoying warning message to try to get people to switch to using gset and gshow.)

The gset and gshow commands allow you to set and show gnuplot parameters. For more information about the gset and gshow commands, see the documentation for set and show in the gnuplot user's guide (also available on line if you run gnuplot directly, instead of running it from Octave).

The replot command allows you to force the plot to be redisplayed. This is useful if you have changed something about the plot, such as the title or axis labels. The replot command also accepts the same arguments as gplot or gsplot (except for data ranges) so you can add additional lines to existing plots.

For example,

```
gset term tek40
gset output "/dev/plotter"
gset title "sine with lines and cosine with impulses"
replot "sin (x) w l"
```

will change the terminal type for plotting, add a title to the current
plot, add a graph of sin($x$) to the plot, and force the new plot to be
sent to the plot device. This last step is normally required in order
to update the plot. This default is reasonable for slow terminals or
hardcopy output devices because even when you are adding additional
lines with a replot command, gnuplot always redraws the entire plot,
and you probably don't want to have a completely new plot generated
every time something as minor as an axis label changes.

The command shg is equivalent to executing `replot` without any arguments.

**automatic_replot**                                    Built-in Variable
You can tell Octave to redisplay the plot each time anything about it
changes by setting the value of the builtin variable `automatic_replot`
to a nonzero value. Since this is fairly inefficient, the default value is
0.

Note that NaN values in the plot data are automatically omitted, and
Inf values are converted to a very large value before calling gnuplot.

The MATLAB-style two-dimensional plotting commands are:

**plot** (*args*)                                       Function File
This function produces two-dimensional plots. Many different combinations of arguments are possible. The simplest form is

```
plot (y)
```

where the argument is taken as the set of $y$ coordinates and the $x$
coordinates are taken to be the indices of the elements, starting with
1.

If more than one argument is given, they are interpreted as

```
plot (x, y, fmt ...)
```

where $y$ and *fmt* are optional, and any number of argument sets may
appear. The $x$ and $y$ values are interpreted as follows:

- If a single data argument is supplied, it is taken as the set of $y$
  coordinates and the $x$ coordinates are taken to be the indices of
  the elements, starting with 1.

- If the first argument is a vector and the second is a matrix, the the vector is plotted versus the columns (or rows) of the matrix. (using whichever combination matches, with columns tried first.)

- If the first argument is a matrix and the second is a vector, the the columns (or rows) of the matrix are plotted versus the vector. (using whichever combination matches, with columns tried first.)

- If both arguments are vectors, the elements of $y$ are plotted versus the elements of $x$.

- If both arguments are matrices, the columns of $y$ are plotted versus the columns of $x$. In this case, both matrices must have the same number of rows and columns and no attempt is made to transpose the arguments to make the number of rows match.

  If both arguments are scalars, a single point is plotted.

The *fmt* argument, if present is interpreted as follows. If *fmt* is missing, the default gnuplot line style is assumed.

| | |
|---|---|
| '-' | Set lines plot style (default). |
| '.' | Set dots plot style. |
| '@' | Set points plot style. |
| '-@' | Set linespoints plot style. |
| '^' | Set impulses plot style. |
| 'L' | Set steps plot style. |
| '#' | Set boxes plot style. |
| '~' | Set errorbars plot style. |
| '#~' | Set boxerrorbars plot style. |
| '$n$' | Interpreted as the plot color if $n$ is an integer in the range 1 to 6. |
| '$nm$' | If $nm$ is a two digit integer and $m$ is an integer in the range 1 to 6, $m$ is interpreted as the point style. This is only valid in combination with the @ or -@ specifiers. |
| '$c$' | If $c$ is one of "r", "g", "b", "m", "c", or "w", it is interpreted as the plot color (red, green, blue, magenta, cyan, or white). |
| '+' | |
| '*' | |
| 'o' | |
| 'x' | Used in combination with the points or linespoints styles, set the point style. |

The color line styles have the following meanings on terminals that support color.

| Number | Gnuplot colors | (lines)points style |
|--------|----------------|---------------------|
| 1 | red | * |
| 2 | green | + |
| 3 | blue | o |
| 4 | magenta | x |
| 5 | cyan | house |
| 6 | brown | there exists |

Here are some plot examples:

    plot (x, y, "@12", x, y2, x, y3, "4", x, y4, "+")

This command will plot y with points of type 2 (displayed as '+') and color 1 (red), y2 with lines, y3 with lines of color 4 (magenta) and y4 with points displayed as '+'.

    plot (b, "*")

This command will plot the data in the variable b will be plotted with points displayed as '*'.

**hold** *args*                                                        Function File
Tell Octave to 'hold' the current data on the plot when executing subsequent plotting commands. This allows you to execute a series of plot commands and have all the lines end up on the same figure. The default is for each new plot command to clear the plot device first. For example, the command

    hold on

turns the hold state on. An argument of off turns the hold state off, and hold with no arguments toggles the current hold state.

**ishold**                                                             Function File
Return 1 if the next line will be added to the current plot, or 0 if the plot device will be cleared before drawing the next line.

**clearplot**                                                          Function File
**clg**                                                                Function File
Clear the plot window and any titles or axis labels. The name clg is aliased to clearplot for compatibility with MATLAB.

The commands *gplot clear*, *gsplot clear*, and *replot clear* are equivalent to clearplot. (Previously, commands like *gplot clear* would evaluate clear as an ordinary expression and clear all the visible variables.)

**closeplot** *Function File*
Close stream to the gnuplot subprocess. If you are using X11, this will close the plot window.

**purge_tmp_files** *Function File*
Delete the temporary files created by the plotting commands.

Octave creates temporary data files for gnuplot and then sends commands to gnuplot through a pipe. Octave will delete the temporary files on exit, but if you are doing a lot of plotting you may want to clean up in the middle of a session.

A future version of Octave will eliminate the need to use temporary files to hold the plot data.

**axis** (*limits*) *Function File*
Sets the axis limits for plots.

The argument *limits* should be a 2, 4, or 6 element vector. The first and second elements specify the lower and upper limits for the x axis. The third and fourth specify the limits for the y axis, and the fifth and sixth specify the limits for the z axis.

With no arguments, axis turns autoscaling on.

If your plot is already drawn, then you need to use replot before the new axis limits will take effect. You can get this to happen automatically by setting the built-in variable automatic_replot to a nonzero value.

# 14.2 Specialized Two-Dimensional Plots

**bar** (*x, y*) *Function File*
Given two vectors of x-y data, bar produces a bar graph.

If only one argument is given, it is taken as a vector of y-values and the x coordinates are taken to be the indices of the elements.

If two output arguments are specified, the data are generated but not plotted. For example,

```
bar (x, y);
```

and

```
[xb, yb] = bar (x, y);
plot (xb, yb);
```

are equivalent.

**contour** (*z, n, x, y*)                                          Function File

Make a contour plot of the three-dimensional surface described by *z*. Someone needs to improve `gnuplot`'s contour routines before this will be very useful.

**hist** (*y, x*)                                                   Function File

Produce histogram counts or plots.

With one vector input argument, plot a histogram of the values with 10 bins. The range of the histogram bins is determined by the range of the data.

Given a second scalar argument, use that as the number of bins.

Given a second vector argument, use that as the centers of the bins, with the width of the bins determined from the adjacent values in the vector.

Extreme values are lumped in the first and last bins.

With two output arguments, produce the values *nn* and *xx* such that `bar` (*xx, nn*) will plot the histogram.

**loglog** (*args*)                                                 Function File

Make a two-dimensional plot using log scales for both axes. See the description of `plot` above for a description of the arguments that `loglog` will accept.

**polar** (*theta, rho*)                                            Function File

Make a two-dimensional plot given polar the coordinates *theta* and *rho*.

**semilogx** (*args*)                                               Function File

Make a two-dimensional plot using a log scale for the *x* axis. See the description of `plot` above for a description of the arguments that `semilogx` will accept.

**semilogy** (*args*)                                               Function File

Make a two-dimensional plot using a log scale for the *y* axis. See the description of `plot` above for a description of the arguments that `semilogy` will accept.

**stairs** (*x, y*)                                                 Function File

Given two vectors of x-y data, bar produces a 'stairstep' plot.

If only one argument is given, it is taken as a vector of y-values and the x coordinates are taken to be the indices of the elements.

If two output arguments are specified, the data are generated but not plotted. For example,

```
    stairs (x, y);
```

and

```
    [xs, ys] = stairs (x, y);
    plot (xs, ys);
```

are equivalent.


## 14.3  Three-Dimensional Plotting


**gsplot** *ranges expression using title style*                    Command
    Generate a 3-dimensional plot.

The *ranges*, *using*, *title*, and *style* arguments are optional, and the
*using*, *title* and *style* qualifiers may appear in any order after the expression. You may plot multiple expressions with a single command
by separating them with commas. Each expression may have its own
set of qualifiers.

The optional item *ranges* has the syntax

```
    [ x_lo : x_up ] [ y_lo : y_up ] [ z_lo : z_up ]
```

and may be used to specify the ranges for the axes of the plot, independent of the actual range of the data. The range for the y and z
axes and any of the individual limits may be omitted. A range [:]
indicates that the default limits should be used. This normally means
that a range just large enough to include all the data points will be
used.

The expression to be plotted must not contain any literal matrices (e.g.
[ 1, 2; 3, 4 ]) since it is nearly impossible to distinguish a plot range
from a matrix of data.

See the help for gnuplot for a description of the syntax for the optional
items.

By default, the gsplot command plots each column of the expression
as the z value, using the row index as the x value, and the column
index as the y value. The indices are counted from zero, not one. For
example,

```
    gsplot rand (5, 2)
```

will plot a random surface, with the x and y values taken from the row
and column indices of the matrix.

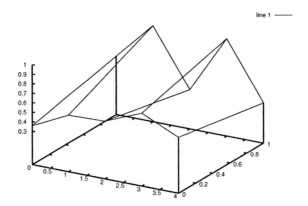

If parametric plotting mode is set (using the command *gset
parametric*, then gsplot takes the columns of the matrix three at a
time as the x, y and z values that define a line in three space. Any
extra columns are ignored, and the x and y values are expected to be
sorted. For example, with parametric set, it makes sense to plot a
matrix like

$$\begin{bmatrix} 1 & 1 & 3 & 2 & 1 & 6 & 3 & 1 & 9 \\ 1 & 2 & 2 & 2 & 2 & 5 & 3 & 2 & 8 \\ 1 & 3 & 1 & 2 & 3 & 4 & 3 & 3 & 7 \end{bmatrix}$$

but not rand (5, 30).

The MATLAB-style three-dimensional plotting commands are:

**mesh** (*x, y, z*)                                        Function File
    Plot a mesh given matrices x, and *y* from meshdom and a matrix *z*
    corresponding to the x and y coordinates of the mesh.

**meshdom** (*x, y*)                                        Function File
    Given vectors of *x* and *y* coordinates, return two matrices correspond-
    ing to the x and y coordinates of the mesh.
    See the file 'sombrero.m' for an example of using mesh and meshdom.

**gnuplot_binary**                                      Built-in Variable
    The name of the program invoked by the plot command. The default
    value is "gnuplot". See Appendix C [Installation], page 259.

**gnuplot_has_frames**                                      Built-in Variable

If the value of this variable is nonzero, Octave assumes that your copy of gnuplot has support for multiple frames that is included in recent 3.6beta releases. It's initial value is determined by configure, but it can be changed in your startup script or at the command line in case configure got it wrong, or if you upgrade your gnuplot installation.

**figure** (*n*)                                          Function File

Set the current plot window to plot window *n*. This function currently requires X11 and a version of gnuplot that supports multiple frames.

**gnuplot_has_multiplot**                                  Built-in Variable

If the value of this variable is nonzero, Octave assumes that your copy of gnuplot has the multiplot support that is included in recent 3.6beta releases. It's initial value is determined by configure, but it can be changed in your startup script or at the command line in case configure got it wrong, or if you upgrade your gnuplot installation.

## 14.4 Plot Annotations

**grid**                                                  Function File

For two-dimensional plotting, force the display of a grid on the plot.

**title** (*string*)                                      Function File

Specify a title for the plot. If you already have a plot displayed, use the command `replot` to redisplay it with the new title.

**xlabel** (*string*)                                     Function File
**ylabel** (*string*)                                     Function File
**zlabel** (*string*)                                     Function File

Specify x, y, and z axis labels for the plot. If you already have a plot displayed, use the command `replot` to redisplay it with the new labels.

## 14.5 Multiple Plots on One Page

The following functions all require a version of gnuplot that supports the multiplot feature.

**mplot** (*x*, *y*)                                      Function File
**mplot** (*x*, *y*, *fmt*)                               Function File
**mplot** (*x1*, *y1*, *x2*, *y2*)                        Function File

This is a modified version of the `plot` function that works with the multiplot version of gnuplot to plot multiple plots per page. This plot

version automatically advances to the next subplot position after each
set of arguments are processed.

See the description of the *plot* function for the various options.

**multiplot** (*xn, yn*)                                           Function File
  Sets and resets multiplot mode.

  If the arguments are non-zero, `multiplot` will set up multiplot mode
  with *xn, yn* subplots along the *x* and *y* axes. If both arguments are
  zero, `multiplot` closes multiplot mode.

**oneplot** ()                                                     Function File
  If in multiplot mode, switches to single plot mode.

**plot_border** (...)                                             Function File
  Multiple arguments allowed to specify the sides on which the border
  is shown. Allowed arguments include:

  "blank"      No borders displayed.

  "all"        All borders displayed

  "north"      North Border

  "south"      South Border

  "east"       East Border

  "west"       West Border

  The arguments may be abbreviated to single characters. Without any
  arguments, `plot_border` turns borders off.

**subplot** (*rows, cols, index*)                                 Function File
**subplot** (*rcn*)                                               Function File
  Sets gnuplot in multiplot mode and plots in location given by index
  (there are *cols* by *rows* subwindows).

  Input:

  *rows*       Number of rows in subplot grid.

  *columns*    Number of columns in subplot grid.

  *index*      Index of subplot where to make the next plot.

  If only one argument is supplied, then it must be a three digit value
  specifying the location in digits 1 (rows) and 2 (columns) and the plot
  index in digit 3.

  The plot index runs row-wise. First all the columns in a row are filled
  and then the next row is filled.

For example, a plot with 4 by 2 grid will have plot indices running as follows:

| 1 | 2 | 3 | 4 |
|---|---|---|---|
| 5 | 6 | 7 | 8 |

**subwindow** (*xn, yn*)                                           Function File
  Sets the subwindow position in multiplot mode for the next plot. The multiplot mode has to be previously initialized using the `multiplot` function, otherwise this command just becomes an alias to `multiplot`

**top_title** (*string*)                                          Function File
**bottom_title** (*string*)                                       Function File
  Makes a title with text *string* at the top (bottom) of the plot.

# 15 Matrix Manipulation

There are a number of functions available for checking to see if the elements of a matrix meet some condition, and for rearranging the elements of a matrix. For example, Octave can easily tell you if all the elements of a matrix are finite, or are less than some specified value. Octave can also rotate the elements, extract the upper- or lower-triangular parts, or sort the columns of a matrix.

## 15.1 Finding Elements and Checking Conditions

The functions any and all are useful for determining whether any or all of the elements of a matrix satisfy some condition. The find function is also useful in determining which elements of a matrix meet a specified condition.

any (x)                                                    Built-in Function
For a vector argument, return 1 if any element of the vector is nonzero.

For a matrix argument, return a row vector of ones and zeros with each element indicating whether any of the elements of the corresponding column of the matrix are nonzero. For example,

```
any (eye (2, 4))
     ⇒ [ 1, 1, 0, 0 ]
```

To see if any of the elements of a matrix are nonzero, you can use a statement like

```
any (any (a))
```

all (x)                                                    Built-in Function
The function all behaves like the function any, except that it returns true only if all the elements of a vector, or all the elements in a column of a matrix, are nonzero.

Since the comparison operators (see Section 8.4 [Comparison Ops], page 78) return matrices of ones and zeros, it is easy to test a matrix for many things, not just whether the elements are nonzero. For example,

```
all (all (rand (5) < 0.9))
     ⇒ 0
```

tests a random 5 by 5 matrix to see if all of its elements are less than 0.9.

Note that in conditional contexts (like the test clause of if and while statements) Octave treats the test as if you had typed all (all (condition)).

[*err*, *y1*, ...] = **common_size** (*x1*, ...)                                          Function File
   Determine if all input arguments are either scalar or of common size.
   If so, *err* is zero, and *yi* is a matrix of the common size with all entries
   equal to *xi* if this is a scalar or *xi* otherwise. If the inputs cannot be
   brought to a common size, errorcode is 1, and *yi* is *xi*. For example,

```
[errorcode, a, b] = common_size ([1 2; 3 4], 5)
    ⇒ errorcode = 0
    ⇒ a = [ 1, 2; 3, 4 ]
    ⇒ b = [ 5, 5; 5, 5 ]
```

   This is useful for implementing functions where arguments can either
   be scalars or of common size.

**diff** (*x*, *k*)                                                                       Function File
   If *x* is a vector of length *n*, diff (*x*) is the vector of first differences
   $x_2 - x_1, \ldots, x_n - x_{n-1}$.

   If *x* is a matrix, diff (*x*) is the matrix of column differences.

   The second argument is optional. If supplied, diff (*x*, *k*), where *k*
   is a nonnegative integer, returns the *k*-th differences.

**isinf** (*x*)                                                                           Mapping Function
   Return 1 for elements of *x* that are infinite and zero otherwise. For
   example,

```
isinf ([13, Inf, NaN])
    ⇒ [ 0, 1, 0 ]
```

**isnan** (*x*)                                                                           Mapping Function
   Return 1 for elements of *x* that are NaN values and zero otherwise.
   For example,

```
isnan ([13, Inf, NaN])
    ⇒ [ 0, 0, 1 ]
```

**finite** (*x*)                                                                          Mapping Function
   Return 1 for elements of *x* that are NaN values and zero otherwise.
   For example,

```
finite ([13, Inf, NaN])
    ⇒ [ 1, 0, 0 ]
```

**find** (*x*)                                                                            Loadable Function
   Return a vector of indices of nonzero elements of a matrix. To obtain a
   single index for each matrix element, Octave pretends that the columns
   of a matrix form one long vector (like Fortran arrays are stored). For
   example,

```
find (eye (2))
    ⇒ [ 1; 4 ]
```

If two outputs are requested, find returns the row and column indices of nonzero elements of a matrix. For example,

```
[i, j] = find (2 * eye (2))
    ⇒ i = [ 1; 2 ]
    ⇒ j = [ 1; 2 ]
```

If three outputs are requested, find also returns a vector containing the nonzero values. For example,

```
[i, j, v] = find (3 * eye (2))
    ⇒ i = [ 1; 2 ]
    ⇒ j = [ 1; 2 ]
    ⇒ v = [ 3; 3 ]
```

# 15.2  Rearranging Matrices

**fliplr** $(x)$                                                   Function File

Return a copy of $x$ with the order of the columns reversed. For example,

```
fliplr ([1, 2; 3, 4])
    ⇒   2   1
        4   3
```

**flipud** $(x)$                                                   Function File

Return a copy of $x$ with the order of the rows reversed. For example,

```
flipud ([1, 2; 3, 4])
    ⇒   3   4
        1   2
```

**rot90** $(x, n)$                                                 Function File

Return a copy of $x$ with the elements rotated counterclockwise in 90-degree increments. The second argument is optional, and specifies how many 90-degree rotations are to be applied (the default value is 1). Negative values of $n$ rotate the matrix in a clockwise direction. For example,

```
rot90 ([1, 2; 3, 4], -1)
    ⇒   3   1
        4   2
```

rotates the given matrix clockwise by 90 degrees. The following are all equivalent statements:

```
rot90 ([1, 2; 3, 4], -1)
≡
rot90 ([1, 2; 3, 4], 3)
≡
rot90 ([1, 2; 3, 4], 7)
```

**reshape** (*a*, *m*, *n*)                                              Function File

Return a matrix with *m* rows and *n* columns whose elements are taken from the matrix *a*. To decide how to order the elements, Octave pretends that the elements of a matrix are stored in column-major order (like Fortran arrays are stored).

For example,

```
reshape ([1, 2, 3, 4], 2, 2)
    ⇒   1   3
        2   4
```

If the variable do_fortran_indexing is nonzero, the reshape function is equivalent to

```
retval = zeros (m, n);
retval (:) = a;
```

but it is somewhat less cryptic to use reshape instead of the colon operator. Note that the total number of elements in the original matrix must match the total number of elements in the new matrix.

**shift** (*x*, *b*)                                                    Function File

If *x* is a vector, perform a circular shift of length *b* of the elements of *x*.

If *x* is a matrix, do the same for each column of *x*.

[*s*, *i*] = **sort** (*x*)                                          Loadable Function

Return a copy of *x* with the elements elements arranged in increasing order. For matrices, sort orders the elements in each column.

For example,

```
sort ([1, 2; 2, 3; 3, 1])
    ⇒   1   1
        2   2
        3   3
```

The sort function may also be used to produce a matrix containing the original row indices of the elements in the sorted matrix. For example,

```
[s, i] = sort ([1, 2; 2, 3; 3, 1])
    ⇒ s = 1   1
          2   2
```

```
                  3   3
    ⇒ i =  1   3
                  2   1
                  3   2
```

Since the sort function does not allow sort keys to be specified, it can't be used to order the rows of a matrix according to the values of the elements in various columns[1] in a single call. Using the second output, however, it is possible to sort all rows based on the values in a given column. Here's an example that sorts the rows of a matrix based on the values in the second column.

```
a = [1, 2; 2, 3; 3, 1];
[s, i] = sort (a (:, 2));
a (i, :)
    ⇒   3   1
              1   2
              2   3
```

**tril** (a, k)                                                    Function File
**triu** (a, k)                                                    Function File

Return a new matrix formed by extracting extract the lower (tril) or upper (triu) triangular part of the matrix a, and setting all other elements to zero. The second argument is optional, and specifies how many diagonals above or below the main diagonal should also be set to zero.

The default value of $k$ is zero, so that triu and tril normally include the main diagonal as part of the result matrix.

If the value of $k$ is negative, additional elements above (for tril) or below (for triu) the main diagonal are also selected.

The absolute value of $k$ must not be greater than the number of sub- or super-diagonals.

For example,

```
tril (ones (3), -1)
    ⇒   0   0   0
              1   0   0
              1   1   0
```

and

```
tril (ones (3), 1)
```

---

[1] For example, to first sort based on the values in column 1, and then, for any values that are repeated in column 1, sort based on the values found in column 2, etc.

```
⇒  1  1  0
   1  1  1
   1  1  1
```

**vec** $(x)$                                                        Function File
    Return the vector obtained by stacking the columns of the matrix $x$
    one above the other.

**vech** $(x)$                                                       Function File
    Return the vector obtained by eliminating all supradiagonal elements
    of the square matrix $x$ and stacking the result one column above the
    other.

## 15.3 Special Utility Matrices

**eye** $(x)$                                                    Built-in Function
**eye** $(n, m)$                                                 Built-in Function
    Return an identity matrix. If invoked with a single scalar argument,
    eye returns a square matrix with the dimension specified. If you supply
    two scalar arguments, eye takes them to be the number of rows and
    columns. If given a vector with two elements, eye uses the values of
    the elements as the number of rows and columns, respectively. For
    example,

```
eye (3)
   ⇒  1  0  0
      0  1  0
      0  0  1
```

The following expressions all produce the same result:

```
eye (2)
≡
eye (2, 2)
≡
eye (size ([1, 2; 3, 4])
```

For compatibility with MATLAB, calling eye with no arguments is
equivalent to calling it with an argument of 1.

**ones** $(x)$                                                   Built-in Function
**ones** $(n, m)$                                                Built-in Function
    Return a matrix whose elements are all 1. The arguments are handled
    the same as the arguments for eye.

If you need to create a matrix whose values are all the same, you should use an expression like

```
val_matrix = val * ones (n, m)
```

**zeros** $(x)$                                            Built-in Function
**zeros** $(n, m)$                                      Built-in Function
Return a matrix whose elements are all 0. The arguments are handled the same as the arguments for eye.

**rand** $(x)$                                          Loadable Function
**rand** $(n, m)$                                     Loadable Function
**rand** ("seed", $x$)                                Loadable Function
Return a matrix with random elements uniformly distributed on the interval $(0, 1)$. The arguments are handled the same as the arguments for eye. In addition, you can set the seed for the random number generator using the form

```
rand ("seed", x)
```

where $x$ is a scalar value. If called as

```
rand ("seed")
```

rand returns the current value of the seed.

**randn** $(x)$                                        Loadable Function
**randn** $(n, m)$                                   Loadable Function
**randn** ("seed", $x$)                            Loadable Function
Return a matrix with normally distributed random elements. The arguments are handled the same as the arguments for eye. In addition, you can set the seed for the random number generator using the form

```
randn ("seed", x)
```

where $x$ is a scalar value. If called as

```
randn ("seed")
```

randn returns the current value of the seed.

The rand and randn functions use separate generators. This ensures that

```
rand ("seed", 13);
randn ("seed", 13);
u = rand (100, 1);
n = randn (100, 1);
```

and

```
rand ("seed", 13);
randn ("seed", 13);
```

```
u = zeros (100, 1);
n = zeros (100, 1);
for i = 1:100
  u(i) = rand ();
  n(i) = randn ();
end
```
produce equivalent results.

Normally, rand and randn obtain their initial seeds from the system clock, so that the sequence of random numbers is not the same each time you run Octave. If you really do need for to reproduce a sequence of numbers exactly, you can set the seed to a specific value.

If it is invoked without arguments, rand and randn return a single element of a random sequence.

The rand and randn functions use Fortran code from RANLIB, a library of fortran routines for random number generation, compiled by Barry W. Brown and James Lovato of the Department of Biomathematics at The University of Texas, M.D. Anderson Cancer Center, Houston, TX 77030.

**diag** (*v*, *k*)                                          Built-in Function
Return a diagonal matrix with vector *v* on diagonal *k*. The second argument is optional. If it is positive, the vector is placed on the *k*-th super-diagonal. If it is negative, it is placed on the -*k*-th sub-diagonal. The default value of *k* is 0, and the vector is placed on the main diagonal. For example,

```
diag ([1, 2, 3], 1)
   ⇒   0   1   0   0
       0   0   2   0
       0   0   0   3
       0   0   0   0
```

The functions linspace and logspace make it very easy to create vectors with evenly or logarithmically spaced elements. See Section 4.2 [Ranges], page 45.

**linspace** (*base*, *limit*, *n*)                              Function File
Return a row vector with *n* linearly spaced elements between *base* and *limit*. The number of elements, *n*, must be greater than 1. The *base* and *limit* are always included in the range. If *base* is greater than *limit*, the elements are stored in decreasing order. If the number of points is not specified, a value of 100 is used.

The linspace function always returns a row vector, regardless of the value of prefer_column_vectors.

**logspace** (*base*, *limit*, *n*)                           Function File
Similar to `linspace` except that the values are logarithmically spaced from $10^{base}$ to $10^{limit}$.

If *limit* is equal to $\pi$, the points are between $10^{base}$ and $\pi$, *not* $10^{base}$ and $10^{\pi}$, in order to be compatible with the corresponding MATLAB function.

**treat_neg_dim_as_zero**                           Built-in Variable
If the value of `treat_neg_dim_as_zero` is nonzero, expressions like

    eye (-1)

produce an empty matrix (i.e., row and column dimensions are zero). Otherwise, an error message is printed and control is returned to the top level. The default value is 0.

# 15.4 Famous Matrices

The following functions return famous matrix forms.

**hankel** (*c*, *r*)                           Function File
Return the Hankel matrix constructed given the first column *c*, and (optionally) the last row *r*. If the last element of *c* is not the same as the first element of *r*, the last element of *c* is used. If the second argument is omitted, the last row is taken to be the same as the first column.

A Hankel matrix formed from an m-vector *c*, and an n-vector *r*, has the elements

$$H(i,j) = \begin{cases} c_{i+j-1}, & i+j-1 \le m; \\ r_{i+j-m}, & \text{otherwise.} \end{cases}$$

**hilb** (*n*)                           Function File
Return the Hilbert matrix of order *n*. The *i, j* element of a Hilbert matrix is defined as

$$H(i,j) = \frac{1}{(i+j-1)}$$

**invhilb** (*n*)                           Function File
Return the inverse of a Hilbert matrix of order *n*. This is exact. Compare with the numerical calculation of `inverse (hilb (n))`, which suffers from the ill-conditioning of the Hilbert matrix, and the finite precision of your computer's floating point arithmetic.

**sylvester_matrix** $(k)$                                    *Function File*
    Return the Sylvester matrix of order $n = 2^k$.

**toeplitz** $(c, r)$                                         *Function File*
    Return the Toeplitz matrix constructed given the first column $c$, and
(optionally) the first row $r$. If the first element of $c$ is not the same
as the first element of $r$, the first element of $c$ is used. If the second
argument is omitted, the first row is taken to be the same as the first
column.

    A square Toeplitz matrix has the form

$$\begin{bmatrix} c_0 & r_1 & r_2 & \cdots & r_n \\ c_1 & c_0 & r_1 & & c_{n-1} \\ c_2 & c_1 & c_0 & & c_{n-2} \\ \vdots & & & & \vdots \\ c_n & c_{n-1} & c_{n-2} & \cdots & c_0 \end{bmatrix}.$$

**vander** $(c)$                                             *Function File*
    Return the Vandermonde matrix whose next to last column is $c$.

    A Vandermonde matrix has the form

$$\begin{bmatrix} c_0^n & \cdots & c_0^2 & c_0 & 1 \\ c_1^n & \cdots & c_1^2 & c_1 & 1 \\ \vdots & & \vdots & \vdots & \vdots \\ c_n^n & \cdots & c_n^2 & c_n & 1 \end{bmatrix}.$$

# 16 Arithmetic

Unless otherwise noted, all of the functions described in this chapter will work for real and complex scalar or matrix arguments.

## 16.1 Utility Functions

The following functions are available for working with complex numbers. Each expects a single argument. They are called *mapping functions* because when given a matrix argument, they apply the given function to each element of the matrix.

**ceil** ($x$)                                                Mapping Function
> Return the smallest integer not less than $x$. If $x$ is complex, return
> ceil (real ($x$)) + ceil (imag ($x$)) * I.

**exp** ($x$)                                                Mapping Function
> Compute the exponential of $x$. To compute the matrix exponential, see Chapter 17 [Linear Algebra], page 183.

**fix** ($x$)                                                Mapping Function
> Truncate $x$ toward zero. If $x$ is complex, return fix (real ($x$)) + fix (imag ($x$)) * I.

**floor** ($x$)                                                Mapping Function
> Return the largest integer not greater than $x$. If $x$ is complex, return
> floor (real ($x$)) + floor (imag ($x$)) * I.

**gcd** ($x$, ...)                                                Mapping Function
> Compute the greatest common divisor of the elements of $x$, or the list of all the arguments. For example,
>
>     gcd (a1, ..., ak)
>
> is the same as
>
>     gcd ([a1, ..., ak])
>
> An optional second return value, $v$ contains an integer vector such that
>
>     g = v(1) * a(k) + ... + v(k) * a(k)

**lcm** ($x$, ...)                                                Mapping Function
> Compute the least common multiple of the elements elements of $x$, or the list of all the arguments. For example,

```
    lcm (a1, ..., ak)
```
is the same as
```
    lcm ([a1, ..., ak]).
```

**log** $(x)$                                                   Mapping Function
    Compute the natural logarithm of $x$. To compute the matrix logarithm, see Chapter 17 [Linear Algebra], page 183.

**log10** $(x)$                                                 Mapping Function
    Compute the base-10 logarithm of $x$.

$y$ = **log2** $(x)$                                            Mapping Function
$[f, e]$ **log2** $(x)$                                         Mapping Function
    Compute the base-2 logarithm of $x$. With two outputs, returns $f$ and $e$ such that $1/2 <= |f| < 1$ and $x = f \cdot 2^e$.

**max** $(x)$                                                   Loadable Function
    For a vector argument, return the maximum value. For a matrix argument, return the maximum value from each column, as a row vector. Thus,
```
    max (max (x))
```
    returns the largest element of $x$.

    For complex arguments, the magnitude of the elements are used for comparison.

**min** $(x)$                                                   Loadable Function
    Like max, but return the minimum value.

**nextpow2** $(x)$                                              Function File
    If $x$ is a scalar, returns the first integer $n$ such that $2^n \geq |x|$.

    If $x$ is a vector, return nextpow2 (length $(x)$).

**pow2** $(x)$                                                  Mapping Function
**pow2** $(f, e)$                                               Mapping Function
    With one argument, computes $2^x$ for each element of $x$. With two arguments, returns $f \cdot 2^e$.

**rem** $(x, y)$                                                Mapping Function
    Return the remainder of $x / y$, computed using the expression
```
    x - y .* fix (x ./ y)
```
    An error message is printed if the dimensions of the arguments do not agree, or if either of the arguments is complex.

**round** (x)                                                   Mapping Function
   Return the integer nearest to x. If x is complex, return round (real
   (x)) + round (imag (x)) * I.

**sign** (x)                                                    Mapping Function
   Compute the *signum* function, which is defined as

$$\text{sign}(x) = \begin{cases} 1, & x > 0; \\ 0, & x = 0; \\ -1, & x < 0. \end{cases}$$

   For complex arguments, sign returns x ./ abs (x).

**sqrt** (x)                                                    Mapping Function
   Compute the square root of x. If x is negative, a complex result is
   returned. To compute the matrix square root, see Chapter 17 [Linear
   Algebra], page 183.

**xor** (x, y)                                                  Mapping Function
   Return the 'exclusive or' of the entries of x and y. For boolean expressions x and y, xor (x, y) is true if and only if x or y is true, but not
   if both x and y are true.

## 16.2 Complex Arithmetic

   The following functions are available for working with complex numbers. Each expects a single argument. Given a matrix they work on an
element by element basis. In the descriptions of the following functions,
z is the complex number $x + iy$, where i is defined as $\sqrt{-1}$.

**abs** (z)                                                     Mapping Function
   Compute the magnitude of z, defined as $|z| = \sqrt{x^2 + y^2}$.
   For example,

       abs (3 + 4i)
          ⇒ 5

**arg** (z)                                                     Mapping Function
**angle** (z)                                                   Mapping Function
   Compute the argument of z, defined as $\theta = \tan^{-1}(y/x)$.
   in radians.
   For example,

       arg (3 + 4i)
          ⇒ 0.92730

**conj** (*z*)                                              Mapping Function
    Return the complex conjugate of *z*, defined as $\bar{z} = x - iy$.


**imag** (*z*)                                              Mapping Function
    Return the imaginary part of *z* as a real number.


**real** (*z*)                                              Mapping Function
    Return the real part of *z*.


# 16.3  Trigonometry

Octave provides the following trigonometric functions.  Angles are specified in radians. To convert from degrees to radians multiply by $\pi/180$ (e.g. sin (30 * pi/180) returns the sine of 30 degrees).


**sin** (*z*)                                              Mapping Function
**cos** (*z*)                                              Mapping Function
**tan** (*z*)                                              Mapping Function
**sec** (*z*)                                              Mapping Function
**csc** (*z*)                                              Mapping Function
**cot** (*z*)                                              Mapping Function
    The ordinary trigonometric functions.


**asin** (*z*)                                             Mapping Function
**acos** (*z*)                                             Mapping Function
**atan** (*z*)                                             Mapping Function
**asec** (*z*)                                             Mapping Function
**acsc** (*z*)                                             Mapping Function
**acot** (*z*)                                             Mapping Function
    The ordinary inverse trigonometric functions.


**sinh** (*z*)                                             Mapping Function
**cosh** (*z*)                                             Mapping Function
**tanh** (*z*)                                             Mapping Function
**sech** (*z*)                                             Mapping Function
**csch** (*z*)                                             Mapping Function
**coth** (*z*)                                             Mapping Function
    Hyperbolic trigonometric functions.

| asinh $(z)$ | Mapping Function |
| acosh $(z)$ | Mapping Function |
| atanh $(z)$ | Mapping Function |
| asech $(z)$ | Mapping Function |
| acsch $(z)$ | Mapping Function |
| acoth $(z)$ | Mapping Function |

Inverse hyperbolic trigonometric functions.

Each of these functions expect a single argument. For matrix arguments, they work on an element by element basis. For example,

```
sin ([1, 2; 3, 4])
   ⇒   0.84147    0.90930
       0.14112   -0.75680
```

atan2 $(y, x)$                                            Mapping Function

Return the arctangent of $y/x$. The signs of the arguments are used to determine the quadrant of the result, which is in the range $\pi$ to $-\pi$.

# 16.4 Sums and Products

sum $(x)$                                                 Built-in Function

For a vector argument, return the sum of all the elements. For a matrix argument, return the sum of the elements in each column, as a row vector. The sum of an empty matrix is 0 if it has no columns, or a vector of zeros if it has no rows (see Section 4.1.1 [Empty Matrices], page 43).

prod $(x)$                                                Built-in Function

For a vector argument, return the product of all the elements. For a matrix argument, return the product of the elements in each column, as a row vector. The product of an empty matrix is 1 if it has no columns, or a vector of ones if it has no rows (see Section 4.1.1 [Empty Matrices], page 43).

cumsum $(x)$                                              Built-in Function

Return the cumulative sum of each column of x. For example,

```
cumsum ([1, 2; 3, 4])
   ⇒   1   2
       4   6
```

cumprod $(x)$                                             Built-in Function

Return the cumulative product of each column of x. For example,

```
cumprod ([1, 2; 3, 4])
    ⇒   1   2
        3   8
```

**sumsq** (*x*)                                                    Built-in Function
  For a vector argument, return the sum of the squares of all the elements. For a matrix argument, return the sum of the squares of the
  elements in each column, as a row vector.

# 16.5 Special Functions

**besseli** (*alpha*, *x*)                                        Mapping Function
**besselj** (*alpha*, *x*)                                        Mapping Function
**besselk** (*alpha*, *x*)                                        Mapping Function
**bessely** (*alpha*, *x*)                                        Mapping Function
  Compute Bessel functions of the following types:

  besselj     Bessel functions of the first kind.

  bessely     Bessel functions of the second kind.

  besseli     Modified Bessel functions of the first kind.

  besselk     Modified Bessel functions of the second kind.

  The second argument, *x*, must be a real matrix, vector, or scalar.

  The first argument, *alpha*, must be greater than or equal to zero. If
  *alpha* is a range, it must have an increment equal to one.

  If *alpha* is a scalar, the result is the same size as *x*.

  If *alpha* is a range, *x* must be a vector or scalar, and the result is a
  matrix with length(*x*) rows and length(*alpha*) columns.

**beta** (*a*, *b*)                                                Mapping Function
  Return the Beta function,

  $$B(a,b) = \frac{\Gamma(a)\Gamma(b)}{\Gamma(a+b)}.$$

**betai** (*a*, *b*, *x*)                                          Mapping Function
  Return the incomplete Beta function,

  $$\beta(a,b,x) = B(a,b)^{-1} \int_0^x t^{(a-z)}(1-t)^{(b-1)}dt.$$

  If *x* has more than one component, both *a* and *b* must be scalars. If *x*
  is a scalar, *a* and *b* must be of compatible dimensions.

**bincoeff** $(n, k)$                                    Mapping Function

Return the binomial coefficient of $n$ and $k$, defined as

$$\binom{n}{k} = \frac{n(n-1)(n-2)\cdots(n-k+1)}{k!}$$

For example,

```
bincoeff (5, 2)
    ⇒ 10
```

**erf** $(z)$                                            Mapping Function

Computes the error function,

$$\text{erf}(z) = \frac{2}{\sqrt{\pi}} \int_0^z e^{-t^2} dt$$

**erfc** $(z)$                                           Mapping Function

Computes the complementary error function, $1 - \text{erf}(z)$.

**erfinv** $(z)$                                         Mapping Function

Computes the inverse of the error function,

**gamma** $(z)$                                          Mapping Function

Computes the Gamma function,

$$\Gamma(z) = \int_0^\infty t^{z-1} e^{-t} dt.$$

**gammai** $(a, x)$                                      Mapping Function

Computes the incomplete gamma function,

$$\gamma(a, x) = \frac{\displaystyle\int_0^x e^{-t} t^{a-1} dt}{\Gamma(a)}$$

If $a$ is scalar, then gammai $(a, x)$ is returned for each element of $x$ and vice versa.

If neither $a$ nor $x$ is scalar, the sizes of $a$ and $x$ must agree, and *gammai* is applied element-by-element.

**lgamma** $(a, x)$                                      Mapping Function
**gammaln** $(a, x)$                                     Mapping Function

Return the natural logarithm of the gamma function.

**cross** $(x, y)$                                            Function File
    Computes the vector cross product of the two 3-dimensional vectors $x$ and $y$. For example,

```
cross ([1,1,0], [0,1,1])
    ⇒ [ 1; -1; 1 ]
```

**commutation_matrix** $(m, n)$                              Function File
    Return the commutation matrix $K_{m,n}$ which is the unique $mn \times mn$ matrix such that $K_{m,n} \cdot \mathrm{vec}(A) = \mathrm{vec}(A^T)$ for all $m \times n$ matrices $A$.

    If only one argument $m$ is given, $K_{m,m}$ is returned.

    See Magnus and Neudecker (1988), Matrix differential calculus with applications in statistics and econometrics.

**duplication_matrix** $(n)$                                 Function File
    Return the duplication matrix $D_n$ which is the unique $n^2 \times n(n + 1)/2$ matrix such that $D_n * \mathrm{vech}(A) = \mathrm{vec}(A)$ for all symmetric $n \times n$ matrices $A$.

    See Magnus and Neudecker (1988), Matrix differential calculus with applications in statistics and econometrics.

# 16.6 Mathematical Constants

**I**                                                        Built-in Variable
**J**                                                        Built-in Variable
**i**                                                        Built-in Variable
**j**                                                        Built-in Variable
    A pure imaginary number, defined as $\sqrt{-1}$. The I and J forms are true constants, and cannot be modified. The i and j forms are like ordinary variables, and may be used for other purposes. However, unlike other variables, they once again assume their special predefined values if they are cleared See Section 7.2 [Status of Variables], page 61.

**Inf**                                                      Built-in Variable
**inf**                                                      Built-in Variable
    Infinity. This is the result of an operation like $1/0$, or an operation that results in a floating point overflow.

**NaN**                                                      Built-in Variable
**nan**                                                      Built-in Variable
    Not a number. This is the result of an operation like $0/0$, or $\infty - \infty$, or any operation with a NaN.

Note that NaN always compares not equal to NaN. This behavior is specified by the IEEE standard for floating point arithmetic. To find NaN values, you must use the isnan function.

**pi** Built-in Variable

The ratio of the circumference of a circle to its diameter. Internally, pi is computed as '4.0 * atan (1.0)'.

**e** Built-in Variable

The base of natural logarithms. The constant $e$ satisfies the equation $\log(e) = 1$.

**eps** Built-in Variable

The machine precision. More precisely, eps is the largest relative spacing between any two adjacent numbers in the machine's floating point system. This number is obviously system-dependent. On machines that support 64 bit IEEE floating point arithmetic, eps is approximately $2.2204 \times 10^{-16}$.

**realmax** Built-in Variable

The largest floating point number that is representable. The actual value is system-dependent. On machines that support 64 bit IEEE floating point arithmetic, realmax is approximately $1.7977 \times 10^{308}$.

**realmin** Built-in Variable

The smallest floating point number that is representable. The actual value is system-dependent. On machines that support 64 bit IEEE floating point arithmetic, realmin is approximately $2.2251 \times 10^{-308}$.

# 17  Linear Algebra

This chapter documents the linear algebra functions of Octave. Reference material for many of these functions may be found in Golub and Van Loan, *Matrix Computations, 2nd Ed.*, Johns Hopkins, 1989, and in LAPACK *Users' Guide*, SIAM, 1992.

## 17.1  Basic Matrix Functions

aa = **balance** (a, *opt*)                                          Loadable Function
[dd, aa] = **balance** (a, *opt*)                                    Loadable Function
[cc, dd, aa, bb] = **balance** (a, b, *opt*)                         Loadable Function

> [dd, aa] = balance (a) returns aa = dd \ a * dd.  aa is a matrix whose row and column norms are roughly equal in magnitude, and dd = p * d, where p is a permutation matrix and d is a diagonal matrix of powers of two. This allows the equilibration to be computed without roundoff. Results of eigenvalue calculation are typically improved by balancing first.
>
> [cc, dd, aa, bb] = balance (a, b) returns aa = cc*a*dd and bb = cc*b*dd), where aa and bb have non-zero elements of approximately the same magnitude and cc and dd are permuted diagonal matrices as in dd for the algebraic eigenvalue problem.
>
> The eigenvalue balancing option opt is selected as follows:
>
> "N", "n"    No balancing; arguments copied, transformation(s) set to identity.
>
> "P", "p"    Permute argument(s) to isolate eigenvalues where possible.
>
> "S", "s"    Scale to improve accuracy of computed eigenvalues.
>
> "B", "b"    Permute and scale, in that order. Rows/columns of a (and b) that are isolated by permutation are not scaled. This is the default behavior.
>
> Algebraic eigenvalue balancing uses standard LAPACK routines.
>
> Generalized eigenvalue problem balancing uses Ward's algorithm (SIAM Journal on Scientific and Statistical Computing, 1981).

**cond** (a)

> Compute the (two-norm) condition number of a matrix. cond (a) is defined as norm (a) * norm (inv (a)), and is computed via a singular value decomposition.

**det** (a)                                                      Loadable Function
    Compute the determinant of a using LINPACK.

*lambda* = **eig** (a)                                           Loadable Function
[*v*, *lambda*] = **eig** (a)                                    Loadable Function
    The eigenvalues (and eigenvectors) of a matrix are computed in a
several step process which begins with a Hessenberg decomposition,
followed by a Schur decomposition, from which the eigenvalues are
apparent. The eigenvectors, when desired, are computed by further
manipulations of the Schur decomposition.

*G* = **givens** (x, y)                                          Loadable Function
[*c*, *s*] = **givens** (x, y)                                   Loadable Function
    Return a $2 \times 2$ orthogonal matrix

$$G = \begin{bmatrix} c & s \\ -s' & c \end{bmatrix}$$

such that

$$G \begin{bmatrix} x \\ y \end{bmatrix} = \begin{bmatrix} * \\ 0 \end{bmatrix}$$

with $x$ and $y$ scalars.

For example,

```
      givens (1, 1)
         ⇒    0.70711    0.70711
              -0.70711    0.70711
```

**inv** (a)                                                     Loadable Function
**inverse** (a)                                                 Loadable Function
    Compute the inverse of the square matrix a.

**norm** (a, p)                                                   Function File
    Compute the p-norm of the matrix a. If the second argument is miss-
ing, p = 2 is assumed.

If a is a matrix:

$p = 1$         1-norm, the largest column sum of a.

$p = 2$         Largest singular value of a.

$p = \text{Inf}$     Infinity norm, the largest row sum of a.

$p = \text{"fro"}$    Frobenius norm of a, sqrt (sum (diag (a' * a))).

If a is a vector or a scalar:

$p = \text{Inf}$      max (abs (a)).

$p = \text{-Inf}$     min (abs (a)).

other        p-norm of a, (sum (abs (a) .$\hat{}$ p)) $\hat{}$ (1/p).

**null** (a, *tol*)                                   Function File
    Return an orthonormal basis of the null space of a.

The dimension of the null space is taken as the number of singular values of a not greater than *tol*. If the argument *tol* is missing, it is computed as

    max (size (a)) * max (svd (a)) * eps

**orth** (a, *tol*)                                   Function File
    Return an orthonormal basis of the range space of a.

The dimension of the range space is taken as the number of singular values of a greater than *tol*. If the argument *tol* is missing, it is computed as

    max (size (a)) * max (svd (a)) * eps

**pinv** (x, *tol*)                                   Function File
    Return the pseudoinverse of x. Singular values less than *tol* are ignored.

If the second argument is omitted, it is assumed that

    tol = max (size (x)) * sigma_max (x) * eps,

where sigma_max (x) is the maximal singular value of x.

**rank** (a, *tol*)                                   Function File
    Compute the rank of a, using the singular value decomposition. The rank is taken to be the number of singular values of a that are greater than the specified tolerance *tol*. If the second argument is omitted, it is taken to be

    tol = max (size (a)) * sigma (1) * eps;

where eps is machine precision and sigma is the largest singular value of a.

**trace** (a)                                         Function File
    Compute the trace of a, sum (diag (a)).

## 17.2 Matrix Factorizations

**chol** (a)                                                    Loadable Function
  Compute the Cholesky factor, r, of the symmetric positive definite
  matrix a, where $R^T R = A$.

$h$ = **hess** (a)                                              Loadable Function
$[p, h]$ = **hess** (a)                                         Loadable Function
  Compute the Hessenberg decomposition of the matrix a.

  The Hessenberg decomposition is usually used as the first step in an
  eigenvalue computation, but has other applications as well (see Golub,
  Nash, and Van Loan, IEEE Transactions on Automatic Control, 1979.
  The Hessenberg decomposition is

$$A = PHP^T$$

  where $P$ is a square unitary matrix $(P^H P = I)$, and $H$ is upper
  Hessenberg $(H_{i,j} = 0, \forall i \geq j + 1)$.

$[l, u, p]$ = **lu** (a)                                        Loadable Function
  Compute the LU decomposition of a, using subroutines from LAPACK.
  The result is returned in a permuted form, according to the optional
  return value p. For example, given the matrix a = [1, 2; 3, 4],

        [l, u, p] = lu (a)

  returns

     l =

          1.00000    0.00000
          0.33333    1.00000

     u =

          3.00000    4.00000
          0.00000    0.66667

     p =

          0   1
          1   0

$[q, r, p]$ = **qr** (a)                                        Loadable Function
  Compute the QR factorization of a, using standard LAPACK subroutines. For example, given the matrix a = [1, 2; 3, 4],

```
    [q, r] = qr (a)
```
returns
```
    q =

        -0.31623   -0.94868
        -0.94868    0.31623


    r =

        -3.16228   -4.42719
         0.00000   -0.63246
```
The qr factorization has applications in the solution of least squares problems

$$\min_{x} \|Ax - b\|_2$$

for overdetermined systems of equations (i.e., $A$ is a tall, thin matrix). The QR factorization is $QR = A$ where $Q$ is an orthogonal matrix and $R$ is upper triangular.

The permuted QR factorization [q, r, p] = qr (a) forms the QR factorization such that the diagonal entries of r are decreasing in magnitude order. For example, given the matrix a = [1, 2; 3, 4],

```
    [q, r, pi] = qr(a)
```
returns
```
    q =

        -0.44721   -0.89443
        -0.89443    0.44721


    r =

        -4.47214   -3.13050
         0.00000    0.44721


    p =

         0   1
         1   0
```
The permuted qr factorization [q, r, p] = qr (a) factorization allows the construction of an orthogonal basis of span (a).

$s$ = **schur** (a)                                              Loadable Function
[$u$, $s$] = **schur** (a, *opt*)                               Loadable Function
The Schur decomposition is used to compute eigenvalues of a square matrix, and has applications in the solution of algebraic Riccati equations in control (see are and dare). schur always returns $S = U^T A U$ where $U$ is a unitary matrix ($U^T U$ is identity) and $S$ is upper triangular. The eigenvalues of $A$ (and $S$) are the diagonal elements of $S$ If the matrix $A$ is real, then the real Schur decomposition is computed, in which the matrix $U$ is orthogonal and $S$ is block upper triangular with blocks of size at most $2 \times 2$ blocks along the diagonal. The diagonal elements of $S$ (or the eigenvalues of the $2 \times 2$ blocks, when appropriate) are the eigenvalues of $A$ and $S$.

The eigenvalues are optionally ordered along the diagonal according to the value of opt. opt = "a" indicates that all eigenvalues with negative real parts should be moved to the leading block of $S$ (used in are), opt = "d" indicates that all eigenvalues with magnitude less than one should be moved to the leading block of $S$ (used in dare), and opt = "u", the default, indicates that no ordering of eigenvalues should occur. The leading $k$ columns of $U$ always span the $A$-invariant subspace corresponding to the $k$ leading eigenvalues of $S$.

$s$ = **svd** (a)                                               Loadable Function
[$u$, $s$, $v$] = **svd** (a)                                   Loadable Function
Compute the singular value decomposition of a

$$A = U \Sigma V^H$$

The function svd normally returns the vector of singular values. If asked for three return values, it computes $U$, $S$, and $V$. For example,

        svd (hilb (3))

returns

        ans =

            1.4083189
            0.1223271
            0.0026873

and

        [u, s, v] = svd (hilb (3))

returns

        u =

            -0.82704    0.54745    0.12766

```
        -0.45986   -0.52829   -0.71375
        -0.32330   -0.64901    0.68867

 s =

         1.40832   0.00000   0.00000
         0.00000   0.12233   0.00000
         0.00000   0.00000   0.00269

 v =

        -0.82704    0.54745    0.12766
        -0.45986   -0.52829   -0.71375
        -0.32330   -0.64901    0.68867
```

If given a second argument, svd returns an economy-sized decomposition, eliminating the unnecessary rows or columns of *u* or *v*.

## 17.3  Functions of a Matrix

expm (a)                                         Loadable Function
    Return the exponential of a matrix, defined as the infinite Taylor series

$$\exp(A) = I + A + \frac{A^2}{2!} + \frac{A^3}{3!} + \cdots$$

The Taylor series is *not* the way to compute the matrix exponential; see Moler and Van Loan, *Nineteen Dubious Ways to Compute the Exponential of a Matrix*, SIAM Review, 1978. This routine uses Ward's diagonal Padé approximation method with three step preconditioning (SIAM Journal on Numerical Analysis, 1977). Diagonal Padé approximations are rational polynomials of matrices $D_q(a)^{-1}N_q(a)$ whose Taylor series matches the first $2q + 1$ terms of the Taylor series above; direct evaluation of the Taylor series (with the same preconditioning steps) may be desirable in lieu of the Padé approximation when $D_q(a)$ is ill-conditioned.

logm (a)                                         Loadable Function
    Compute the matrix logarithm of the square matrix a. Note that this is currently implemented in terms of an eigenvalue expansion and needs to be improved to be more robust.

**sqrtm** (a)                                          Loadable Function
Compute the matrix square root of the square matrix a.  Note that
this is currently implemented in terms of an eigenvalue expansion and
needs to be improved to be more robust.

**kron** (a, b)                                             Function File
Form the kronecker product of two matrices, defined block by block as

        x = [a(i, j) b]

For example,

        kron (1:4, ones (3, 1))
           ⇒   1   2   3   4
               1   2   3   4
               1   2   3   4

[aa, bb, q, z] = **qzhess** (a, b)                         Function File
Compute the Hessenberg-triangular decomposition of the matrix pencil (a, b), returning aa = $q * a * z$, bb = $q * b * z$, with q and z orthogonal. For example,

        [aa, bb, q, z] = qzhess ([1, 2; 3, 4], [5, 6; 7, 8])
           ⇒ aa = [ -3.02244, -4.41741;  0.92998,  0.69749 ]
           ⇒ bb = [ -8.60233, -9.99730;  0.00000, -0.23250 ]
           ⇒  q = [ -0.58124, -0.81373; -0.81373,  0.58124 ]
           ⇒  z = [ 1, 0; 0, 1 ]

The Hessenberg-triangular decomposition is the first step in Moler and
Stewart's QZ decomposition algorithm.

Algorithm taken from Golub and Van Loan, *Matrix Computations*,
*2nd edition*.

**qzval** (a, b)                                       Loadable Function
Compute generalized eigenvalues of the matrix pencil $a - \lambda b$.

The arguments a and b must be real matrices.

x = **syl** (a, b, c)                                  Loadable Function
Solve the Sylvester equation

$$AX + XB + C = 0$$

using standard LAPACK subroutines. For example,

        syl ([1, 2; 3, 4], [5, 6; 7, 8], [9, 10; 11, 12])
           ⇒ [ -0.50000, -0.66667; -0.66667, -0.50000 ]

# 18 Nonlinear Equations

Octave can solve sets of nonlinear equations of the form

$$f(x) = 0$$

using the function fsolve, which is based on the MINPACK subroutine hybrd.

[*x*, *info*] = fsolve (*fcn*, *x0*)                                          Loadable Function
> Given *fcn*, the name of a function of the form f (*x*) and an initial starting point *x0*, fsolve solves the set of equations such that f (*x*) == 0.

fsolve_options (*opt*, *val*)                                        Loadable Function
> When called with two arguments, this function allows you set options parameters for the function fsolve. Given one argument, fsolve_options returns the value of the corresponding option. If no arguments are supplied, the names of all the available options and their current values are displayed.

> Here is a complete example. To solve the set of equations

$$-2x^2 + 3xy + 4\sin(y) - 6 = 0$$
$$3x^2 - 2xy^2 + 3\cos(x) + 4 = 0$$

> you first need to write a function to compute the value of the given function. For example:

```
function y = f (x)
   y(1) = -2*x(1)^2 + 3*x(1)*x(2)   + 4*sin(x(2)) - 6;
   y(2) =  3*x(1)^2 - 2*x(1)*x(2)^2 + 3*cos(x(1)) + 4;
endfunction
```

> Then, call fsolve with a specified initial condition to find the roots of the system of equations. For example, given the function f defined above,

```
   [x, info] = fsolve ("f", [1; 2])
```

> results in the solution

```
   x =

      0.57983
      2.54621

   info = 1
```

A value of info = 1 indicates that the solution has converged.

The function perror may be used to print English messages corresponding to the numeric error codes. For example,

```
perror ("fsolve", 1)
     ⊣ solution converged to requested tolerance
```

# 19 Quadrature

## 19.1 Functions of One Variable

[v, *ier*, *nfun*, *err*] = **quad** (*f*, *a*, *b*, *tol*, *sing*)            Loadable Function
Integrate a nonlinear function of one variable using Quadpack. The first argument is the name of the function to call to compute the value of the integrand. It must have the form

    y = f (x)

where *y* and *x* are scalars.

The second and third arguments are limits of integration. Either or both may be infinite.

The optional argument *tol* is a vector that specifies the desired accuracy of the result. The first element of the vector is the desired absolute tolerance, and the second element is the desired relative tolerance. To choose a relative test only, set the absolute tolerance to zero. To choose an absolute test only, set the relative tolerance to zero.

The optional argument *sing* is a vector of values at which the integrand is known to be singular.

The result of the integration is returned in *v* and *ier* contains an integer error code (0 indicates a successful integration). The value of *nfun* indicates how many function evaluations were required, and *err* contains an estimate of the error in the solution.

**quad_options** (*opt*, *val*)                        Loadable Function
When called with two arguments, this function allows you set options parameters for the function quad. Given one argument, quad_options returns the value of the corresponding option. If no arguments are supplied, the names of all the available options and their current values are displayed.

Here is an example of using quad to integrate the function

$$f(x) = x \sin(1/x)\sqrt{|1 - x|}$$

from $x = 0$ to $x = 3$.

This is a fairly difficult integration (plot the function over the range of integration to see why).

The first step is to define the function:

```
function y = f (x)
  y = x .* sin (1 ./ x) .* sqrt (abs (1 - x));
endfunction
```

Note the use of the 'dot' forms of the operators. This is not necessary for the call to quad, but it makes it much easier to generate a set of points for plotting (because it makes it possible to call the function with a vector argument to produce a vector result).

Then we simply call quad:

```
[v, ier, nfun, err] = quad ("f", 0, 3)
    ⇒ 1.9819
    ⇒ 1
    ⇒ 5061
    ⇒ 1.1522e-07
```

Although quad returns a nonzero value for *ier*, the result is reasonably accurate (to see why, examine what happens to the result if you move the lower bound to 0.1, then 0.01, then 0.001, etc.).

## 19.2 Orthogonal Collocation

[*r*, *A*, *B*, *q*] = **colloc** (*n*, "left", "right")               Loadable Function
  Compute derivative and integral weight matrices for orthogonal collocation using the subroutines given in J. Villadsen and M. L. Michelsen, *Solution of Differential Equation Models by Polynomial Approximation*.

Here is an example of using `colloc` to generate weight matrices for solving the second order differential equation $u' - \alpha u'' = 0$ with the boundary conditions $u(0) = 0$ and $u(1) = 1$.

First, we can generate the weight matrices for *n* points (including the endpoints of the interval), and incorporate the boundary conditions in the right hand side (for a specific value of $\alpha$).

```
n = 7;
alpha = 0.1;
[r, a, b] = colloc (n-2, "left", "right");
at = a(2:n-1,2:n-1);
bt = b(2:n-1,2:n-1);
rhs = alpha * b(2:n-1,n) - a(2:n-1,n);
```

Then the solution at the roots *r* is

```
u = [ 0; (at - alpha * bt) \ rhs; 1]
    ⇒ [ 0.00; 0.004; 0.01 0.00; 0.12; 0.62; 1.00 ]
```

# 20  Differential Equations

Octave has two built-in functions for solving differential equations. Both are based on reliable ODE solvers written in Fortran.

## 20.1  Ordinary Differential Equations

The function lsode can be used to solve ODEs of the form

$$\frac{dx}{dt} = f(x, t)$$

using Hindmarsh's ODE solver LSODE.

**lsode** (*fcn*, *x0*, *t*, *t_crit*)                                   Loadable Function
Return a matrix of *x* as a function of *t*, given the initial state of the system *x0*. Each row in the result matrix corresponds to one of the elements in the vector *t*. The first element of *t* corresponds to the initial state *x0*, so that the first row of the output is *x0*.

The first argument, *fcn*, is a string that names the function to call to compute the vector of right hand sides for the set of equations. It must have the form

    xdot = f (x, t)

where *xdot* and *x* are vectors and *t* is a scalar.

The fourth argument is optional, and may be used to specify a set of times that the ODE solver should not integrate past. It is useful for avoiding difficulties with singularities and points where there is a discontinuity in the derivative.

Here is an example of solving a set of three differential equations using lsode. Given the function

```
function xdot = f (x, t)

  xdot = zeros (3,1);

  xdot(1) = 77.27 * (x(2) - x(1)*x(2) + x(1) \
          - 8.375e-06*x(1)^2);
  xdot(2) = (x(3) - x(1)*x(2) - x(2)) / 77.27;
  xdot(3) = 0.161*(x(1) - x(3));

endfunction
```

and the initial condition x0 = [ 4; 1.1; 4 ], the set of equations can be integrated using the command

```
t = linspace (0, 500, 1000);
```

```
y = lsode ("f", x0, t);
```

If you try this, you will see that the value of the result changes dramatically between $t = 0$ and 5, and again around $t = 305$. A more efficient set of output points might be

```
t = [0, logspace (-1, log10(303), 150), \
        logspace (log10(304), log10(500), 150)];
```

**lsode_options** (*opt*, *val*)                                  Loadable Function
When called with two arguments, this function allows you set options parameters for the function lsode. Given one argument, lsode_ options returns the value of the corresponding option. If no arguments are supplied, the names of all the available options and their current values are displayed.

See Alan C. Hindmarsh, *ODEPACK, A Systematized Collection of ODE Solvers*, in Scientific Computing, R. S. Stepleman, editor, (1983) for more information about the inner workings of lsode.

## 20.2 Differential-Algebraic Equations

The function dassl can be used to solve DAEs of the form

$$0 = f(\dot{x}, x, t), \qquad x(t = 0) = x_0, \dot{x}(t = 0) = \dot{x}_0$$

using Petzold's DAE solver DASSL.

[*x, xdot*] = **dassl** (*fcn*, *x0*, *xdot0*, *t*, *t_crit*)            Loadable Function
Return a matrix of states and their first derivatives with respect to *t*. Each row in the result matrices correspond to one of the elements in the vector *t*. The first element of *t* corresponds to the initial state *x0* and derivative *xdot0*, so that the first row of the output *x* is *x0* and the first row of the output *xdot* is *xdot0*.

The first argument, *fcn*, is a string that names the function to call to compute the vector of residuals for the set of equations. It must have the form

```
res = f (x, xdot, t)
```

where *x*, *xdot*, and *res* are vectors, and *t* is a scalar.

The second and third arguments to dassl specify the initial condition of the states and their derivatives, and the fourth argument specifies a vector of output times at which the solution is desired, including the time corresponding to the initial condition.

The set of initial states and derivatives are not strictly required to be consistent. In practice, however, DASSL is not very good at determining a consistent set for you, so it is best if you ensure that the initial values result in the function evaluating to zero.

The fifth argument is optional, and may be used to specify a set of times that the DAE solver should not integrate past. It is useful for avoiding difficulties with singularities and points where there is a discontinuity in the derivative.

**dassl_options** (*opt, val*)                                   Loadable Function
When called with two arguments, this function allows you set options parameters for the function lsode. Given one argument, dassl_options returns the value of the corresponding option. If no arguments are supplied, the names of all the available options and their current values are displayed.

See K. E. Brenan, et al., *Numerical Solution of Initial-Value Problems in Differential-Algebraic Equations*, North-Holland (1989) for more information about the implementation of DASSL.

# 21 Optimization

## 21.1 Quadratic Programming

There are no functions available in this section at the moment. Check the development version of Octave for possible additions.

## 21.2 Nonlinear Programming

There are no functions available in this section at the moment. Check the development version of Octave for possible additions.

## 21.3 Linear Least Squares

[*beta*, *v*, *r*] = **gls** (*y*, *x*, *o*)                                      Function File
  Generalized least squares estimation for the multivariate model $y = xb + e$ with $\bar{e} = 0$ and $\mathrm{cov}(\mathrm{vec}(e)) = (s^2)o$, where $y$ is a $t \times p$ matrix, $x$ is a $t \times k$ matrix, $b$ is a $k \times p$ matrix, $e$ is a $t \times p$ matrix, and $o$ is a $tp \times tp$ matrix.

  Each row of Y and X is an observation and each column a variable.

  The return values *beta*, *v*, and *r* are defined as follows.

  *beta*          The GLS estimator for *b*.

  *v*             The GLS estimator for $s\hat{}2$.

  *r*             The matrix of GLS residuals, *r* = *y* - *x* * *beta*.

[*beta*, *sigma*, *r*] = **ols** (*y*, *x*)                                   Function File
  Ordinary least squares estimation for the multivariate model $y = xb + e$ with $\bar{e} = 0$, and $\mathrm{cov}(\mathrm{vec}(e)) = \mathrm{kron}(s, I)$ where $y$ is a $t \times p$ matrix, $x$ is a $t \times k$ matrix, $b$ is a $k \times p$ matrix, and $e$ is a $t \times p$ matrix.

  Each row of *y* and *x* is an observation and each column a variable.

  The return values *beta*, *sigma*, and *r* are defined as follows.

  *beta*          The OLS estimator for *b*, *beta* = pinv (*x*) * *y*, where pinv (*x*) denotes the pseudoinverse of *x*.

  *sigma*         The OLS estimator for the matrix *s*,

                  *sigma* = *r*' * *r* / (*t*-rank(*x*))

                  where *r* = *y*-*x*\**beta*.

  *r*             The matrix of OLS residuals, *r* = *y* - *x* * *beta*.

# 22 Statistics

The development version of Octave includes additional statistics functions not described in this chapter.

**mean** $(x)$                                                      Function File

If $x$ is a vector, compute the mean of the elements of $x$

$$\text{mean}(x) = \bar{x} = \frac{1}{N} \sum_{i=1}^{N} x_i$$

If $x$ is a matrix, compute the mean for each column and return them in a row vector.

**median** $(x)$                                                    Function File

If $x$ is a vector, compute the median value of the elements of $x$.

$$\text{median}(x) = \begin{cases} x(\lceil N/2 \rceil), & N \text{ odd}; \\ (x(N/2) + x(N/2+1))/2, & N \text{ even}. \end{cases}$$

If $x$ is a matrix, compute the median value for each column and return them in a row vector.

**std** $(x)$                                                       Function File

If $x$ is a vector, compute the standard deviation of the elements of $x$.

$$\text{std}(x) = \sigma(x) = \sqrt{\frac{\sum_{i=1}^{N}(x_i - \bar{x})}{N-1}}$$

If $x$ is a matrix, compute the standard deviation for each column and return them in a row vector.

**cov** $(x, y)$                                                    Function File

If each row of $x$ and $y$ is an observation and each column is a variable, the $(i,j)$-th entry of cov $(x, y)$ is the covariance between the $i$-th variable in $x$ and the $j$-th variable in $y$. If called with one argument, compute cov $(x, x)$.

**corrcoef** $(x, y)$                                               Function File

If each row of $x$ and $y$ is an observation and each column is a variable, the $(i,j)$-th entry of corrcoef $(x, y)$ is the correlation between the $i$-th variable in $x$ and the $j$-th variable in $y$. If called with one argument, compute corrcoef $(x, x)$.

**kurtosis** (*x*)                                          Function File

If *x* is a vector of length $N$, return the kurtosis

$$\text{kurtosis}(x) = \frac{1}{N\sigma(x)^4} \sum_{i=1}^{N} (x_i - \bar{x})^4 - 3$$

of *x*. If *x* is a matrix, return the row vector containing the kurtosis of each column.

**mahalanobis** (*x*, *y*)                                  Function File

Return the Mahalanobis' D-square distance between the multivariate samples *x* and *y*, which must have the same number of components (columns), but may have a different number of observations (rows).

**skewness** (*x*)                                          Function File

If *x* is a vector of length $N$, return the skewness

$$\text{skewness}(x) = \frac{1}{N\sigma(x)^3} \sum_{i=1}^{N} (x_i - \bar{x})^3$$

of *x*. If *x* is a matrix, return the row vector containing the skewness of each column.

# 23 Sets

Octave has a limited set of functions for managing sets of data, where a set is defined as a collection unique elements.

**create_set** ($x$)                                                                    Function File
  Return a row vector containing the unique values in $x$, sorted in ascending order. For example,

```
create_set ([ 1, 2; 3, 4; 4, 2 ])
     ⇒ [ 1, 2, 3, 4 ]
```

**union** ($x$, $y$)                                                                    Function File
  Return the set of elements that are in either of the sets $x$ and $y$. For example,

```
union ([ 1, 2, 4 ], [ 2, 3, 5 ])
     ⇒ [ 1, 2, 3, 4, 5 ]
```

**intersection** ($x$, $y$)                                                             Function File
  Return the set of elements that are in both sets $x$ and $y$. For example,

```
intersection ([ 1, 2, 3 ], [ 2, 3, 5 ])
     ⇒ [ 2, 3 ]
```

**complement** ($x$, $y$)                                                               Function File
  Return the elements of set $y$ that are not in set $x$. For example,

```
complement ([ 1, 2, 3 ], [ 2, 3, 5 ])
     ⇒ 5
```

# 24 Polynomial Manipulations

In Octave, a polynomial is represented by its coefficients (arranged in descending order). For example, a vector of length $N + 1$ corresponds to the following polynomial of order $N$

$$p(x) = c_1 x^N + \ldots + c_N x + c_{N+1}.$$

**compan** $(c)$ — Function File

Compute the companion matrix corresponding to polynomial coefficient vector $c$.

The companion matrix is

$$A = \begin{bmatrix} -c_2/c_1 & -c_3/c_1 & \cdots & -c_N/c_1 & -c_{N+1}/c_1 \\ 1 & 0 & \cdots & 0 & 0 \\ 0 & 1 & \cdots & 0 & 0 \\ \vdots & \vdots & \ddots & \vdots & \vdots \\ 0 & 0 & \cdots & 1 & 0 \end{bmatrix}.$$

The eigenvalues of the companion matrix are equal to the roots of the polynomial.

**conv** $(a,\ b)$ — Function File

Convolve two vectors.

y = conv (a, b) returns a vector of length equal to length (a) + length (b) - 1. If a and b are polynomial coefficient vectors, conv returns the coefficients of the product polynomial.

**deconv** $(y,\ a)$ — Function File

Deconvolve two vectors.

[b, r] = deconv (y, a) solves for $b$ and $r$ such that y = conv (a, b) + r.

If $y$ and $a$ are polynomial coefficient vectors, $b$ will contain the coefficients of the polynomial quotient and $r$ will be a remainder polynomial of lowest order.

**poly** $(a)$ — Function File

If a is a square $N$-by-$N$ matrix, poly (a) is the row vector of the coefficients of det (z * eye (N) - a), the characteristic polynomial of a. If x is a vector, poly (x) is a vector of coefficients of the polynomial whose roots are the elements of $x$.

**polyderiv** (*c*)                                              Function File
  Return the coefficients of the derivative of the polynomial whose coefficients are given by vector *c*.

[*p*, *yf*] = **polyfit** (*x*, *y*, *n*)                        Function File
  Return the coefficients of a polynomial $p(x)$ of degree *n* that minimizes

$$\sum_{i=1}^{N}(p(x_i) - y_i)^2$$

to best fit the data in the least squares sense.

  If two output arguments are requested, the second contains the values of the polynomial for each value of *x*.

**polyinteg** (*c*)                                             Function File
  Return the coefficients of the integral of the polynomial whose coefficients are represented by the vector *c*.
  The constant of integration is set to zero.

**polyreduce** (*c*)                                            Function File
  Reduces a polynomial coefficient vector to a minimum number of terms by stripping off any leading zeros.

**polyval** (*c*, *x*)                                          Function File
  Evaluate a polynomial.
  polyval (*c*, *x*) will evaluate the polynomial at the specified value of *x*.
  If *x* is a vector or matrix, the polynomial is evaluated at each of the elements of *x*.

**polyvalm** (*c*, *x*)                                         Function File
  Evaluate a polynomial in the matrix sense.
  polyvalm (*c*, *x*) will evaluate the polynomial in the matrix sense, i.e. matrix multiplication is used instead of element by element multiplication as is used in polyval.
  The argument *x* must be a square matrix.

**residue** (*b*, *a*, *tol*)                                   Function File
  If *b* and *a* are vectors of polynomial coefficients, then residue calculates the partial fraction expansion corresponding to the ratio of the two polynomials.

The function residue returns $r$, $p$, $k$, and $e$, where the vector $r$ contains the residue terms, $p$ contains the pole values, $k$ contains the coefficients of a direct polynomial term (if it exists) and $e$ is a vector containing the powers of the denominators in the partial fraction terms.

Assuming $b$ and $a$ represent polynomials $P(s)$ and $Q(s)$ we have:

$$\frac{P(s)}{Q(s)} = \sum_{m=1}^{M} \frac{r_m}{(s - p_m)_m^e} + \sum_{i=1}^{N} k_i s^{N-i}.$$

where $M$ is the number of poles (the length of the $r$, $p$, and $e$ vectors) and $N$ is the length of the $k$ vector.

The argument *tol* is optional, and if not specified, a default value of 0.001 is assumed. The tolerance value is used to determine whether poles with small imaginary components are declared real. It is also used to determine if two poles are distinct. If the ratio of the imaginary part of a pole to the real part is less than *tol*, the imaginary part is discarded. If two poles are farther apart than *tol* they are distinct. For example,

```
b = [1, 1, 1];
a = [1, -5, 8, -4];
[r, p, k, e] = residue (b, a);
    ⇒ r = [-2, 7, 3]
    ⇒ p = [2, 2, 1]
    ⇒ k = [] (0x0)
    ⇒ e = [1, 2, 1]
```

which implies the following partial fraction expansion

$$\frac{s^2 + s + 1}{s^3 - 5s^2 + 8s - 4} = \frac{-2}{s - 2} + \frac{7}{(s - 2)^2} + \frac{3}{s - 1}$$

**roots** $(v)$          Function File

For a vector $v$ with $N$ components, return the roots of the polynomial

$$v_1 z^{N-1} + \cdots + v_{N-1} z + v_N.$$

# 25  Control Theory

Most of the functions described in this chapter were contributed by A. Scottedward Hodel A.S.Hodel@eng.auburn.edu and R. Bruce Tenison Bruce.Tenison@eng.auburn.edu. They have also written a larger collection of functions for solving linear control problems. It is currently being updated for Octave version 2, with snapshots of the sources available from ftp://ftp.eng.auburn.edu/pub/hodel.

[n, m, p] = abcddim (a, b, c, d)                                   Function File
    Check for compatibility of the dimensions of the matrices defining the linear system $[A, B, C, D]$ corresponding to

$$\frac{dx}{dt} = Ax + Bu$$
$$y = Cx + Du$$

or a similar discrete-time system.

If the matrices are compatibly dimensioned, then abcddim returns

n          The number of system states.

m          The number of system inputs.

p          The number of system outputs.

Otherwise abcddim returns $n = m = p = -1$.

are (a, b, c, opt)                                                 Function File
    Return the solution, $x$, of the algebraic Riccati equation

$$A^T X + XA - XBX + C = 0$$

for identically dimensioned square matrices a, b, and c. If b is not square, are attempts to use b*b' instead. If c is not square, are attempts to use c'*c) instead.

To form the solution, Laub's Schur method (IEEE Transactions on Automatic Control, 1979) is applied to the appropriate Hamiltonian matrix.

The optional argument opt is passed to the eigenvalue balancing routine. If it is omitted, a value of "B" is assumed.

c2d (a, b, t)                                                      Function File
    Convert the continuous time system described by:

$$\frac{dx}{dt} = Ax + Bu$$

into a discrete time equivalent model

$$x_{k+1} = A_d x_k + B_d u_k$$

via the matrix exponential assuming a zero-order hold on the input and sample time $t$.

**dare** (a, b, c, r, opt)                                         Function File
    Return the solution, $x$ of the discrete-time algebraic Riccati equation

$$A^T X A - X + A^T X B (R + B^T X B)^{-1} B^T X A + C = 0$$

for matrices with dimensions:

a           $n$ by $n$.

b           $n$ by $m$.

c           $n$ by $n$, symmetric positive semidefinite.

r           $m$ by $m$, symmetric positive definite (invertible).

If $c$ is not square, then the function attempts to use $c'*c$ instead.

To form the solution, Laub's Schur method (IEEE Transactions on Automatic Control, 1979) is applied to the appropriate symplectic matrix.

See also Ran and Rodman, *Stable Hermitian Solutions of Discrete Algebraic Riccati Equations*, Mathematics of Control, Signals and Systems, Volume 5, Number 2 (1992).

The optional argument *opt* is passed to the eigenvalue balancing routine. If it is omitted, a value of "B" is assumed.

**dgram** (a, b)                                                   Function File
    Return the discrete controllability or observability gramian for the discrete time system described by

$$x_{k+1} = A x_k + B u_k$$

$$y_k = C x_k + D u_k$$

For example, dgram (a, b) returns the discrete controllability gramian and dgram (a', c') returns the observability gramian.

[l, m, p, e] = **dlqe** (a, g, c, sigw, sigv, z)                   Function File
    Construct the linear quadratic estimator (Kalman filter) for the discrete time system

$$x_{k+1} = A x_k + B u_k + G w_k$$

$$y_k = Cx_k + Du_k + w_k$$

where $w$, $v$ are zero-mean gaussian noise processes with respective intensities *sigw* = cov $(w, w)$ and *sigv* = cov $(v, v)$.

If specified, $z$ is cov $(w, v)$. Otherwise cov $(w, v) = 0$.

The observer structure is

$$z_{k+1} = Az_k + Bu_k + k(y_k - Cz_k - Du_k)$$

The following values are returned:

| | |
|---|---|
| $l$ | The observer gain, $(A - ALC)$. is stable. |
| $m$ | The Riccati equation solution. |
| $p$ | The estimate error covariance after the measurement update. |
| $e$ | The closed loop poles of $(A - ALC)$. |

$[k, p, e]$ = **dlqr** $(a, b, q, r, z)$                                    Function File

Construct the linear quadratic regulator for the discrete time system

$$x_{k+1} = Ax_k + Bu_k$$

to minimize the cost functional

$$J = \sum x^T Qx + u^T Ru$$

$z$ omitted or

$$J = \sum x^T Qx + u^T Ru + 2x^T Zu$$

$z$ included.

The following values are returned:

| | |
|---|---|
| $k$ | The state feedback gain, $(A - BK)$ is stable. |
| $p$ | The solution of algebraic Riccati equation. |
| $e$ | The closed loop poles of $(A - BK)$. |

**dlyap** $(a, b)$                                                  Function File

Solve the discrete-time Lyapunov equation $AXA^T - X + B = 0$ for square matrices a, b. If $b$ is not square, then the function attempts to solve either $AXA^T - X + BB^T = 0$ or $A^TXA - X + B^TB = 0$, whichever is appropriate.

Uses Schur decomposition method as in Kitagawa *An Algorithm for Solving the Matrix Equation* $X = FXF' + S$, International Journal of Control, Volume 25, Number 5, pages 745–753 (1977); column-by-column solution method as suggested in Hammerling, *Numerical Solution of the Stable, Non-Negative Definite Lyapunov Equation*, IMA Journal of Numerical Analysis, Volume 2, pages 303–323 (1982).

**is_controllable** (a, b, *tol*)                                    Function File
   Return 1 if the pair (a, b) is controllable. Otherwise, return 0.

   The optional argument *tol* is a roundoff parameter. If it is omitted, a
   value of 2*eps is used.

   Currently, is_controllable just constructs the controllability matrix
   and checks rank.

**is_observable** (a, c, *tol*)                                      Function File
   Return 1 if the pair (a, c) is observable. Otherwise, return 0.

   The optional argument *tol* is a roundoff parameter. If it is omitted, a
   value of 2*eps is used.

[k, p, e] = **lqe** (a, g, c, *sigw*, *sigv*, *z*)                   Function File
   Construct the linear quadratic estimator (Kalman filter) for the continuous time system

$$\frac{dx}{dt} = Ax + Bu$$

$$y = Cx + Du$$

   where w and v are zero-mean gaussian noise processes with respective
   intensities

       sigw = cov (w, w)
       sigv = cov (v, v)

   The optional argument z is the cross-covariance cov (w, v). If it is
   omitted, cov (w, v) = 0 is assumed.

   Observer structure is dz/dt = A z + B u + k (y - C z - D u)

   The following values are returned:

   k              The observer gain, $(A - KC)$ is stable.

   p              The solution of algebraic Riccati equation.

   e              The vector of closed loop poles of $(A - KC)$.

[k, p, e] = **lqr** (a, b, q, r, z)                                  Function File
   construct the linear quadratic regulator for the continuous time system

$$\frac{dx}{dt} = Ax + Bu$$

   to minimize the cost functional

$$J = \int_0^\infty x^T Q x + u^T R u$$

$z$ omitted or

$$J = \int_0^\infty x^T Q x + u^T R u + 2 x^T Z u$$

$z$ included.

The following values are returned:

k            The state feedback gain, $(A - BK)$ is stable.

p            The stabilizing solution of appropriate algebraic Riccati
             equation.

e            The vector of the closed loop poles of $(A - BK)$.

**lyap** (a, b, c)                                         Function File
   Solve the Lyapunov (or Sylvester) equation via the Bartels-Stewart
   algorithm (Communications of the ACM, 1972).

   If a, b, and c are specified, then lyap returns the solution of the
   Sylvester equation
$$AX + XB + C = 0$$

   If only (a, b) are specified, then lyap returns the solution of the
   Lyapunov equation

$$A^T X + X A + B = 0$$

   If b is not square, then lyap returns the solution of either

$$A^T X + X A + B^T B = 0$$

   or

$$AX + X A^T + B B^T = 0$$

   whichever is appropriate.

**tzero** (a, b, c, d, opt)                                Function File
   Compute the transmission zeros of $[A, B, C, D]$.

   The optional argument *opt* is passed to the eigenvalue balancing routine. If it is omitted, a value of "B" is assumed.

# 26 Signal Processing

The development version of Octave includes additional signal processing functions not described in this chapter.

detrend (x, p)                                              Function File

If x is a vector, detrend (x, p) removes the best fit of a polynomial of order p from the data x.

If x is a matrix, detrend (x, p) does the same for each column in x.

The second argument is optional. If it is not specified, a value of 1 is assumed. This corresponds to removing a linear trend.

fft (a, n)                                                     Function

Compute the FFT of a using subroutines from FFTPACK. If a is a matrix, fft computes the FFT for each column of a.

If called with two arguments, n is expected to be an integer specifying the number of elements of a to use. If a is a matrix, n specifies the number of rows of a to use. If n is larger than the size of a, a is resized and padded with zeros.

ifft (a, n)                                          Loadable Function

Compute the inverse FFT of a using subroutines from FFTPACK. If a is a matrix, fft computes the inverse FFT for each column of a.

If called with two arguments, n is expected to be an integer specifying the number of elements of a to use. If a is a matrix, n specifies the number of rows of a to use. If n is larger than the size of a, a is resized and padded with zeros.

fft2 (a, n, m)                                       Loadable Function

Compute the two dimensional FFT of a.

The optional arguments n and m may be used specify the number of rows and columns of a to use. If either of these is larger than the size of a, a is resized and padded with zeros.

ifft2 (a, n, m)                                      Loadable Function

Compute the two dimensional inverse FFT of a.

The optional arguments n and m may be used specify the number of rows and columns of a to use. If either of these is larger than the size of a, a is resized and padded with zeros.

**fftconv** (*a*, *b*, *n*)                                      Built-in Function
Return the convolution of the vectors *a* and *b*, as a vector with length equal to the length (a) + length (b) - 1. If *a* and *b* are the coefficient vectors of two polynomials, the returned value is the coefficient vector of the product polynomial.

The computation uses the FFT by calling the function fftfilt. If the optional argument *n* is specified, an N-point FFT is used.

**fftfilt** (*b*, *x*, *n*)                                      Function File
With two arguments, fftfilt filters *x* with the FIR filter *b* using the FFT.

Given the optional third argument, *n*, fftfilt uses the overlap-add method to filter *x* with *b* using an N-point FFT.

y = **filter** (*b*, *a*, *x*)                                  Loadable Function
Return the solution to the following linear, time-invariant difference equation:

$$\sum_{k=0}^{N} a_{k+1} y_{n-k} = \sum_{k=0}^{M} b_{k+1} x_{n-k}, \qquad 1 \le n \le P$$

where $a \in \Re^{N-1}$, $b \in \Re^{M-1}$, and $x \in \Re^{P}$. An equivalent form of this equation is:

$$y_n = -\sum_{k=1}^{N} c_{k+1} y_{n-k} + \sum_{k=0}^{M} d_{k+1} x_{n-k}, \qquad 1 \le n \le P$$

where $c = a/a_1$ and $d = b/a_1$.

In terms of the z-transform, y is the result of passing the discrete-time signal x through a system characterized by the following rational system function:

$$H(z) = \frac{\displaystyle\sum_{k=0}^{M} d_{k+1} z^{-k}}{1 + \displaystyle\sum_{k+1}^{N} c_{k+1} z^{-k}}$$

[*y*, *sf*] = **filter** (*b*, *a*, *x*, *si*)                  Loadable Function
This is the same as the filter function described above, except that *si* is taken as the initial state of the system and the final state is returned as *sf*. The state vector is a column vector whose length is equal to the length of the longest coefficient vector minus one. If *si* is not set, the initial state vector is set to all zeros.

[*h*, *w*] = **freqz** (*b*, *a*, *n*, "whole")                                    Function File

Return the complex frequency response *h* of the rational IIR filter whose numerator and denominator coefficients are *b* and *a*, respectively. The response is evaluated at *n* angular frequencies between 0 and $2\pi$.

The output value *w* is a vector of the frequencies.

If the fourth argument is omitted, the response is evaluated at frequencies between 0 and $\pi$.

If *n* is omitted, a value of 512 is assumed.

If *a* is omitted, the denominator is assumed to be 1 (this corresponds to a simple FIR filter).

For fastest computation, *n* should factor into a small number of small primes.

**sinc** (*x*)                                                         Function File

Return $\sin(\pi x)/(\pi x)$.

# 27 Image Processing

Octave can display images with the X Window System using the xloadimage program. You do not need to be running X in order to manipulate images, however, so some of these functions may be useful even if you are not able to view the results.

Loading images only works with Octave's image format (a file with a matrix containing the image data, and a matrix containing the colormap). Contributions of robust, well-written functions to read other image formats are welcome. If you can provide them, or would like to improve Octave's image processing capabilities in other ways, please contact bug@octave.org.

**colormap** (*map*)                                           Function File
**colormap** ("default")                                       Function File
> Set the current colormap.
>
> colormap (*map*) sets the current colormap to *map*. The color map should be an *n* row by 3 column matrix. The columns contain red, green, and blue intensities respectively. All entries should be between 0 and 1 inclusive. The new colormap is returned.
>
> colormap ("default") restores the default colormap (a gray scale colormap with 64 entries). The default colormap is returned.
>
> With no arguments, colormap returns the current color map.

**gray** (*n*)                                                 Function File
> Return a gray colormap with *n* entries corresponding to values from 0 to *n*-1. The argument *n* should be a scalar. If it is omitted, 64 is assumed.

[*img*, *map*] = **gray2ind** ()                               Function File
> Convert a gray scale intensity image to an Octave indexed image.

**image** (*x*, *zoom*)                                        Function File
> Display a matrix as a color image. The elements of *x* are indices into the current colormap and should have values between 1 and the length of the colormap. If *zoom* is omitted, a value of 4 is assumed.

**imagesc** (*x*, *zoom*)                                      Function File
> Display a scaled version of the matrix *x* as a color image. The matrix is scaled so that its entries are indices into the current colormap. The scaled matrix is returned. If *zoom* is omitted, a value of 4 is assumed.

imshow (*x*, *map*)                                          Function File
imshow (*x*, *n*)                                            Function File
imshow (*i*, *n*)                                            Function File
imshow (*r*, *g*, *b*)                                       Function File
    Display images.

    imshow (*x*) displays an indexed image using the current colormap.

    imshow (*x*, *map*) displays an indexed image using the specified colormap.

    imshow (*i*, *n*) displays a gray scale intensity image.

    imshow (*r*, *g*, *b*) displays an RGB image.

ind2gray (*x*, *map*)                                        Function File
    Convert an Octave indexed image to a gray scale intensity image. If *map* is omitted, the current colormap is used to determine the intensities.

[*r*, *g*, *b*] = ind2rgb (*x*, *map*)                       Function File
    Convert an indexed image to red, green, and blue color components. If *map* is omitted, the current colormap is used for the conversion.

[*x*, *map*] = loadimage (*file*)                            Function File
    Load an image file and it's associated color map from the specified *file*. The image must be stored in Octave's image format.

rgb2ntsc (*rgb*)                                             Function File
    Image format conversion.

ntsc2rgb (*yiq*)                                             Function File
    Image format conversion.

ocean (*n*)                                                  Function File
    Create color colormap. The argument *n* should be a scalar. If it is omitted, 64 is assumed.

[*x*, *map*] = rgb2ind (*r*, *g*, *b*)                       Function File
    Convert and RGB image to an Octave indexed image.

saveimage (*file*, *x*, *fmt*, *map*)                        Function File
    Save the matrix *x* to *file* in image format *fmt*. Valid values for *fmt* are

    "img"      Octave's image format. The current colormap is also saved in the file.

"ppm"        Portable pixmap format.

"ps"         PostScript format. Note that images saved in PostScript
             format can not be read back into Octave with loadimage.

If the fourth argument is supplied, the specified colormap will also be
saved along with the image.

Note: if the colormap contains only two entries and these entries are
black and white, the bitmap ppm and PostScript formats are used.
If the image is a gray scale image (the entries within each row of the
colormap are equal) the gray scale ppm and PostScript image formats
are used, otherwise the full color formats are used.

**IMAGEPATH**                                          Built-in Variable
A colon separated list of directories in which to search for image files.

# 28 Audio Processing

Octave provides a few functions for dealing with audio data. An audio 'sample' is a single output value from an A/D converter, i.e., a small integer number (usually 8 or 16 bits), and audio data is just a series of such samples. It can be characterized by three parameters: the sampling rate (measured in samples per second or Hz, e.g. 8000 or 44100), the number of bits per sample (e.g. 8 or 16), and the number of channels (1 for mono, 2 for stereo, etc.).

There are many different formats for representing such data. Currently, only the two most popular, *linear encoding* and *mu-law encoding*, are supported by Octave. There is an excellent FAQ on audio formats by Guido van Rossum <guido@cwi.nl> which can be found at any FAQ ftp site, in particular in the directory '/pub/usenet/news.answers/audio-fmts' of the archive site rtfm.mit.edu.

Octave simply treats audio data as vectors of samples (non-mono data are not supported yet). It is assumed that audio files using linear encoding have one of the extensions 'lin' or 'raw', and that files holding data in mu-law encoding end in 'au', 'mu', or 'snd'.

**lin2mu** (*x*)                                                    Function File
   If the vector *x* represents mono audio data in 8- or 16-bit linear encoding, lin2mu (*x*) is the corresponding mu-law encoding.

**mu2lin** (*x*, *bps*)                                             Function File
   If the vector *x* represents mono audio data in mu-law encoding, mu2lin converts it to linear encoding. The optional argument *bps* specifies whether the input data uses 8 bit per sample (default) or 16 bit.

**loadaudio** (*name*, *ext*, *bps*)                               Function File
   Loads audio data from the file '*name.ext*' into the vector *x*.

   The extension *ext* determines how the data in the audio file is interpreted; the extensions 'lin' (default) and 'raw' correspond to linear, the extensions 'au', 'mu', or 'snd' to mu-law encoding.

   The argument *bps* can be either 8 (default) or 16, and specifies the number of bits per sample used in the audio file.

**saveaudio** (*name*, *x*, *ext*, *bps*)                          Function File
   Saves a vector *x* of audio data to the file '*name.ext*'. The optional parameters *ext* and *bps* determine the encoding and the number of bits per sample used in the audio file (see loadaudio); defaults are 'lin' and 8, respectively.

The following functions for audio I/O require special A/D hardware
and operating system support. It is assumed that audio data in linear
encoding can be played and recorded by reading from and writing to
'/dev/dsp', and that similarly '/dev/audio' is used for mu-law encoding.
These file names are system-dependent. Improvements so that these functions will work without modification on a wide variety of hardware are
welcome.

**playaudio** (*name, ext*)                                   Function File
**playaudio** (*x*)                                           Function File
> Plays the audio file '*name.ext*' or the audio data stored in the vector
> *x*.

**record** (*sec, sampling_rate*)                             Function File
> Records *sec* seconds of audio input into the vector *x*. The default value
> for *sampling_rate* is 8000 samples per second, or 8kHz. The program
> waits until the user types (RET) and then immediately starts to record.

**setaudio** (*type*)                                         Function File
**setaudio** (*type, value*)                                  Function File
> Set or display various properties of your mixer hardware.
>
> For example, if `vol` corresponds to the volume property, you can set
> it to 50 (percent) by `setaudio ("vol", 50)`.
>
> This is an simple experimental program to control the audio hardware
> settings. It assumes that there is a `mixer` program which can be used as
> `mixer type value`, and simply executes `system ("mixer type value")`.
> Future releases might get rid of this assumption by using the `fcntl`
> interface.

# 29  System Utilities

This chapter describes the functions that are available to allow you to get information about what is happening outside of Octave, while it is still running, and use this information in your program. For example, you can get information about environment variables, the current time, and even start other programs from the Octave prompt.

## 29.1  Timing Utilities

Octave's core set of functions for manipulating time values are patterned after the corresponding functions from the standard C library. Several of these functions use a data structure for time that includes the following elements:

usec      Microseconds after the second (0-999999).

sec       Seconds after the minute (0-61). This number can be 61 to account for leap seconds.

min       Minutes after the hour (0-59).

hour      Hours since midnight (0-23).

mday      Day of the month (1-31).

mon       Months since January (0-11).

year      Years since 1900.

wday      Days since Sunday (0-6).

yday      Days since January 1 (0-365).

isdst     Daylight Savings Time flag.

zone      Time zone.

In the descriptions of the following functions, this structure is referred to as a *tm_struct*.

**time ()**                                        Loadable Function
    Return the current time as the number of seconds since the epoch. The epoch is referenced to 00:00:00 CUT (Coordinated Universal Time) 1 Jan 1970. For example, on Monday February 17, 1997 at 07:15:06 CUT, the value returned by time was 856163706.

**ctime** (*t*)                                                    Function File

  Convert a value returned from time (or any other nonnegative integer),
  to the local time and return a string of the same form as asctime. The
  function ctime (time) is equivalent to asctime (localtime (time)).
  For example,

```
ctime (time ())
    ⇒ "Mon Feb 17 01:15:06 1997"
```

**gmtime** (*t*)                                               Loadable Function

  Given a value returned from time (or any nonnegative integer), return
  a time structure corresponding to CUT. For example,

```
gmtime (time ())
    ⇒ {
            usec = 0
            year = 97
            mon = 1
            mday = 17
            sec = 6
            zone = CST
            min = 15
            wday = 1
            hour = 7
            isdst = 0
            yday = 47
       }
```

**localtime** (*t*)                                            Loadable Function

  Given a value returned from time (or any nonnegative integer), return
  a time structure corresponding to the local time zone.

```
localtime (time ())
    ⇒ {
            usec = 0
            year = 97
            mon = 1
            mday = 17
            sec = 6
            zone = CST
            min = 15
            wday = 1
            hour = 1
            isdst = 0
            yday = 47
```

                              }

**mktime** (*tm_struct*)                                    Loadable Function
   Convert a time structure corresponding to the local time to the number
   of seconds since the epoch. For example,

```
mktime (localtime (time ())
   ⇒ 856163706
```

**asctime** (*tm_struct*)                                       Function File
   Convert a time structure to a string using the following five-field format: Thu Mar 28 08:40:14 1996. For example,

```
asctime (localtime (time ())
   ⇒ "Mon Feb 17 01:15:06 1997\n"
```

   This is equivalent to ctime (time ()).

**strftime** (*tm_struct*)                                  Loadable Function
   Format a time structure in a flexible way using '%' substitutions similar
   to those in printf. Except where noted, substituted fields have a fixed
   size; numeric fields are padded if necessary. Padding is with zeros by
   default; for fields that display a single number, padding can be changed
   or inhibited by following the '%' with one of the modifiers described
   below. Unknown field specifiers are copied as normal characters. All
   other characters are copied to the output without change. For example,

```
strftime ("%r (%Z) %A %e %B %Y", localtime (time ())
   ⇒ "01:15:06 AM (CST) Monday 17 February 1997"
```

   Octave's strftime function supports a superset of the ANSI C field
   specifiers.
   Literal character fields:

%            % character.

n            Newline character.

t            Tab character.

   Numeric modifiers (a nonstandard extension):

- (dash)     Do not pad the field.

_ (underscore)
             Pad the field with spaces.

   Time fields:

%H           Hour (00-23).

%I           Hour (01-12).

%k          Hour (0-23).

%l          Hour (1-12).

%M          Minute (00-59).

%p          Locale's AM or PM.

%r          Time, 12-hour (hh:mm:ss [AP]M).

%R          Time, 24-hour (hh:mm).

%s          Time in seconds since 00:00:00, Jan 1, 1970 (a nonstan-
            dard extension).

%S          Second (00-61).

%T          Time, 24-hour (hh:mm:ss).

%X          Locale's time representation (%H:%M:%S).

%Z          Time zone (EDT), or nothing if no time zone is deter-
            minable.

Date fields:

%a          Locale's abbreviated weekday name (Sun-Sat).

%A          Locale's full weekday name, variable length (Sunday-
            Saturday).

%b          Locale's abbreviated month name (Jan-Dec).

%B          Locale's full month name, variable length (January-
            December).

%c          Locale's date and time (Sat Nov 04 12:02:33 EST 1989).

%C          Century (00-99).

%d          Day of month (01-31).

%e          Day of month ( 1-31).

%D          Date (mm/dd/yy).

%h          Same as %b.

%j          Day of year (001-366).

%m          Month (01-12).

%U          Week number of year with Sunday as first day of week
            (00-53).

%w          Day of week (0-6).

%W          Week number of year with Monday as first day of week
            (00-53).

%x          Locale's date representation (mm/dd/yy).

%y          Last two digits of year (00-99).

%Y          Year (1970-).

Most of the remaining functions described in this section are not patterned after the standard C library. Some are available for compatibility
with MATLAB and others are provided because they are useful.

**clock ()**                                            Function File
    Return a vector containing the current year, month (1-12), day (1-31),
    hour (0-23), minute (0-59) and second (0-61). For example,

        clock ()
            ⇒ [ 1993, 8, 20, 4, 56, 1 ]

    The function clock is more accurate on systems that have the
    gettimeofday function.

**date ()**                                             Function File
    Return the date as a character string in the form DD-MMM-YY. For
    example,

        date ()
            ⇒ "20-Aug-93"

**etime** (*t1, t2*)                                    Function File
    Return the difference (in seconds) between two time values returned
    from clock. For example:

        t0 = clock ();
        # many computations later...
        elapsed_time = etime (clock (), t0);

    will set the variable elapsed_time to the number of seconds since the
    variable t0 was set.

**[*total, user, system*] = cputime ();**               Built-in Function
    Return the CPU time used by your Octave session. The first output
    is the total time spent executing your process and is equal to the sum
    of second and third outputs, which are the number of CPU seconds
    spent executing in user mode and the number of CPU seconds spent
    executing in system mode, respectively. If your system does not have a
    way to report CPU time usage, cputime returns 0 for each of its output
    values. Note that because Octave used some CPU time to start, it is

reasonable to check to see if cputime works by checking to see if the total CPU time used is nonzero.

**is_leap_year** (*year*)                                          Function File
Return 1 if the given year is a leap year and 0 otherwise. If no arguments are provided, is_leap_year will use the current year. For example,

```
is_leap_year (2000)
    ⇒ 1
```

**tic** ()                                                        Function File
**toc** ()                                                        Function File
These functions set and check a wall-clock timer. For example,

```
tic ();
# many computations later...
elapsed_time = toc ();
```

will set the variable elapsed_time to the number of seconds since the most recent call to the function tic.

If you are more interested in the CPU time that your process used, you should use the cputime function instead. The tic and toc functions report the actual wall clock time that elapsed between the calls. This may include time spent processing other jobs or doing nothing at all. For example,

```
tic (); sleep (5); toc ()
    ⇒ 5
t = cputime (); sleep (5); cputime () - t
    ⇒ 0
```

(This example also illustrates that the CPU timer may have a fairly coarse resolution.)

**pause** (*seconds*)                                          Built-in Function
Suspend the execution of the program. If invoked without any arguments, Octave waits until you type a character. With a numeric argument, it pauses for the given number of seconds. For example, the following statement prints a message and then waits 5 seconds before clearing the screen.

```
fprintf (stderr, "wait please...\n");
pause (5);
clc;
```

**sleep** (*seconds*)                                          Built-in Function
Suspend the execution of the program for the given number of seconds.

**usleep** (*microseconds*)                                    Built-in Function
  Suspend the execution of the program for the given number of microseconds. On systems where it is not possible to sleep for periods of time less than one second, usleep will pause the execution for round (*microseconds* / 1e6) seconds.

## 29.2 Filesystem Utilities

  Octave includes the following functions for renaming and deleting files, creating, deleting, and reading directories, and for getting information about the status of files.

[*err*, *msg*] = **rename** (*old*, *new*)                                    Built-in Function
  Change the name of file *old* to *new*.

  If successful, *err* is 0 and *msg* is an empty string. Otherwise, *err* is nonzero and *msg* contains a system-dependent error message.

[*err*, *msg*] = **unlink** (*file*)                                    Built-in Function
  Delete *file*.

  If successful, *err* is 0 and *msg* is an empty string. Otherwise, *err* is nonzero and *msg* contains a system-dependent error message.

[*files*, *err*, *msg*] = **readdir** (*dir*)                                    Built-in Function
  Return names of the files in the directory *dir* as an array of strings. If an error occurs, return an empty matrix in *files*.

  If successful, *err* is 0 and *msg* is an empty string. Otherwise, *err* is nonzero and *msg* contains a system-dependent error message.

[*err*, *msg*] = **mkdir** (*dir*)                                    Built-in Function
  Create a directory named *dir*.

  If successful, *err* is 0 and *msg* is an empty string. Otherwise, *err* is nonzero and *msg* contains a system-dependent error message.

[*err*, *msg*] = **rmdir** (*dir*)                                    Built-in Function
  Remove the directory named *dir*.

  If successful, *err* is 0 and *msg* is an empty string. Otherwise, *err* is nonzero and *msg* contains a system-dependent error message.

[*err*, *msg*] = **mkfifo** (*name*)                                    Built-in Function
  Create a FIFO special file.

  If successful, *err* is 0 and *msg* is an empty string. Otherwise, *err* is nonzero and *msg* contains a system-dependent error message.

umask (*mask*)                                                     Built-in Function

Set the permission mask for file creation. The parameter *mask* is interpreted as an octal number.

[*info*, *err*, *msg*] = stat (*file*)                            Built-in Function
[*info*, *err*, *msg*] = lstat (*file*)                           Built-in Function

Return a structure *s* containing the following information about *file*.

dev          ID of device containing a directory entry for this file.

ino          File number of the file.

modestr      File mode, as a string of ten letters or dashes as would be returned by *ls -l*.

nlink        Number of links.

uid          User ID of file's owner.

gid          Group ID of file's group.

rdev         ID of device for block or character special files.

size         Size in bytes.

atime        Time of last access in the same form as time values returned from time. See Section 29.1 [Timing Utilities], page 225.

mtime        Time of last modification in the same form as time values returned from time. See Section 29.1 [Timing Utilities], page 225.

ctime        Time of last file status change in the same form as time values returned from time. See Section 29.1 [Timing Utilities], page 225.

blksize      Size of blocks in the file.

blocks       Number of blocks allocated for file.

If the call is successful *err* is 0 and *msg* is an empty string. If the file does not exist, or some other error occurs, *s* is an empty matrix, *err* is −1, and *msg* contains the corresponding system error message.

If *file* is a symbolic link, stat will return information about the actual file the is referenced by the link. Use lstat if you want information about the symbolic link itself.

For example,

```
[s, err, msg] = stat ("/vmlinuz")
    ⇒ s =
      {
          atime = 855399756
          rdev = 0
          ctime = 847219094
          uid = 0
          size = 389218
          blksize = 4096
          mtime = 847219094
          gid = 6
          nlink = 1
          blocks = 768
          modestr = -rw-r--r--
          ino = 9316
          dev = 2049
      }
    ⇒ err = 0
    ⇒ msg =
```

**glob** (*pattern*)                                              Built-in Function

Given an array of strings in *pattern*, return the list of file names that any of them, or an empty string if no patterns match. Tilde expansion is performed on each of the patterns before looking for matching file names. For example,

```
glob ("/vm*")
    ⇒ "/vmlinuz"
```

Note that multiple values are returned in a string matrix with the fill character set to ASCII NUL.

**fnmatch** (*pattern*, *string*)                                 Built-in Function

Return 1 or zero for each element of *string* that matches any of the elements of the string array *pattern*, using the rules of filename pattern matching. For example,

```
fnmatch ("a*b", ["ab"; "axyzb"; "xyzab"])
    ⇒ [ 1; 1; 0 ]
```

**file_in_path** (*path*, *file*)                                 Built-in Function

Return the absolute name name of *file* if it can be found in *path*. The value of *path* should be a colon-separated list of directories in the format described for the built-in variable LOADPATH.

If the file cannot be found in the path, an empty matrix is returned. For example,

```
file_in_path (LOADPATH, "nargchk.m")
    ⇒ "/usr/local/share/octave/2.0/m/general/nargchk.m"
```

**tilde_expand** (*string*)                                    Built-in Function
Performs tilde expansion on *string*. If *string* begins with a tilde character, ('˜'), all of the characters preceding the first slash (or all characters, if there is no slash) are treated as a possible user name, and the tilde and the following characters up to the slash are replaced by the home directory of the named user. If the tilde is followed immediately by a slash, the tilde is replaced by the home directory of the user running Octave. For example,

```
tilde_expand ("˜joeuser/bin")
    ⇒ "/home/joeuser/bin"
tilde_expand ("˜/bin")
    ⇒ "/home/jwe/bin"
```

## 29.3 Controlling Subprocesses

Octave includes some high-level commands like system and popen for starting subprocesses. If you want to run another program to perform some task and then look at its output, you will probably want to use these functions.

Octave also provides several very low-level Unix-like functions which can also be used for starting subprocesses, but you should probably only use them if you can't find any way to do what you need with the higher-level functions.

**system** (*string*, *return_output*, *type*)                Built-in Function
Execute a shell command specified by *string*. The second argument is optional. If *type* is "async", the process is started in the background and the process id of the child process is returned immediately. Otherwise, the process is started, and Octave waits until it exits. If *type* argument is omitted, a value of "sync" is assumed.

If two input arguments are given (the actual value of *return_output* is irrelevant) and the subprocess is started synchronously, or if *system* is called with one input argument and one or more output arguments, the output from the command is returned. Otherwise, if the subprocess is executed synchronously, it's output is sent to the standard output. To send the output of a command executed with *system* through the pager, use a command like

```
     disp (system (cmd, 1));
```
or
```
     printf ("%s\n", system (cmd, 1));
```
The system function can return two values. The first is any output
from the command that was written to the standard output stream,
and the second is the output status of the command. For example,
```
     [output, status] = system ("echo foo; exit 2");
```
will set the variable output to the string 'foo', and the variable status
to the integer '2'.

**fid = popen** (*command, mode*)                          Built-in Function
Start a process and create a pipe. The name of the command to run
is given by *command*. The file identifier corresponding to the input or
output stream of the process is returned in *fid*. The argument *mode*
may be

"r"         The pipe will be connected to the standard output of the
            process, and open for reading.

"w"         The pipe will be connected to the standard input of the
            process, and open for writing.

For example,
```
     fid = popen ("ls -ltr / | tail -3", "r");
     while (isstr (s = fgets (fid)))
       fputs (stdout, s);
     endwhile
          ⊣ drwxr-xr-x 33 root root 3072 Feb 15 13:28 etc
          ⊣ drwxr-xr-x  3 root root 1024 Feb 15 13:28 lib
          ⊣ drwxrwxrwt 15 root root 2048 Feb 17 14:53 tmp
```

**pclose** (*fid*)                                        Built-in Function
Close a file identifier that was opened by popen. You may also use
fclose for the same purpose.

[*in, out, pid*] = **popen2** (*command, args*)           Built-in Function
Start a subprocess with two-way communication. The name of the
process is given by *command*, and *args* is an array of strings containing
options for the command. The file identifiers for the input and output
streams of the subprocess are returned in *in* and *out*. If execution of the
command is successful, *pid* contains the process ID of the subprocess.
Otherwise, *pid* is −1.
For example,

```
[in, out, pid] = popen2 ("sort", "-nr");
fputs (in, "these\nare\nsome\nstrings\n");
fclose (in);
while (isstr (s = fgets (out)))
  fputs (stdout, s);
endwhile
fclose (out);
        ⊣ are
        ⊣ some
        ⊣ strings
        ⊣ these
```

## EXEC_PATH                                            Built-in Variable

The variable EXEC_PATH is a colon separated list of directories to search
when executing subprograms. Its initial value is taken from the environment variable OCTAVE_EXEC_PATH (if it exists) or PATH, but that
value can be overridden by the command line argument --exec-path
PATH, or by setting the value of EXEC_PATH in a startup script. If the
value of EXEC_PATH begins (ends) with a colon, the directories

*octave-home*/libexec/octave/site/exec/*arch*

*octave-home*/libexec/octave/*version*/exec/*arch*

are prepended (appended) to EXEC_PATH, where *octave-home* is the
top-level directory where all of Octave is installed (the default value is
'/usr/local'). If you don't specify a value for EXEC_PATH explicitly,
these special directories are prepended to your shell path.

In most cases, the following functions simply decode their arguments
and make the corresponding Unix system calls. For a complete example
of how they can be used, look at the definition of the function popen2.

## [*pid*, *msg*] = fork ()                                Built-in Function

Create a copy of the current process.

Fork can return one of the following values:

> 0          You are in the parent process. The value returned from
            fork is the process id of the child process. You should
            probably arrange to wait for any child processes to exit.

0           You are in the child process. You can call exec to start
            another process. If that fails, you should probably call
            exit.

< 0         The call to fork failed for some reason. You must take
            evasive action. A system dependent error message will
            be waiting in *msg*.

[err, *msg*] = **exec** (*file*, *args*)                              Built-in Function
Replace current process with a new process. Calling exec without first calling fork will terminate your current Octave process and replace it with the program named by *file*. For example,

    exec ("ls" "-1")

will run ls and return you to your shell prompt.

If successful, exec does not return. If exec does return, *err* will be nonzero, and *msg* will contain a system-dependent error message.

[*file_ids*, *err*, *msg*] = **pipe** ()                              Built-in Function
Create a pipe and return the vector *file_ids*, which corresponding to the reading and writing ends of the pipe.

If successful, *err* is 0 and *msg* is an empty string. Otherwise, *err* is nonzero and *msg* contains a system-dependent error message.

[*fid*, *msg*] = **dup2** (*old*, *new*)                              Built-in Function
Duplicate a file descriptor.

If successful, *fid* is greater than zero and contains the new file ID. Otherwise, *fid* is negative and *msg* contains a system-dependent error message.

[*pid*, *msg*] = **waitpid** (*pid*, *options*)                       Built-in Function
Wait for process *pid* to terminate. The *pid* argument can be:

−1          Wait for any child process.

0           Wait for any child process whose process group ID is equal to that of the Octave interpreter process.

> 0         Wait for termination of the child process with ID *pid*.

The *options* argument can be:

0           Wait until signal is received or a child process exits (this is the default if the *options* argument is missing).

1           Do not hang if status is not immediately available.

2           Report the status of any child processes that are stopped, and whose status has not yet been reported since they stopped.

3           Implies both 1 and 2.

If the returned value of *pid* is greater than 0, it is the process ID of the child process that exited. If an error occurs, *pid* will be less than zero and *msg* will contain a system-dependent error message.

[err, msg] = fcntl (fid, request, arg)                    Built-in Function
    Change the properties of the open file fid. The following values may
    be passed as request:

F_DUPFD      Return a duplicate file descriptor.

F_GETFD      Return the file descriptor flags for fid.

F_SETFD      Set the file descriptor flags for fid.

F_GETFL      Return the file status flags for fid. The following codes
             may be returned (some of the flags may be undefined on
             some systems).

             O_RDONLY      Open for reading only.

             O_WRONLY      Open for writing only.

             O_RDWR        Open for reading and writing.

             O_APPEND      Append on each write.

             O_NONBLOCK
                           Nonblocking mode.

             O_SYNC        Wait for writes to complete.

             O_ASYNC       Asynchronous I/O.

F_SETFL      Set the file status flags for fid to the value specified by
             arg. The only flags that can be changed are O_APPEND
             and O_NONBLOCK.

    If successful, err is 0 and msg is an empty string. Otherwise, err is
    nonzero and msg contains a system-dependent error message.

# 29.4 Process, Group, and User IDs

getpgrp ()                                                Built-in Function
    Return the process group id of the current process.

getpid ()                                                 Built-in Function
    Return the process id of the current process.

getppid ()                                                Built-in Function
    Return the process id of the parent process.

**geteuid ()**                                          Built-in Function
    Return the effective user id of the current process.

**getuid ()**                                           Built-in Function
    Return the real user id of the current process.

**getegid ()**                                          Built-in Function
    Return the effective group id of the current process.

**getgid ()**                                           Built-in Function
    Return the real group id of the current process.

# 29.5  Environment Variables

**getenv** (*var*)                                      Built-in Function
    Return the value of the environment variable *var*. For example,

```
getenv ("PATH")
```

returns a string containing the value of your path.

**putenv** (*var, value*)                              Built-in Function
    Set the value of the environment variable *var* to *value*.

# 29.6  Current Working Directory

**cd** *dir*                                                  Command
**chdir** *dir*                                               Command
    Change the current working directory to *dir*. For example,

```
cd ~/octave
```

Changes the current working directory to '~/octave'. If the directory
does not exist, an error message is printed and the working directory
is not changed.

**pwd ()**                                             Built-in Function
    Return the current working directory.

**ls** *options*                                             Command
**dir** *options*                                            Command
    List directory contents. For example,

```
ls -1
     ⊣ total 12
     ⊣ -rw-r--r-- 1 jwe users 4488 Aug 19 04:02 foo.m
     ⊣ -rw-r--r-- 1 jwe users 1315 Aug 17 23:14 bar.m
```

The dir and ls commands are implemented by calling your system's
directory listing command, so the available options may vary from
system to system.

# 29.7 Password Database Functions

Octave's password database functions return information in a structure with the following fields.

name        The user name.

passwd      The encrypted password, if available.

uid         The numeric user id.

gid         The numeric group id.

gecos       The GECOS field.

dir         The home directory.

shell       The initial shell.

In the descriptions of the following functions, this data structure is
referred to as a *pw_struct*.

*pw_struct* = **getpwent** ()                              Loadable Function
  Return a structure containing an entry from the password database,
  opening it if necessary. Once the end of the data has been reached,
  getpwent returns 0.

*pw_struct* = **getpwuid** (*uid*).                        Loadable Function
  Return a structure containing the first entry from the password
  database with the user ID *uid*. If the user ID does not exist in the
  database, getpwuid returns 0.

*pw_struct* = **getpwnam** (*name*)                        Loadable Function
  Return a structure containing the first entry from the password
  database with the user name *name*. If the user name does not exist in the database, getpwname returns 0.

**setpwent** ()                                            Loadable Function
  Return the internal pointer to the beginning of the password database.

**endpwent** ()                                                    Loadable Function
    Close the password database.

## 29.8  Group Database Functions

Octave's group database functions return information in a structure with the following fields.

name         The user name.

passwd       The encrypted password, if available.

gid           The numeric group id.

mem         The members of the group.

In the descriptions of the following functions, this data structure is referred to as a *grp_struct*.

*grp_struct* = **getgrent** ()                                    Loadable Function
    Return an entry from the group database, opening it if necessary. Once the end of the data has been reached, getgrent returns 0.

*grp_struct* = **getgrgid** (*gid*).                              Loadable Function
    Return the first entry from the group database with the group ID *gid*. If the group ID does not exist in the database, getgrgid returns 0.

*grp_struct* = **getgrnam** (*name*)                              Loadable Function
    Return the first entry from the group database with the group name *name*. If the group name does not exist in the database, getgrname returns 0.

**setgrent** ()                                                   Loadable Function
    Return the internal pointer to the beginning of the group database.

**endgrent** ()                                                   Loadable Function
    Close the group database.

## 29.9  System Information

**computer** ()                                                   Built-in Function
    Print or return a string of the form *cpu-vendor-os* that identifies the kind of computer Octave is running on. If invoked with an output argument, the value is returned instead of printed. For example,

```
computer ()
     ⊣ i586-pc-linux-gnu

x = computer ()
     ⇒ x = "i586-pc-linux-gnu"
```

**isieee ()**                                                  Built-in Function

Return 1 if your computer claims to conform to the IEEE standard for floating point calculations.

**version ()**                                                 Built-in Function

Return Octave's version number as a string. This is also the value of the built-in variable OCTAVE_VERSION.

**OCTAVE_VERSION**                                             Built-in Variable

The version number of Octave, as a string.

**octave_config_info ()**                                      Built-in Function

Return a structure containing configuration and installation information.

**getrusage ()**                                               Loadable Function

Return a structure containing a number of statistics about the current Octave process. Not all fields are available on all systems. If it is not possible to get CPU time statistics, the CPU time slots are set to zero. Other missing data are replaced by NaN. Here is a list of all the possible fields that can be present in the structure returned by getrusage:

| | |
|---|---|
| idrss | Unshared data size. |
| inblock | Number of block input operations. |
| isrss | Unshared stack size. |
| ixrss | Shared memory size. |
| majflt | Number of major page faults. |
| maxrss | Maximum data size. |
| minflt | Number of minor page faults. |
| msgrcv | Number of messages received. |
| msgsnd | Number of messages sent. |

nivcsw      Number of involuntary context switches.

nsignals    Number of signals received.

nswap       Number of swaps.

nvcsw       Number of voluntary context switches.

oublock     Number of block output operations.

stime       A structure containing the system CPU time used. The
            structure has the elements sec (seconds) usec (microsec-
            onds).

utime       A structure containing the user CPU time used. The
            structure has the elements sec (seconds) usec (microsec-
            onds).

# Appendix A  Tips and Standards

This chapter describes no additional features of Octave. Instead it gives advice on making effective use of the features described in the previous chapters.

## A.1  Writing Clean Octave Programs

Here are some tips for avoiding common errors in writing Octave code intended for widespread use:

- Since all global variables share the same name space, and all functions share another name space, you should choose a short word to distinguish your program from other Octave programs. Then take care to begin the names of all global variables, constants, and functions with the chosen prefix. This helps avoid name conflicts.

  If you write a function that you think ought to be added to Octave under a certain name, such as `fiddle_matrix`, don't call it by that name in your program. Call it `mylib_fiddle_matrix` in your program, and send mail to bug@octave.org suggesting that it be added to Octave. If and when it is, the name can be changed easily enough.

  If one prefix is insufficient, your package may use two or three alternative common prefixes, so long as they make sense.

  Separate the prefix from the rest of the symbol name with an underscore '_'. This will be consistent with Octave itself and with most Octave programs.

- When you encounter an error condition, call the function `error` (or `usage`). The `error` and `usage` functions do not return. See Section 2.5 [Errors], page 31.

- Please put a copyright notice on the file if you give copies to anyone. Use the same lines that appear at the top of the function files distributed with Octave. If you have not signed papers to assign the copyright to anyone else, then place your name in the copyright notice.

## A.2  Tips for Making Code Run Faster.

Here are some ways of improving the execution speed of Octave programs.

- Avoid looping wherever possible.
- Use iteration rather than recursion whenever possible. Function calls are slow in Octave.

- Avoid resizing matrices unnecessarily. When building a single result matrix from a series of calculations, set the size of the result matrix first, then insert values into it. Write

```
result = zeros (big_n, big_m)
for i = over:and_over
  r1 = ...
  r2 = ...
  result (r1, r2) = new_value ();
endfor
```

instead of

```
result = [];
for i = ever:and_ever
  result = [ result, new_value() ];
endfor
```

- Avoid calling `eval` or `feval` whenever possible, because they require Octave to parse input or look up the name of a function in the symbol table.

  If you are using `eval` as an exception handling mechanism and not because you need to execute some arbitrary text, use the `try` statement instead. See Section 10.8 [The try Statement], page 99.

- If you are calling lots of functions but none of them will need to change during your run, set the variable `ignore_function_time_stamp` to `"all"` so that Octave doesn't waste a lot of time checking to see if you have updated your function files.

## A.3 Tips for Documentation Strings

Here are some tips for the writing of documentation strings.

- Every command, function, or variable intended for users to know about should have a documentation string.

- An internal variable or subroutine of an Octave program might as well have a documentation string.

- The first line of the documentation string should consist of one or two complete sentences that stand on their own as a summary.

  The documentation string can have additional lines that expand on the details of how to use the function or variable. The additional lines should also be made up of complete sentences.

- For consistency, phrase the verb in the first sentence of a documentation string as an infinitive with "to" omitted. For instance, use "Return the frob of A and B." in preference to "Returns the frob of

A and B." Usually it looks good to do likewise for the rest of the first paragraph. Subsequent paragraphs usually look better if they have proper subjects.

- Write documentation strings in the active voice, not the passive, and in the present tense, not the future. For instance, use "Return a list containing A and B." instead of "A list containing A and B will be returned."

- Avoid using the word "cause" (or its equivalents) unnecessarily. Instead of, "Cause Octave to display text in boldface," write just "Display text in boldface."

- Do not start or end a documentation string with whitespace.

- Format the documentation string so that it fits in an Emacs window on an 80-column screen. It is a good idea for most lines to be no wider than 60 characters.

  However, rather than simply filling the entire documentation string, you can make it much more readable by choosing line breaks with care. Use blank lines between topics if the documentation string is long.

- **Do not** indent subsequent lines of a documentation string so that the text is lined up in the source code with the text of the first line. This looks nice in the source code, but looks bizarre when users view the documentation. Remember that the indentation before the starting double-quote is not part of the string!

- The documentation string for a variable that is a yes-or-no flag should start with words such as "Nonzero means...", to make it clear that all nonzero values are equivalent and indicate explicitly what zero and nonzero mean.

- When a function's documentation string mentions the value of an argument of the function, use the argument name in capital letters as if it were a name for that value. Thus, the documentation string of the operator / refers to its second argument as 'DIVISOR', because the actual argument name is divisor.

  Also use all caps for meta-syntactic variables, such as when you show the decomposition of a list or vector into subunits, some of which may vary.

## A.4  Tips on Writing Comments

Here are the conventions to follow when writing comments.

'#'               Comments that start with a single sharp-sign, '#', should all be aligned to the same column on the right of the source code. Such comments usually explain how the code on the same line does its job. In the Emacs mode for Octave, the *M-;* (indent-for-comment) command automatically inserts such a '#' in the right place, or aligns such a comment if it is already present.

'##'                Comments that start with two semicolons, '##', should be aligned to the same level of indentation as the code. Such comments usually describe the purpose of the following lines or the state of the program at that point.

The indentation commands of the Octave mode in Emacs, such as *M-; (indent-for-comment)* and *TAB* (octave-indent-line) automatically indent comments according to these conventions, depending on the number of semicolons. See section "Manipulating Comments" in *The GNU Emacs Manual*.

# A.5 Conventional Headers for Octave Functions

Octave has conventions for using special comments in function files to give information such as who wrote them. This section explains these conventions.

The top of the file should contain a copyright notice, followed by a block of comments that can be used as the help text for the function. Here is an example:

```
## Copyright (C) 1996, 1997 John W. Eaton
##
## This file is part of Octave.
##
## Octave is free software; you can redistribute it and/or
## modify it under the terms of the GNU General Public
## License as published by the Free Software Foundation;
## either version 2, or (at your option) any later version.
##
## Octave is distributed in the hope that it will be useful,
## but WITHOUT ANY WARRANTY; without even the implied
## warranty of MERCHANTABILITY or FITNESS FOR A PARTICULAR
## PURPOSE.  See the GNU General Public License for more
## details.
##
## You should have received a copy of the GNU General Public
## License along with Octave; see the file COPYING.  If not,
```

```
## write to the Free Software Foundation, 59 Temple Place -
## Suite 330, Boston, MA 02111-1307, USA.

## usage: [IN, OUT, PID] = popen2 (COMMAND, ARGS)
##
## Start a subprocess with two-way communication.  COMMAND
## specifies the name of the command to start.  ARGS is an
## array of strings containing options for COMMAND.  IN and
## OUT are the file ids of the input and streams for the
## subprocess, and PID is the process id of the subprocess,
## or -1 if COMMAND could not be executed.
##
## Example:
##
##   [in, out, pid] = popen2 ("sort", "-nr");
##   fputs (in, "these\nare\nsome\nstrings\n");
##   fclose (in);
##   while (isstr (s = fgets (out)))
##     fputs (stdout, s);
##   endwhile
##   fclose (out);
```

Octave uses the first block of comments in a function file that do not
appear to be a copyright notice as the help text for the file. For Octave
to recognize the first comment block as a copyright notice, it must match
the regular expression

   ^ Copyright (C).*\n\n This file is part of Octave.

or

   ^ Copyright (C).*\n\n This program is free softwar

(after stripping the leading comment characters). This is a fairly strict
requirement, and may be relaxed somewhat in the future.

After the copyright notice and help text come several *header comment*
lines, each beginning with '## *header-name*:'. For example,

```
## Author: jwe
## Keywords: subprocesses input-output
## Maintainer: jwe
```

Here is a table of the conventional possibilities for *header-name*:

'Author'     This line states the name and net address of at least the
             principal author of the library.

```
## Author: John W. Eaton <jwe@bevo.che.wisc.edu>
```

'Maintainer'

>   This line should contain a single name/address as in the Author line, or an address only, or the string 'jwe'. If there is no maintainer line, the person(s) in the Author field are presumed to be the maintainers. The example above is mildly bogus because the maintainer line is redundant.
>
>   The idea behind the 'Author' and 'Maintainer' lines is to make possible a function to "send mail to the maintainer" without having to mine the name out by hand.
>
>   Be sure to surround the network address with '<...>' if you include the person's full name as well as the network address.

'Created'   This optional line gives the original creation date of the file. For historical interest only.

'Version'   If you wish to record version numbers for the individual Octave program, put them in this line.

'Adapted-By'

>   In this header line, place the name of the person who adapted the library for installation (to make it fit the style conventions, for example).

'Keywords'   This line lists keywords. Eventually, it will be used by an apropos command to allow people will find your package when they're looking for things by topic area. To separate the keywords, you can use spaces, commas, or both.

Just about every Octave function ought to have the 'Author' and 'Keywords' header comment lines. Use the others if they are appropriate. You can also put in header lines with other header names—they have no standard meanings, so they can't do any harm.

# Appendix B Known Causes of Trouble

This section describes known problems that affect users of Octave. Most of these are not Octave bugs per se—if they were, we would fix them. But the result for a user may be like the result of a bug.

Some of these problems are due to bugs in other software, some are missing features that are too much work to add, and some are places where people's opinions differ as to what is best.

## B.1 Actual Bugs We Haven't Fixed Yet

- Output that comes directly from Fortran functions is not sent through the pager and may appear out of sequence with other output that is sent through the pager. One way to avoid this is to force pending output to be flushed before calling a function that will produce output from within Fortran functions. To do this, use the command

      fflush (stdout)

  Another possible workaround is to use the command

      page_screen_output = "false"

  to turn the pager off.

- If you get messages like

      Input line too long

  when trying to plot many lines on one graph, you have probably generated a plot command that is too larger for gnuplot's fixed-length buffer for commands. Splitting up the plot command doesn't help because replot is implemented in gnuplot by simply appending the new plotting commands to the old command line and then evaluating it again.

  You can demonstrate this 'feature' by running gnuplot and doing something like

      plot sin (x), sin (x), ... lots more ..., sin (x)

  and then

      replot sin (x), sin (x), ... lots more ..., sin (x)

  after repeating the replot command a few times, gnuplot will give you an error.

  Also, it doesn't help to use backslashes to enter a plot command over several lines, because the limit is on the overall command line length, once the backslashed lines are all pasted together.

Because of this, Octave tries to use as little of the command-line length as possible by using the shortest possible abbreviations for all the plot commands and options. Unfortunately, the length of the temporary file names is probably what is taking up the most space on the command line.

You can buy a little bit of command line space by setting the environment variable TMPDIR to be "." before starting Octave, or you can increase the maximum command line length in gnuplot by changing the following limits in the file plot.h in the gnuplot distribution and recompiling gnuplot.

```
#define MAX_LINE_LEN 32768   /* originally 1024 */
#define MAX_TOKENS 8192      /* originally 400 */
```

Of course, this doesn't really fix the problem, but it does make it much less likely that you will run into trouble unless you are putting a very large number of lines on a given plot.

A list of ideas for future enhancements is distributed with Octave. See the file 'PROJECTS' in the top level directory in the source distribution.

## B.2 Reporting Bugs

Your bug reports play an essential role in making Octave reliable.

When you encounter a problem, the first thing to do is to see if it is already known. See Appendix B [Trouble], page 251. If it isn't known, then you should report the problem.

Reporting a bug may help you by bringing a solution to your problem, or it may not. In any case, the principal function of a bug report is to help the entire community by making the next version of Octave work better. Bug reports are your contribution to the maintenance of Octave.

In order for a bug report to serve its purpose, you must include the information that makes it possible to fix the bug.

If you have Octave working at all, the easiest way to prepare a complete bug report is to use the Octave function bug_report. When you execute this function, Octave will prompt you for a subject and then invoke the editor on a file that already contains all the configuration information. When you exit the editor, Octave will mail the bug report for you.

## B.3 Have You Found a Bug?

If you are not sure whether you have found a bug, here are some guidelines:

- If Octave gets a fatal signal, for any input whatever, that is a bug. Reliable interpreters never crash.

- If Octave produces incorrect results, for any input whatever, that is a bug.

- Some output may appear to be incorrect when it is in fact due to a program whose behavior is undefined, which happened by chance to give the desired results on another system. For example, the range operator may produce different results because of differences in the way floating point arithmetic is handled on various systems.

- If Octave produces an error message for valid input, that is a bug.

- If Octave does not produce an error message for invalid input, that is a bug. However, you should note that your idea of "invalid input" might be my idea of "an extension" or "support for traditional practice".

- If you are an experienced user of programs like Octave, your suggestions for improvement are welcome in any case.

## B.4  Where to Report Bugs

If you have Octave working at all, the easiest way to prepare a complete bug report is to use the Octave function `bug_report`. When you execute this function, Octave will prompt you for a subject and then invoke the editor on a file that already contains all the configuration information. When you exit the editor, Octave will mail the bug report for you.

If for some reason you cannot use Octave's `bug_report` function, send bug reports for Octave to bug@octave.org.

**Do not send bug reports to** 'help@octave.org'. Most users of Octave do not want to receive bug reports. Those that do have asked to be on the mailing list.

As a last resort, send bug reports on paper to:

```
Octave Bugs c/o John W. Eaton
University of Wisconsin-Madison
Department of Chemical Engineering
1415 Engineering Drive
Madison, Wisconsin 53706   USA
```

## B.5  How to Report Bugs

Send bug reports for Octave to one of the addresses listed in Section B.4 [Bug Lists], page 253.

The fundamental principle of reporting bugs usefully is this: **report all the facts**. If you are not sure whether to state a fact or leave it out, state it!

Often people omit facts because they think they know what causes the problem and they conclude that some details don't matter. Thus, you might assume that the name of the variable you use in an example does not matter. Well, probably it doesn't, but one cannot be sure. Perhaps the bug is a stray memory reference which happens to fetch from the location where that name is stored in memory; perhaps, if the name were different, the contents of that location would fool the interpreter into doing the right thing despite the bug. Play it safe and give a specific, complete example.

Keep in mind that the purpose of a bug report is to enable someone to fix the bug if it is not known. Always write your bug reports on the assumption that the bug is not known.

Sometimes people give a few sketchy facts and ask, "Does this ring a bell?" This cannot help us fix a bug. It is better to send a complete bug report to begin with.

Try to make your bug report self-contained. If we have to ask you for more information, it is best if you include all the previous information in your response, as well as the information that was missing.

To enable someone to investigate the bug, you should include all these things:

- The version of Octave. You can get this by noting the version number that is printed when Octave starts, or running it with the '-v' option.

- A complete input file that will reproduce the bug.

  A single statement may not be enough of an example—the bug might depend on other details that are missing from the single statement where the error finally occurs.

- The command arguments you gave Octave to execute that example and observe the bug. To guarantee you won't omit something important, list all the options.

  If we were to try to guess the arguments, we would probably guess wrong and then we would not encounter the bug.

- The type of machine you are using, and the operating system name and version number.

- The command-line arguments you gave to the `configure` command when you installed the interpreter.

- A complete list of any modifications you have made to the interpreter source.

  Be precise about these changes—show a context diff for them.

- Details of any other deviations from the standard procedure for installing Octave.

- A description of what behavior you observe that you believe is incorrect. For example, "The interpreter gets a fatal signal," or, "The output produced at line 208 is incorrect."

  Of course, if the bug is that the interpreter gets a fatal signal, then one can't miss it. But if the bug is incorrect output, we might not notice unless it is glaringly wrong.

  Even if the problem you experience is a fatal signal, you should still say so explicitly. Suppose something strange is going on, such as, your copy of the interpreter is out of synch, or you have encountered a bug in the C library on your system. Your copy might crash and the copy here would not. If you said to expect a crash, then when the interpreter here fails to crash, we would know that the bug was not happening. If you don't say to expect a crash, then we would not know whether the bug was happening. We would not be able to draw any conclusion from our observations.

  Often the observed symptom is incorrect output when your program is run. Unfortunately, this is not enough information unless the program is short and simple. It is very helpful if you can include an explanation of the expected output, and why the actual output is incorrect.

- If you wish to suggest changes to the Octave source, send them as context diffs. If you even discuss something in the Octave source, refer to it by context, not by line number, because the line numbers in the development sources probably won't match those in your sources.

Here are some things that are not necessary:

- A description of the envelope of the bug.

  Often people who encounter a bug spend a lot of time investigating which changes to the input file will make the bug go away and which changes will not affect it. Such information is usually not necessary to enable us to fix bugs in Octave, but if you can find a simpler example to report *instead* of the original one, that is a convenience. Errors in the output will be easier to spot, running under the debugger will take less time, etc. Most Octave bugs involve just one function, so the most straightforward way to simplify an example is to delete all the function definitions except the one in which the bug occurs.

  However, simplification is not vital; if you don't want to do this, report the bug anyway and send the entire test case you used.

- A patch for the bug. Patches can be helpful, but if you find a bug, you should report it, even if you cannot send a fix for the problem.

# B.6  Sending Patches for Octave

If you would like to write bug fixes or improvements for Octave, that is very helpful. When you send your changes, please follow these guidelines to avoid causing extra work for us in studying the patches.

If you don't follow these guidelines, your information might still be useful, but using it will take extra work. Maintaining Octave is a lot of work in the best of circumstances, and we can't keep up unless you do your best to help.

- Send an explanation with your changes of what problem they fix or what improvement they bring about. For a bug fix, just include a copy of the bug report, and explain why the change fixes the bug.

- Always include a proper bug report for the problem you think you have fixed. We need to convince ourselves that the change is right before installing it. Even if it is right, we might have trouble judging it if we don't have a way to reproduce the problem.

- Include all the comments that are appropriate to help people reading the source in the future understand why this change was needed.

- Don't mix together changes made for different reasons. Send them *individually*.

  If you make two changes for separate reasons, then we might not want to install them both. We might want to install just one.

- Use 'diff -c' to make your diffs. Diffs without context are hard for us to install reliably. More than that, they make it hard for us to study the diffs to decide whether we want to install them. Unidiff format is better than contextless diffs, but not as easy to read as '-c' format.

  If you have GNU diff, use 'diff -cp', which shows the name of the function that each change occurs in.

- Write the change log entries for your changes.

  Read the 'ChangeLog' file to see what sorts of information to put in, and to learn the style that we use. The purpose of the change log is to show people where to find what was changed. So you need to be specific about what functions you changed; in large functions, it's often helpful to indicate where within the function the change was made.

  On the other hand, once you have shown people where to find the change, you need not explain its purpose. Thus, if you add a new function, all you need to say about it is that it is new. If you feel that the purpose needs explaining, it probably does—but the explanation will be much more useful if you put it in comments in the code.

If you would like your name to appear in the header line for who made the change, send us the header line.

# B.7 How To Get Help with Octave

The mailing list `help@octave.org` exists for the discussion of matters related to using and installing Octave. If would like to join the discussion, please send an email to `help-subscribe@octave.org`.

**Please do not** send requests to be added or removed from the mailing list, or other administrative trivia to the list itself.

If you think you have found a bug in the installation procedure, however, you should send a complete bug report for the problem to `bug@octave.org`. See Section B.5 [Bug Reporting], page 253 for information that will help you to submit a useful report.

# Appendix C  Installing Octave

Here is the procedure for installing Octave from scratch on a Unix system. For instructions on how to install the binary distributions of Octave, see Section C.3 [Binary Distributions], page 266.

- Run the shell script 'configure'. This will determine the features your system has (or doesn't have) and create a file named 'Makefile' from each of the files named 'Makefile.in'.

Here is a summary of the configure options that are most frequently used when building Octave:

--prefix=*prefix*
> Install Octave in subdirectories below *prefix*. The default value of *prefix* is '/usr/local'.

--srcdir=*dir*
> Look for Octave sources in the directory *dir*.

--with-f2c
> Use f2c even if a Fortran compiler is available.

--with-g77
> Use g77 to compile Fortran code.

--enable-shared
> Create shared libraries. If you are planning to use --enable-lite-kernel or the dynamic loading features, you will probably want to use this option. It will make your '.oct' files much smaller and on some systems it may be necessary to build shared libraries in order to use dynamically linked functions.
>
> You may also want to build a shared version of libstdc++, if your system doesn't already have one. Note that a patch is needed to build shared versions of version 2.7.2 of libstdc++ on the HP-PA architecture. You can find the patch at ftp://ftp.cygnus.com/pub/g++/libg++-2.7.2-hppa-gcc-fix.

--enable-dl
> Use dlopen and friends to make Octave capable of dynamically linking externally compiled functions. This only works on systems that actually have these functions. If you plan on using this feature, you should probably also use --enable-shared to reduce the size of your '.oct' files.

`--enable-shl`

> Use `shl_load` and friends to make Octave capable
> of dynamically linking externally compiled functions.
> This only works on systems that actually have these
> functions (only HP-UX systems). If you plan on using
> this feature, you should probably also use `--enable-shared` to reduce the size of your '.oct' files.

`--enable-lite-kernel`

> Compile smaller kernel. This currently requires the dy-
> namic linking functions `dlopen` or `shl_load` and friends
> so that Octave can load functions at run time that are
> not loaded at compile time.

`--help`     Print a summary of the options recognized by the configure script.

See the file 'INSTALL' for more information about the command line
options used by configure. That file also contains instructions for
compiling in a directory other than where the source is located.

- Run make.

You will need a recent version of GNU Make. Modifying Octave's
makefiles to work with other make programs is probably not worth
your time. We recommend you get and compile GNU Make instead.

For plotting, you will need to have gnuplot installed on your system.
Gnuplot is a command-driven interactive function plotting program.
Gnuplot is copyrighted, but freely distributable. The 'gnu' in gnuplot
is a coincidence—it is not related to the GNU project or the FSF in
any but the most peripheral sense.

To compile Octave, you will need a recent version of GNU Make.
You will also need g++ 2.7.2 or later. Version 2.8.0 or egcs 1.0.x
should work. Later versions may work, but C++ is still evolving, so
don't be too surprised if you run into some trouble.

It is no longer necessary to have libg++, but you do need to have
the GNU implementation of libstdc++. If you are using g++ 2.7.2,
libstdc++ is distributed along with libg++, but for later versions,
libstdc++ is distributed separately. For egcs, libstdc++ is included
with the compiler distribution.

If you plan to modify the parser you will also need GNU bison and
flex. If you modify the documentation, you will need GNU Texinfo,
along with the patch for the makeinfo program that is distributed
with Octave.

GNU Make, gcc, and libstdc++, gnuplot, bison, flex, and Texinfo
are all available from many anonymous ftp archives. The primary

site is ftp.gnu.org, but it is often very busy. A list of sites that
mirror the software on ftp.gnu.org is available by anonymous ftp
from ftp://ftp.gnu.org/pub/gnu/GNUinfo/FTP.

If you don't have a Fortran compiler, or if your Fortran compiler
doesn't work like the traditional Unix f77, you will need to have the
Fortran to C translator f2c. You can get f2c from any number of
anonymous ftp archives. The most recent version of f2c is always
available from netlib.att.com.

On an otherwise idle Pentium 133 running Linux, it will take somewhere between 1-1/2 to 3 hours to compile everything, depending on
whether you are building shared libraries. You will need about 100
megabytes of disk storage to work with (considerably less if you don't
compile with debugging symbols). To do that, use the command

```
make CFLAGS=-O CXXFLAGS=-O LDFLAGS=
```

instead of just 'make'.

- If you encounter errors while compiling Octave, first check the list
  of known problems below to see if there is a workaround or solution
  for your problem. If not, see Appendix B [Trouble], page 251, for
  information about how to report bugs.

- Once you have successfully compiled Octave, run 'make install'.

  This will install a copy of octave, its libraries, and its documentation in the destination directory. As distributed, Octave is installed
  in the following directories. In the table below, *prefix* defaults to
  '/usr/local', *version* stands for the current version number of the
  interpreter, and *arch* is the type of computer on which Octave is
  installed (for example, 'i586-unknown-gnu').

'*prefix*/bin'
> Octave and other binaries that people will want to run
> directly.

'*prefix*/lib'
> Libraries like libcruft.a and liboctave.a.

'*prefix*/share'
> Architecture-independent data files.

'*prefix*/include/octave'
> Include files distributed with Octave.

'*prefix*/man/man1'
> Unix-style man pages describing Octave.

'*prefix*/info'
> Info files describing Octave.

'*prefix*/share/octave/*version*/m'
>    Function files distributed with Octave. This includes
>    the Octave version, so that multiple versions of Octave
>    may be installed at the same time.

'*prefix*/lib/octave/*version*/exec/*arch*'
>    Executables to be run by Octave rather than the user.

'*prefix*/lib/octave/*version*/oct/*arch*'
>    Object files that will be dynamically loaded.

'*prefix*/share/octave/*version*/imagelib'
>    Image files that are distributed with Octave.

# C.1 Notes

- You must use the version of GNU Info distributed with Octave, because it includes some changes to allow Octave to search the indices of
  the info files. If you would like, you should be able to replace other
  copies of the Info browser that you have with the one distributed
  with Octave. Patches relative to a recent release of the GNU Info
  browser are included in the file 'INFO.PATCH' in the Octave source
  distribution. This modification has been submitted to the GNU Info
  maintainer, and should appear in some future release. Once that
  happens, the GNU Info browser will no longer be distributed with
  Octave.

# C.2 Installation Problems

This section contains a list of problems (and some apparent problems
that don't really mean anything is wrong) that may show up during installation of Octave.

- On some SCO systems, info fails to compile if HAVE_TERMIOS_
  H is defined int 'config.h'. Simply removing the definition from
  'info/config.h' should allow it to compile.

- If configure finds dlopen, dlsym, dlclose, and dlerror, but not
  the header file 'dlfcn.h', you need to find the source for the header
  file and install it in the directory 'usr/include'. This is reportedly
  a problem with Slackware 3.1. For Linux/GNU systems, the source
  for 'dlfcn.h' is in the ldso package.

- Building '.oct' files doesn't work.

  You should probably have a shared version of libstdc++. A patch is
  needed to build shared versions of version 2.7.2 of libstdc++ on the

HP-PA architecture. You can find the patch at `ftp://ftp.cygnus.com/pub/g++/libg++-2.7.2-hppa-gcc-fix`.

- On some alpha systems there may be a problem with the `libdxml` library, resulting in floating point errors and/or segmentation faults in the linear algebra routines called by Octave. If you encounter such problems, then you should modify the configure script so that `SPECIAL_MATH_LIB` is not set to `-ldxml`.

- On FreeBSD systems Octave may hang while initializing some internal constants. The fix appears to be to use

      options        GPL_MATH_EMULATE

  rather than

      options        MATH_EMULATE

  in the kernel configuration files (typically found in the directory '/sys/i386/conf'. After making this change, you'll need to rebuild the kernel, install it, and reboot.

- If you encounter errors like

      passing 'void (*)()' as argument 2 of
        'octave_set_signal_handler(int, void (*)(int))'

  or

      warning: ANSI C++ prohibits conversion from
              '(int)' to '(...)'

  while compiling 'sighandlers.cc', you may need to edit some files in the gcc include subdirectory to add proper prototypes for functions there. For example, Ultrix 4.2 needs proper declarations for the signal function and the `SIG_IGN` macro in the file 'signal.h'.

  On some systems the `SIG_IGN` macro is defined to be something like this:

      #define  SIG_IGN  (void (*)())1

  when it should really be something like:

      #define  SIG_IGN  (void (*)(int))1

  to match the prototype declaration for the `signal` function. This change should also be made for the `SIG_DFL` and `SIG_ERR` symbols. It may be necessary to change the definitions in 'sys/signal.h' as well.

  The gcc `fixincludes` and `fixproto` scripts should probably fix these problems when gcc installs its modified set of header files, but I don't think that's been done yet.

  **You should not change the files in '/usr/include'.** You can find the gcc include directory tree by running the command

```
gcc -print-libgcc-file-name
```

The directory of gcc include files normally begins in the same directory that contains the file 'libgcc.a'.

- There is a bug with the makeinfo program that is distributed with Texinfo (through version 3.9) that causes the indices in Octave's on-line manual to be generated incorrectly. If you need to recreate the on-line documentation, you should get the makeinfo program that is distributed with texinfo-3.9 and apply the patch for makeinfo that is distributed with Octave. See the file 'MAKEINFO.PATCH' for more details.

- Some of the Fortran subroutines may fail to compile with older versions of the Sun Fortran compiler. If you get errors like

```
zgemm.f:
zgemm:
warning: unexpected parent of complex expression subtree
zgemm.f, line 245: warning: unexpected parent of complex
  expression subtree
warning: unexpected parent of complex expression subtree
zgemm.f, line 304: warning: unexpected parent of complex
  expression subtree
warning: unexpected parent of complex expression subtree
zgemm.f, line 327: warning: unexpected parent of complex
  expression subtree
pcc_binval: missing IR_CONV in complex op
make[2]: *** [zgemm.o] Error 1
```

when compiling the Fortran subroutines in the 'libcruft' subdirectory, you should either upgrade your compiler or try compiling with optimization turned off.

- On NeXT systems, if you get errors like this:

```
/usr/tmp/cc007458.s:unknown:Undefined local symbol LBB7656
/usr/tmp/cc007458.s:unknown:Undefined local symbol LBE7656
```

when compiling 'Array.cc' and 'Matrix.cc', try recompiling these files without -g.

- Some people have reported that calls to shell_cmd and the pager do not work on SunOS systems. This is apparently due to having G_HAVE_SYS_WAIT defined to be 0 instead of 1 when compiling libstdc++.

- On NeXT systems, linking to 'libsys_s.a' may fail to resolve the following functions

```
_tcgetattr
```

```
_tcsetattr
_tcflow
```

which are part of 'libposix.a'. Unfortunately, linking Octave with
-posix results in the following undefined symbols.

```
.destructors_used
.constructors_used
_objc_msgSend
_NXGetDefaultValue
_NXRegisterDefaults
.objc_class_name_NXStringTable
.objc_class_name_NXBundle
```

One kluge around this problem is to extract 'termios.o' from
'libposix.a', put it in Octave's 'src' directory, and add it to the
list of files to link together in the makefile. Suggestions for better
ways to solve this problem are welcome!

- If Octave crashes immediately with a floating point exception, it is
  likely that it is failing to initialize the IEEE floating point values for
  infinity and NaN.

  If your system actually does support IEEE arithmetic, you should
  be able to fix this problem by modifying the function octave_ieee_
  init in the file 'lo-ieee.cc' to correctly initialize Octave's internal
  infinity and NaN variables.

  If your system does not support IEEE arithmetic but Octave's configure script incorrectly determined that it does, you can work around
  the problem by editing the file 'config.h' to not define HAVE_ISINF,
  HAVE_FINITE, and HAVE_ISNAN.

  In any case, please report this as a bug since it might be possible to
  modify Octave's configuration script to automatically determine the
  proper thing to do.

- After installing the binary distribution of Octave in an alternate
  directory, the Emacs command run-octave doesn't work. Emacs
  hangs in accept-process-output in inferior-octave-startup.

  This seems to be a problem with executing a shell script using the
  comint package. You can avoid the problem by changing the way
  Octave is installed to eliminate the need for the shell script. You
  can either compile and install Octave using the source distribution,
  reinstall the binary distribution in the default directory, or copy the
  commands in the octave shell script wrapper to your shell startup
  files (and the shell startup files for anyone else who is using Octave)
  and then rename the file 'octave.bin' to be 'octave'.

# C.3 Binary Distributions

Although Octave is not very difficult to build from its sources, it is a relatively large program that does require a significant amount of time and disk space to compile and install. Because of this, many people want to be able to obtain binary distributions so they can start using Octave immediately, without having to bother with the details of compiling it first. This is understandable, so I try to maintain a current collection of binary distributions at ftp://ftp.che.wisc.edu/pub/octave/BINARIES.

Please understand, however, that there is only a limited amount of time available to devote to making binaries, so binaries may not be immediately available for some platforms. (Please contact bug@octave.org if you are interested in helping make a binary distribution available for your system.)

## C.3.1 Installing Octave from a Binary Distribution

To install Octave from a binary distribution, execute the command

```
sh ./install-octave
```

in the top level directory of the distribution.

Binary distributions are normally compiled assuming that Octave will be installed in the following subdirectories of '/usr/local'.

'bin'          Octave and other binaries that people will want to run directly.

'lib'          Shared libraries that Octave needs in order to run. These files are not included if you are installing a statically linked version of Octave.

'man/man1'     Unix-style man pages describing Octave.

'info'         Info files describing Octave.

'share/octave/version/m'
               Function files distributed with Octave. This includes the Octave version, so that multiple versions of Octave may be installed at the same time.

'libexec/octave/version/exec/arch'
               Executables to be run by Octave rather than the user.

'libexec/octave/version/oct/arch'
               Object files that will be dynamically loaded.

'share/octave/version/imagelib'
               Image files that are distributed with Octave.

where *version* stands for the current version number of the interpreter, and *arch* is the type of computer on which Octave is installed (for example, 'i586-pc-linux-gnu').

If these directories don't exist, the script install-octave will create them for you. The installation script also creates the following subdirectories of '/usr/local' that are intended for locally installed functions:

'share/octave/site/m'
> Locally installed M-files.

'libexec/octave/site/exec/*arch*'
> Locally installed binaries intended to be run by Octave rather than by the user.

'libexec/octave/site/octave/*arch*'
> Local object files that will be dynamically linked.

If it is not possible for you to install Octave in '/usr/local', or if you would prefer to install it in a different directory, you can specify the name of the top level directory as an argument to the 'install-octave' script. For example:

```
sh ./install-octave /some/other/directory
```
will install Octave in subdirectories of the given directory.

## C.3.2 Creating a Binary Distribution

Here is how to build a binary distribution for others to use. If you want to make a binary distribution for your system available along with the Octave sources and binaries on ftp.che.wisc.edu, please follow this procedure. For directions explaining how to make the binary available on the ftp site, please contact bug@octave.org.

- Unpack the source distribution:
  ```
  gunzip -c octave-2.0.17.tar.gz | tar xf -
  ```
- Change your current directory to the top-level directory of the source distribution:
  ```
  cd octave-2.0.17
  ```
- Make the binary distribution:
  ```
  make binary-dist
  ```
  This will create a compressed tar file ready for distribution. It will have a name like 'octave-2.0.17-i586-pc-linux-gnu.tar.gz'

# Appendix D  Emacs Octave Support

The development of Octave code can greatly be facilitated using Emacs with Octave mode, a major mode for editing Octave files which can e.g. automatically indent the code, do some of the typing (with Abbrev mode) and show keywords, comments, strings, etc. in different faces (with Font-lock mode on devices that support it).

It is also possible to run Octave from within Emacs, either by directly entering commands at the prompt in a buffer in Inferior Octave mode, or by interacting with Octave from within a file with Octave code. This is useful in particular for debugging Octave code.

Finally, you can convince Octave to use the Emacs info reader for *help -i*.

All functionality is provided by the Emacs Lisp package EOS (for "Emacs Octave Support"). This chapter describes how to set up and use this package.

Please contact <Kurt.Hornik@ci.tuwien.ac.at> if you have any questions or suggestions on using EOS.

## D.1  Installing EOS

The Emacs package EOS consists of the three files 'octave-mod.el', 'octave-inf.el', and 'octave-hlp.el'. These files, or better yet their byte-compiled versions, should be somewhere in your Emacs load-path.

If you have GNU Emacs with a version number at least as high as 19.35, you are all set up, because EOS is respectively will be part of GNU Emacs as of version 19.35.

Otherwise, copy the three files from the 'emacs' subdirectory of the Octave distribution to a place where Emacs can find them (this depends on how your Emacs was installed). Byte-compile them for speed if you want.

## D.2  Using Octave Mode

If you are lucky, your sysadmins have already arranged everything so that Emacs automatically goes into Octave mode whenever you visit an Octave code file as characterized by its extension '.m'. If not, proceed as follows.

1. To begin using Octave mode for all '.m' files you visit, add the following lines to a file loaded by Emacs at startup time, typically your '~/.emacs' file:

```
(autoload 'octave-mode "octave-mod" nil t)
(setq auto-mode-alist
     (cons '("\\.m$" . octave-mode) auto-mode-alist))
```

2. Finally, to turn on the abbrevs, auto-fill and font-lock features automatically, also add the following lines to one of the Emacs startup files:

```
(add-hook 'octave-mode-hook
         (lambda ()
           (abbrev-mode 1)
           (auto-fill-mode 1)
           (if (eq window-system 'x)
               (font-lock-mode 1))))
```

See the Emacs manual for more information about how to customize Font-lock mode.

In Octave mode, the following special Emacs commands can be used in addition to the standard Emacs commands.

C-h m         Describe the features of Octave mode.

LFD            Reindent the current Octave line, insert a newline and indent the new line (octave-reindent-then-newline-and-indent). An abbrev before point is expanded if abbrev-mode is non-nil.

TAB            Indents current Octave line based on its contents and on previous lines (indent-according-to-mode).

;               Insert an "electric" semicolon (octave-electric-semi). If octave-auto-indent is non-nil, reindent the current line. If octave-auto-newline is non-nil, automagically insert a newline and indent the new line.

'               Start entering an abbreviation (octave-abbrev-start). If Abbrev mode is turned on, typing 'C-h or '? lists all abbrevs. Any other key combination is executed normally. Note that all Octave abbrevs start with a grave accent.

M-LFD        Break line at point and insert continuation marker and alignment (octave-split-line).

M-TAB        Perform completion on Octave symbol preceding point, comparing that symbol against Octave's reserved words and builtin variables (octave-complete-symbol).

M-C-a        Move backward to the beginning of a function (octave-beginning-of-defun). With prefix argument $N$, do it that many times if $N$ is positive; otherwise, move forward to the $N$-th following beginning of a function.

M-C-e    Move forward to the end of a function (octave-end-of-defun). With prefix argument $N$, do it that many times if $N$ is positive; otherwise, move back to the $N$-th preceding end of a function.

M-C-h    Puts point at beginning and mark at the end of the current Octave function, i.e., the one containing point or following point (octave-mark-defun).

M-C-q    Properly indents the Octave function which contains point (octave-indent-defun).

M-;      If there is no comment already on this line, create a code-level comment (started by two comment characters) if the line is empty, or an in-line comment (started by one comment character) otherwise (octave-indent-for-comment). Point is left after the start of the comment which is properly aligned.

C-c ;    Puts the comment character '#' (more precisely, the string value of octave-comment-start) at the beginning of every line in the region (octave-comment-region). With just C-u prefix argument, uncomment each line in the region. A numeric prefix argument $N$ means use $N$ comment characters.

C-c :    Uncomments every line in the region (octave-uncomment-region).

C-c C-p  Move one line of Octave code backward, skipping empty and comment lines (octave-previous-code-line). With numeric prefix argument $N$, move that many code lines backward (forward if $N$ is negative).

C-c C-n  Move one line of Octave code forward, skipping empty and comment lines (octave-next-code-line). With numeric prefix argument $N$, move that many code lines forward (backward if $N$ is negative).

C-c C-a  Move to the 'real' beginning of the current line (octave-beginning-of-line). If point is in an empty or comment line, simply go to its beginning; otherwise, move backwards to the beginning of the first code line which is not inside a continuation statement, i.e., which does not follow a code line ending in '...' or '\', or is inside an open parenthesis list.

*C-c C-e*     Move to the 'real' end of the current line (`octave-end-of-line`). If point is in a code line, move forward to the end of the first Octave code line which does not end in '...' or '\' or is inside an open parenthesis list. Otherwise, simply go to the end of the current line.

*C-c M-C-n*   Move forward across one balanced begin-end block of Octave code (`octave-forward-block`). With numeric prefix argument *N*, move forward across *n* such blocks (backward if *N* is negative).

*C-c M-C-p*   Move back across one balanced begin-end block of Octave code (`octave-backward-block`). With numeric prefix argument *N*, move backward across *N* such blocks (forward if *N* is negative).

*C-c M-C-d*   Move forward down one begin-end block level of Octave code (`octave-down-block`). With numeric prefix argument, do it that many times; a negative argument means move backward, but still go down one level.

*C-c M-C-u*   Move backward out of one begin-end block level of Octave code (`octave-backward-up-block`). With numeric prefix argument, do it that many times; a negative argument means move forward, but still to a less deep spot.

*C-c M-C-h*   Put point at the beginning of this block, mark at the end (`octave-mark-block`). The block marked is the one that contains point or follows point.

*C-c ]*       Close the current block on a separate line (`octave-close-block`). An error is signaled if no block to close is found.

*C-c f*       Insert a function skeleton, prompting for the function's name, arguments and return values which have to be entered without parens (`octave-insert-defun`).

*C-c C-h*     Search the function, operator and variable indices of all info files with documentation for Octave for entries (`octave-help`). If used interactively, the entry is prompted for with completion. If multiple matches are found, one can cycle through them using the standard ',' (`Info-index-next`) command of the Info reader.

              The variable `octave-help-files` is a list of files to search through and defaults to `'("octave")`. If there is also an Octave Local Guide with corresponding info file, say, 'octave-LG', you can have `octave-help` search both files by

```
(setq octave-help-files '("octave" "octave-LG"))
```
in one of your Emacs startup files.

A common problem is that the (RET) key does *not* indent the line to where the new text should go after inserting the newline. This is because the standard Emacs convention is that (RET) (aka *C-m*) just adds a newline, whereas (LFD) (aka *C-j*) adds a newline and indents it. This is particularly inconvenient for users with keyboards which do not have a special (LFD) key at all; in such cases, it is typically more convenient to use (RET) as the (LFD) key (rather than typing *C-j*).

You can make (RET) do this by adding

```
(define-key octave-mode-map "\C-m"
  'octave-reindent-then-newline-and-indent)
```
to one of your Emacs startup files. Another, more generally applicable solution is

```
(defun RET-behaves-as-LFD ()
  (let ((x (key-binding "\C-j")))
    (local-set-key "\C-m" x)))
(add-hook 'octave-mode-hook 'RET-behaves-as-LFD)
```
(this works for all modes by adding to the startup hooks, without having to know the particular binding of (RET) in that mode!). Similar considerations apply for using (M-RET) as (M-LFD). As Barry A. Warsaw <bwarsaw@cnri.reston.va.us> says in the documentation for his cc-mode, "This is a very common question. :-) If you want this to be the default behavior, don't lobby me, lobby RMS!"

The following variables can be used to customize Octave mode.

octave-auto-indent
> Non-nil means auto-indent the current line after a semicolon or space. Default is nil.

octave-auto-newline
> Non-nil means auto-insert a newline and indent after semicolons are typed. The default value is nil.

octave-blink-matching-block
> Non-nil means show matching begin of block when inserting a space, newline or ';' after an else or end keyword. Default is t. This is an extremely useful feature for automatically verifying that the keywords match—if they don't, an error message is displayed.

octave-block-offset
> Extra indentation applied to statements in block structures. Default is 2.

`octave-continuation-offset`
> Extra indentation applied to Octave continuation lines. Default is 4.

`octave-continuation-string`
> String used for Octave continuation lines. Normally '\'.

`octave-mode-startup-message`
> If t (default), a startup message is displayed when Octave mode is called.

If Font Lock mode is enabled, Octave mode will display

- strings in `font-lock-string-face`
- comments in `font-lock-comment-face`
- the Octave reserved words (such as all block keywords) and the text functions (such as 'cd' or 'who') which are also reserved using `font-lock-keyword-face`
- the builtin operators ('&&', '<>', . . .) using `font-lock-reference-face`
- the builtin variables (such as 'prefer_column_vectors', 'NaN' or 'LOADPATH') in `font-lock-variable-name-face`
- and the function names in function declarations in `font-lock-function-name-face`.

There is also rudimentary support for Imenu (currently, function names can be indexed).

You can generate TAGS files for Emacs from Octave '.m' files using the shell script `otags` that is installed alongside your copy of Octave.

Customization of Octave mode can be performed by modification of the variable `octave-mode-hook`. If the value of this variable is non-`nil`, turning on Octave mode calls its value.

If you discover a problem with Octave mode, you can conveniently send a bug report using `C-c C-b` (`octave-submit-bug-report`). This automatically sets up a mail buffer with version information already added. You just need to add a description of the problem, including a reproducible test case and send the message.

# D.3 Running Octave From Within Emacs

The package 'octave' provides commands for running an inferior Octave process in a special Emacs buffer. Use

`M-x run-octave`

to directly start an inferior Octave process. If Emacs does not know about this command, add the line

```
(autoload 'run-octave "octave-inf" nil t)
```
to your '.emacs' file.

This will start Octave in a special buffer the name of which is specified by the variable `inferior-octave-buffer` and defaults to `"*Inferior Octave*"`. From within this buffer, you can interact with the inferior Octave process 'as usual', i.e., by entering Octave commands at the prompt. The buffer is in Inferior Octave mode, which is derived from the standard Comint mode, a major mode for interacting with an inferior interpreter. See the documentation for `comint-mode` for more details, and use *C-h b* to find out about available special keybindings.

You can also communicate with an inferior Octave process from within files with Octave code (i.e., buffers in Octave mode), using the following commands.

*C-c i l*    Send the current line to the inferior Octave process (`octave-send-line`). With positive prefix argument *N*, send that many lines. If `octave-send-line-auto-forward` is non-nil, go to the next unsent code line.

*C-c i b*    Send the current block to the inferior Octave process (`octave-send-block`).

*C-c i f*    Send the current function to the inferior Octave process (`octave-send-defun`).

*C-c i r*    Send the region to the inferior Octave process (`octave-send-region`).

*C-c i s*    Make sure that 'inferior-octave-buffer' is displayed (`octave-show-process-buffer`).

*C-c i h*    Delete all windows that display the inferior Octave buffer (`octave-hide-process-buffer`).

*C-c i k*    Kill the inferior Octave process and its buffer (`octave-kill-process`).

The effect of the commands which send code to the Octave process can be customized by the following variables.

`octave-send-echo-input`
> Non-nil means echo input sent to the inferior Octave process. Default is t.

`octave-send-show-buffer`
> Non-nil means display the buffer running the Octave process after sending a command (but without selecting it). Default is t.

If you send code and there is no inferior Octave process yet, it will be started automatically.

The startup of the inferior Octave process is highly customizable. The variable `inferior-octave-startup-args` can be used for specifying command lines arguments to be passed to Octave on startup as a list of strings. For example, to suppress the startup message and use 'traditional' mode, set this to `'("-q" "--traditional")`. You can also specify a startup file of Octave commands to be loaded on startup; note that these commands will not produce any visible output in the process buffer. Which file to use is controlled by the variable `inferior-octave-startup-file`. If this is nil, the file '`~/.emacs-octave`' is used if it exists.

And finally, `inferior-octave-mode-hook` is run after starting the process and putting its buffer into Inferior Octave mode. Hence, if you like the up and down arrow keys to behave in the interaction buffer as in the shell, and you want this buffer to use nice colors, add

```
(add-hook 'inferior-octave-mode-hook
          (lambda ()
            (turn-on-font-lock)
            (define-key inferior-octave-mode-map [up]
              'comint-previous-input)
            (define-key inferior-octave-mode-map [down]
              'comint-next-input)))
```

to your '`.emacs`' file. You could also swap the roles of *C*-a (beginning-of-line) and C-c C-a (comint-bol) using this hook.

> **Note:** If you set your Octave prompts to something different from the defaults, make sure that `inferior-octave-prompt` matches them. Otherwise, *nothing* will work, because Emacs will have no idea when Octave is waiting for input, or done sending output.

# D.4 Using the Emacs Info Reader for Octave

You can also set up the Emacs Info reader for dealing with the results of Octave's 'help -i'. For this, the package 'gnuserv' needs to be installed, which unfortunately still does not come with GNU Emacs (it does with XEmacs). It can be retrieved from any GNU Emacs Lisp Code Directory archive, e.g. `ftp://ftp.cis.ohio-state.edu/pub/gnu/emacs/elisp-archive`, in the 'packages' subdirectory. The alpha version of an enhanced version of gnuserv is available at `ftp://ftp.wellfleet.com/netman/psmith/emacs/gnuserv-2.1alpha.tar.gz`.

If 'gnuserv' is installed, add the lines

```
(autoload 'octave-help "octave-hlp" nil t)
(require 'gnuserv)
(gnuserv-start)
```

to your '.emacs' file.

You can use either 'plain' Emacs Info or the function octave-help as your Octave info reader (for 'help -i'). In the former case, set the Octave variable INFO_PROGRAM to "info-emacs-info". The latter is perhaps more attractive because it allows to look up keys in the indices of *several* info files related to Octave (provided that the Emacs variable octave-help-files is set correctly). In this case, set INFO_PROGRAM to "info-emacs-octave-help".

If you use Octave from within Emacs, these settings are best done in the '~/.emacs-octave' startup file (or the file pointed to by the Emacs variable inferior-octave-startup-file).

# 30  Grammar

Someday I hope to expand this to include a semi-formal description of Octave's language.

## 30.1  Keywords

The following identifiers are keywords, and may not be used as variable or function names:

| | |
|---|---|
| all_va_args | endwhile |
| break | for |
| case | function |
| catch | global |
| continue | gplot |
| else | gsplot |
| elseif | if |
| end | otherwise |
| end_try_catch | return |
| end_unwind_protect | switch |
| endfor | try |
| endfunction | unwind_protect |
| endif | unwind_protect_cleanup |
| endswitch | while |

The following command-like functions are also special. They may be used as simple variable names, but not as formal parameters for functions, or as the names of structure variables. Failed assignments leave them undefined (you can recover the original definition as a function using clear).

| | | | |
|---|---|---|---|
| casesen | echo | load | show |
| cd | edit_history | ls | type |
| chdir | format | more | which |
| clear | help | run_history | who |
| diary | history | save | whos |
| dir | hold | set | |

# Appendix E GNU GENERAL PUBLIC LICENSE

Version 2, June 1991

Copyright © 1989, 1991 Free Software Foundation, Inc.
59 Temple Place - Suite 330, Boston, MA  02111-1307, USA

## E.1 Preamble

The licenses for most software are designed to take away your freedom to share and change it. By contrast, the GNU General Public License is intended to guarantee your freedom to share and change free software— to make sure the software is free for all its users. This General Public License applies to most of the Free Software Foundation's software and to any other program whose authors commit to using it. (Some other Free Software Foundation software is covered by the GNU Library General Public License instead.) You can apply it to your programs, too.

When we speak of free software, we are referring to freedom, not price. Our General Public Licenses are designed to make sure that you have the freedom to distribute copies of free software (and charge for this service if you wish), that you receive source code or can get it if you want it, that you can change the software or use pieces of it in new free programs; and that you know you can do these things.

To protect your rights, we need to make restrictions that forbid anyone to deny you these rights or to ask you to surrender the rights. These restrictions translate to certain responsibilities for you if you distribute copies of the software, or if you modify it.

For example, if you distribute copies of such a program, whether gratis or for a fee, you must give the recipients all the rights that you have. You must make sure that they, too, receive or can get the source code. And you must show them these terms so they know their rights.

We protect your rights with two steps: (1) copyright the software, and (2) offer you this license which gives you legal permission to copy, distribute and/or modify the software.

Also, for each author's protection and ours, we want to make certain that everyone understands that there is no warranty for this free software. If the software is modified by someone else and passed on, we want its recipients to know that what they have is not the original, so that any problems introduced by others will not reflect on the original authors' reputations.

Finally, any free program is threatened constantly by software patents. We wish to avoid the danger that redistributors of a free program will individually obtain patent licenses, in effect making the program proprietary. To prevent this, we have made it clear that any patent must be licensed for everyone's free use or not licensed at all.

The precise terms and conditions for copying, distribution and modification follow.

## E.2  TERMS AND CONDITIONS FOR COPYING, DISTRIBUTION AND MODIFICATION

0. This License applies to any program or other work which contains a notice placed by the copyright holder saying it may be distributed under the terms of this General Public License. The "Program", below, refers to any such program or work, and a "work based on the Program" means either the Program or any derivative work under copyright law: that is to say, a work containing the Program or a portion of it, either verbatim or with modifications and/or translated into another language. (Hereinafter, translation is included without limitation in the term "modification".) Each licensee is addressed as "you".

   Activities other than copying, distribution and modification are not covered by this License; they are outside its scope. The act of running the Program is not restricted, and the output from the Program is covered only if its contents constitute a work based on the Program (independent of having been made by running the Program). Whether that is true depends on what the Program does.

1. You may copy and distribute verbatim copies of the Program's source code as you receive it, in any medium, provided that you conspicuously and appropriately publish on each copy an appropriate copyright notice and disclaimer of warranty; keep intact all the notices that refer to this License and to the absence of any warranty; and give any other recipients of the Program a copy of this License along with the Program.

   You may charge a fee for the physical act of transferring a copy, and you may at your option offer warranty protection in exchange for a fee.

2. You may modify your copy or copies of the Program or any portion of it, thus forming a work based on the Program, and copy and

distribute such modifications or work under the terms of Section 1 above, provided that you also meet all of these conditions:

a.  You must cause the modified files to carry prominent notices stating that you changed the files and the date of any change.

b.  You must cause any work that you distribute or publish, that in whole or in part contains or is derived from the Program or any part thereof, to be licensed as a whole at no charge to all third parties under the terms of this License.

c.  If the modified program normally reads commands interactively when run, you must cause it, when started running for such interactive use in the most ordinary way, to print or display an announcement including an appropriate copyright notice and a notice that there is no warranty (or else, saying that you provide a warranty) and that users may redistribute the program under these conditions, and telling the user how to view a copy of this License. (Exception: if the Program itself is interactive but does not normally print such an announcement, your work based on the Program is not required to print an announcement.)

These requirements apply to the modified work as a whole. If identifiable sections of that work are not derived from the Program, and can be reasonably considered independent and separate works in themselves, then this License, and its terms, do not apply to those sections when you distribute them as separate works. But when you distribute the same sections as part of a whole which is a work based on the Program, the distribution of the whole must be on the terms of this License, whose permissions for other licensees extend to the entire whole, and thus to each and every part regardless of who wrote it.

Thus, it is not the intent of this section to claim rights or contest your rights to work written entirely by you; rather, the intent is to exercise the right to control the distribution of derivative or collective works based on the Program.

In addition, mere aggregation of another work not based on the Program with the Program (or with a work based on the Program) on a volume of a storage or distribution medium does not bring the other work under the scope of this License.

3.  You may copy and distribute the Program (or a work based on it, under Section 2) in object code or executable form under the terms of Sections 1 and 2 above provided that you also do one of the following:

a.  Accompany it with the complete corresponding machine-readable source code, which must be distributed under the terms of Sections 1 and 2 above on a medium customarily used for software interchange; or,

b. Accompany it with a written offer, valid for at least three years, to give any third party, for a charge no more than your cost of physically performing source distribution, a complete machine-readable copy of the corresponding source code, to be distributed under the terms of Sections 1 and 2 above on a medium customarily used for software interchange; or,

c. Accompany it with the information you received as to the offer to distribute corresponding source code. (This alternative is allowed only for noncommercial distribution and only if you received the program in object code or executable form with such an offer, in accord with Subsection b above.)

The source code for a work means the preferred form of the work for making modifications to it. For an executable work, complete source code means all the source code for all modules it contains, plus any associated interface definition files, plus the scripts used to control compilation and installation of the executable. However, as a special exception, the source code distributed need not include anything that is normally distributed (in either source or binary form) with the major components (compiler, kernel, and so on) of the operating system on which the executable runs, unless that component itself accompanies the executable.

If distribution of executable or object code is made by offering access to copy from a designated place, then offering equivalent access to copy the source code from the same place counts as distribution of the source code, even though third parties are not compelled to copy the source along with the object code.

4. You may not copy, modify, sublicense, or distribute the Program except as expressly provided under this License. Any attempt otherwise to copy, modify, sublicense or distribute the Program is void, and will automatically terminate your rights under this License. However, parties who have received copies, or rights, from you under this License will not have their licenses terminated so long as such parties remain in full compliance.

5. You are not required to accept this License, since you have not signed it. However, nothing else grants you permission to modify or distribute the Program or its derivative works. These actions are prohibited by law if you do not accept this License. Therefore, by modifying or distributing the Program (or any work based on the Program), you indicate your acceptance of this License to do so, and

all its terms and conditions for copying, distributing or modifying the Program or works based on it.

6. Each time you redistribute the Program (or any work based on the Program), the recipient automatically receives a license from the original licensor to copy, distribute or modify the Program subject to these terms and conditions. You may not impose any further restrictions on the recipients' exercise of the rights granted herein. You are not responsible for enforcing compliance by third parties to this License.

7. If, as a consequence of a court judgment or allegation of patent infringement or for any other reason (not limited to patent issues), conditions are imposed on you (whether by court order, agreement or otherwise) that contradict the conditions of this License, they do not excuse you from the conditions of this License. If you cannot distribute so as to satisfy simultaneously your obligations under this License and any other pertinent obligations, then as a consequence you may not distribute the Program at all. For example, if a patent license would not permit royalty-free redistribution of the Program by all those who receive copies directly or indirectly through you, then the only way you could satisfy both it and this License would be to refrain entirely from distribution of the Program.

If any portion of this section is held invalid or unenforceable under any particular circumstance, the balance of the section is intended to apply and the section as a whole is intended to apply in other circumstances.

It is not the purpose of this section to induce you to infringe any patents or other property right claims or to contest validity of any such claims; this section has the sole purpose of protecting the integrity of the free software distribution system, which is implemented by public license practices. Many people have made generous contributions to the wide range of software distributed through that system in reliance on consistent application of that system; it is up to the author/donor to decide if he or she is willing to distribute software through any other system and a licensee cannot impose that choice.

This section is intended to make thoroughly clear what is believed to be a consequence of the rest of this License.

8. If the distribution and/or use of the Program is restricted in certain countries either by patents or by copyrighted interfaces, the original copyright holder who places the Program under this License may add an explicit geographical distribution limitation excluding those countries, so that distribution is permitted only in or among coun-

tries not thus excluded. In such case, this License incorporates the limitation as if written in the body of this License.

9. The Free Software Foundation may publish revised and/or new versions of the General Public License from time to time. Such new versions will be similar in spirit to the present version, but may differ in detail to address new problems or concerns.

   Each version is given a distinguishing version number. If the Program specifies a version number of this License which applies to it and "any later version", you have the option of following the terms and conditions either of that version or of any later version published by the Free Software Foundation. If the Program does not specify a version number of this License, you may choose any version ever published by the Free Software Foundation.

10. If you wish to incorporate parts of the Program into other free programs whose distribution conditions are different, write to the author to ask for permission. For software which is copyrighted by the Free Software Foundation, write to the Free Software Foundation; we sometimes make exceptions for this. Our decision will be guided by the two goals of preserving the free status of all derivatives of our free software and of promoting the sharing and reuse of software generally.

# NO WARRANTY

11. BECAUSE THE PROGRAM IS LICENSED FREE OF CHARGE, THERE IS NO WARRANTY FOR THE PROGRAM, TO THE EXTENT PERMITTED BY APPLICABLE LAW. EXCEPT WHEN OTHERWISE STATED IN WRITING THE COPYRIGHT HOLDERS AND/OR OTHER PARTIES PROVIDE THE PROGRAM "AS IS" WITHOUT WARRANTY OF ANY KIND, EITHER EXPRESSED OR IMPLIED, INCLUDING, BUT NOT LIMITED TO, THE IMPLIED WARRANTIES OF MERCHANTABILITY AND FITNESS FOR A PARTICULAR PURPOSE. THE ENTIRE RISK AS TO THE QUALITY AND PERFORMANCE OF THE PROGRAM IS WITH YOU. SHOULD THE PROGRAM PROVE DEFECTIVE, YOU ASSUME THE COST OF ALL NECESSARY SERVICING, REPAIR OR CORRECTION.

12. IN NO EVENT UNLESS REQUIRED BY APPLICABLE LAW OR AGREED TO IN WRITING WILL ANY COPYRIGHT HOLDER, OR ANY OTHER PARTY WHO MAY MODIFY AND/OR REDISTRIBUTE THE PROGRAM AS PERMITTED ABOVE, BE LIABLE TO YOU FOR DAMAGES, INCLUDING ANY GEN-

ERAL, SPECIAL, INCIDENTAL OR CONSEQUENTIAL DAM-
AGES ARISING OUT OF THE USE OR INABILITY TO USE
THE PROGRAM (INCLUDING BUT NOT LIMITED TO LOSS
OF DATA OR DATA BEING RENDERED INACCURATE OR
LOSSES SUSTAINED BY YOU OR THIRD PARTIES OR A FAIL-
URE OF THE PROGRAM TO OPERATE WITH ANY OTHER
PROGRAMS), EVEN IF SUCH HOLDER OR OTHER PARTY
HAS BEEN ADVISED OF THE POSSIBILITY OF SUCH DAM-
AGES.

# END OF TERMS AND CONDITIONS

# E.3 Appendix: How to Apply These Terms to Your New Programs

If you develop a new program, and you want it to be of the greatest possible use to the public, the best way to achieve this is to make it free software which everyone can redistribute and change under these terms.

To do so, attach the following notices to the program. It is safest to attach them to the start of each source file to most effectively convey the exclusion of warranty; and each file should have at least the "copyright" line and a pointer to where the full notice is found.

*one line to give the program's name and a brief idea of what it does.*
Copyright (C) 19*yy   name of author*

```
This program is free software; you can redistribute it and/or
modify it under the terms of the GNU General Public License
as published by the Free Software Foundation; either version
2 of the License, or (at your option) any later version.

This program is distributed in the hope that it will be useful,
but WITHOUT ANY WARRANTY; without even the implied warranty of
MERCHANTABILITY or FITNESS FOR A PARTICULAR PURPOSE.  See the
GNU General Public License for more details.

You should have received a copy of the GNU General Public
License along with this program; if not, write to the Free
Software Foundation, Inc., 59 Temple Place - Suite 330,
Boston, MA 02111-1307, USA.
```

Also add information on how to contact you by electronic and paper mail.

If the program is interactive, make it output a short notice like this when it starts in an interactive mode:

```
Gnomovision version 69, Copyright (C) 19yy name of author
Gnomovision comes with ABSOLUTELY NO WARRANTY; for details
type 'show w'.  This is free software, and you are welcome
to redistribute it under certain conditions; type 'show c'
for details.
```

The hypothetical commands 'show w' and 'show c' should show the appropriate parts of the General Public License. Of course, the commands you use may be called something other than 'show w' and 'show c'; they could even be mouse-clicks or menu items—whatever suits your program.

You should also get your employer (if you work as a programmer) or your school, if any, to sign a "copyright disclaimer" for the program, if necessary. Here is a sample; alter the names:

```
Yoyodyne, Inc., hereby disclaims all copyright interest in
the program 'Gnomovision' (which makes passes at compilers)
written by James Hacker.
```

*signature of Ty Coon*, 1 April 1989
Ty Coon, President of Vice

This General Public License does not permit incorporating your program into proprietary programs. If your program is a subroutine library, you may consider it more useful to permit linking proprietary applications with the library. If this is what you want to do, use the GNU Library General Public License instead of this License.

# Other books from the publisher

Network Theory publishes books about free software under free documentation licenses. Our current catalogue includes the following titles:

- **An Introduction to GCC** by Brian J. Gough, foreword by Richard M. Stallman. (ISBN 0-9541617-9-3) $19.95 (£12.95)

  This manual provides a tutorial introduction to the GNU C and C++ compilers, gcc and g++. Many books teach the C and C++ languages, but this book explains how to use the compiler itself. Based on years of observation of questions posted on mailing lists, it guides the reader straight to the important options of GCC.

  Concisely written, with numerous easy-to-follow "Hello World" examples, this book features a special foreword by Richard M. Stallman, principal developer of GCC and founder of the GNU Project.

- **GNU Scientific Library Reference Manual—Revised Second Edition** by M. Galassi, et al (ISBN 0-9541617-3-4) $39.99 (£24.99)

  This reference manual is the definitive guide to the GNU Scientific Library (GSL), a numerical library for C and C++ programmers. The manual documents over 1,000 mathematical routines needed for solving problems in science and engineering. All the money raised from the sale of this book supports the development of the GNU Scientific Library.

- **An Introduction to R** by W.N. Venables, D.M. Smith and the R Development Core Team (ISBN 0-9541617-4-2) $19.95 (£12.95)

  This tutorial manual provides a comprehensive introduction to GNU R, a free software package for statistical computing and graphics.

- **The R Reference Manual—Base Package (Volume 1)** by the R Development Core Team (ISBN 0-9546120-0-0) $69.95 (£39.95)

  This manual is the first volume of the complete reference manual for the base package of GNU R, a free software environment for statistical computing and graphics. The main commands of the base package of R are described in this volume, while the other functions (such as graphics) are described in volume two.

  For each set of manuals sold (volumes 1 & 2), $10 is donated to the R Foundation.

- **The R Reference Manual—Base Package (Volume 2)** by the R Development Core Team (ISBN 0-9546120-1-9) $69.95 (£39.95)

This manual is the second volume of the complete reference manual for the base package of GNU R. The commands for graphics, mathematics, distributions and random numbers, models, time-series and datasets are described in this volume.

- **Comparing and Merging Files with GNU diff and patch** by David MacKenzie, Paul Eggert, and Richard Stallman (ISBN 0-9541617-5-0) $19.95 (£12.95)

  This manual describes how to compare and merge files using GNU diff and patch. It includes an extensive tutorial that guides the reader through all the options of the diff and patch commands. Later chapters cover powerful time-saving techniques such as automatic merging of divergent branches of a source tree.

  This is a printed copy of the official GNU diffutils manual. It documents all the diffutils programs (diff, cmp, sdiff, diff3), plus GNU patch. For each copy of this manual sold, $1 is donated to the Free Software Foundation.

- **Version Management with CVS** by Per Cederqvist et al. (ISBN 0-9541617-1-8) $29.95 (£19.95)

  This manual describes how to use CVS, the concurrent versioning system—one of the most widely-used source-code management systems available today. The manual provides tutorial examples for new users of CVS, as well as the definitive reference documentation for every CVS command and configuration option.

- **GNU Bash Reference Manual** by Chet Ramey and Brian Fox (ISBN 0-9541617-7-7) $29.95 (£19.95)

  This manual is the definitive reference for GNU Bash, the standard GNU command-line interpreter. GNU Bash is a complete implementation of the POSIX.2 Bourne shell specification, with additional features from the C-shell and Korn shell. For each copy of this manual sold, $1 is donated to the Free Software Foundation.

- **An Introduction to Python** by Guido van Rossum and Fred L. Drake, Jr. (ISBN 0-9541617-6-9) $19.95 (£12.95)

  This tutorial provides an introduction to Python, an easy to learn object oriented programming language. For each copy of this manual sold, $1 is donated to the Python Software Foundation.

- **Python Language Reference Manual** by Guido van Rossum and Fred L. Drake, Jr. (ISBN 0-9541617-8-5) $19.95 (£12.95)

  This manual is the official reference for the Python language itself. It describes the syntax of Python and its built-in datatypes in depth, This manual is suitable for readers who need to be familiar with the details and rules of the Python language and its object system. For each copy of this manual sold, $1 is donated to the Python Software Foundation.

All titles are available for order from bookstores worldwide.

Sales of the manuals fund the development of more free software and documentation.

For details, visit the website http://www.network-theory.co.uk/

# Variable Index

## A

# Operator Index

# Function Index

## A

## B

## C

# G

# H

# I

# Concept Index

# C

# D

# E

Printed in the United States
61099LVS00003B/65